Western
Landscaping
Book

Edited by Kathleen Norris Brenzel

LEFT *The simplest of concrete patios, colored to sit comfortably amid natural hues, pays homage to its lovely Napa Valley surroundings.*

RIGHT *Pride of place goes to the Ping-Pong table in an Arizona garden ablaze with gaillardia, red penstemon, and other blooms.*

SUNSET BOOKS
Vice President, General Manager: Richard A. Smeby
Vice President, Editorial Director: Bob Doyle
Production Director: Lory Day
Operations Director: Rosann Sutherland
Marketing Manager: Linda Barker
Art Director: Vasken Guiragossian
Special Sales: Brad Moses

STAFF FOR THIS BOOK
Editor: Kathleen Norris Brenzel
Managing Editor: Fiona Gilsenan
Associate Editor: Tom Wilhite
Senior Writers: Valerie Easton, Philip Edinger

Art Director: Christine Rocha/Hespenheide Design
Photo Editor: Cynthia Del Fava
Illustrators: Sylvia Hofflund, Tracy LaRue Hohn
Prepress Coordinator: Danielle Javier
Production Specialist: Linda M. Bouchard

Copy Editor & Indexer: Erin Hartshorn
Proofreaders: Bridget Neumayr/Hespenheide Design,
Michelle Pollace, David Sweet

Many thanks to the following for their contributions to the *Sunset Western Landscaping Book:* Scott Atkinson, Debra Lee Baldwin, Pamela Cornelison, Sharon Cohoon, Carrie Dodson Davis, Evan Elliot, Jim McCausland, Alice Rogers, Lauren Bonar Swezey, RG Turner Jr., Lance Walheim, Peter O. Whiteley

Cover: photography by Thomas J. Story; landscape design by Paul Harris, Imagine Sonoma; architecture by Diana Marley and Sam Wells, Marley + Wells Architects

10 9 8 7 6 5 4 3 2 1
First Printing January 2006. Copyright ©2006 Sunset Publishing Corporation, Menlo Park, CA 94025. Printed in the United States of America.

Library of Congress Control Number: 2005932444
ISBN-13: 978-0-376-03915-6
ISBN-10: 0-376-03915-9

For additional copies of *Sunset Western Landscaping Book* or any other Sunset book, call 1-800-526-5111 or visit us at www.sunset.com.

contents

Gardens are for Living

In the West, outdoor living is not just a privilege and a passion, it's a way of life. I grew up in Southern California, on the edge of a canyon near the beach. Because the weather there was mostly mild (except for the "June gloom" morning fogs that rolled in off the ocean), we spent all of our time outdoors—climbing trees, chasing butterflies, picking tomatoes fresh off the vine, barbecuing, then watching the sun float down into the Pacific. In summer, we'd drag our sleeping bags out onto the back lawn so we could fall asleep under the stars while frogs serenaded us from the creek and the sweet scents of honeysuckle and dewy sycamore leaves perfumed the air. That garden seemed magical and boundless, and I knew that one day I wanted another just like it.

Each of us has our own idea of what a garden should be, whether a place to grow things, entertain friends, or reconnect with nature. But one thing we probably agree on: Gardens are for living. We plan pocket patios off the bedroom for views or off the kitchen for enjoying morning coffee. Architects and landscape designers use illusion to visually connect our homes to the landscape—flooring that flows from indoors to outdoors through glass walls, for example, or reflecting pools that appear to jut into the house. Our gardens are not built for looks alone; they allow us to extend our lifestyles outside with sleeping porches, built-in pizza ovens, personal retreats, outdoor showers, game courts, cooling pools. And in spite of our busy schedules, we build raised beds for growing herbs, find sunny spots for tomatoes, and cultivate roses for cutting. We've learned to get the most out of every inch of land.

This book offers ideas, inspiration, and practical tips for making your garden all that you want it to be. You don't need a large budget to provide for open-air living: You can build a tiny retreat surrounded with pots in a corner of a perennial bed, bring a portable firepit and a couple of rustic chairs onto a gravel patio, or move a daybed onto a veranda and cover it with outdoor fabrics in soft pastels or vibrant stripes. You can create a private oasis that makes you feel good—one that provides tranquility, soothes the soul, touches hearts, connects you to nature.

In doing so, perhaps you'll discover—as I did—that our instinctive love for a life spent out of doors can be not just a childhood dream, but a reality.

Kathleen N Brenzel

gardens

A gallery of great gardens from all parts of the West, from woodland to tropical, meadowlike to Mediterranean, contemporary to rustic, coastal to desert, and more.

Forest Fusion

CONTEMPLATING NATURE IN THE CITY

Architect Bob Swain loves to hike the peaks of Washington's Cascade mountains, and he has brought the range's rugged aesthetic to his urban garden. When Swain began the remodel, the garden was no more than a concrete driveway and a few overgrown shrubs and trees. Now, mountain hemlocks skirted with native plantings conceal the garden from the street and remind him of Northwest alpine forests. A walkway of cedar planks leads past Douglas fir, quaking aspen, and bamboo to a meadowlike clearing planted with wildflowers such as bleeding heart *(Dicentra formosa)* and trillium. Hunks of granite salvaged from a Chinese village lead through carpets of salal and pave a quiet seating area. Native

ferns and rhododendron (*R. macrophyllum*) soften the stone and clothe the patio in green.

Asian elements and artifacts fit harmoniously into the natural-looking garden, adding style and an air of timelessness. An upright Buddha stone and Japanese-style water basin and fountain set the tone as you walk toward the meditation wing of the house (converted from an old garage). A sliding glass panel reveals an indoor-outdoor shower. Giant timber bamboo and slatted cedar screens create both privacy and an atmosphere of leafy sanctuary on this transformed city property.

ABOVE *A diminutive city lot didn't prevent Swain from creating his own wooded sanctuary with native plantings. A naturalistic grove of mountain hemlocks screens the cedar plank walkway and entry to the garden's inner spaces.*

FACING PAGE, ABOVE *A slab of granite step, ferns, and a Japanese water basin are framed from inside the house in the Asian manner of blurring the lines between exterior and interior.*

FACING PAGE, BELOW *The small dining terrace is made intimate with a surround of house, arbor, breezeway, and giant timber bamboo. The base of the glass-topped table is a Chinese granite mortar.*

RIGHT *A wooden deck extends behind the meditation house. The open arbor carries the roofline of the house out into the garden, and provides support for climbing vines.*

ABOVE *Salvaged metal was used to create this shade arbor; the criss-crossed rafters cast interesting patterns on the scored concrete below. The patio is surrounded with fragrant lavender and rosemary; roses clamber aloft.*

Steeled to Perfection

RUSTED YET RICH

The difference between a good landscape and a great one lies in the details. Steven and Kimberly Cook's garden in Napa Valley, California, designed by Jack Chandler, creates a bold statement with an unusual collection of substantial steel elements—including an arbor, 2-inch-thick steel plate retaining walls, light fixtures, and sculptures. Metal was even used to form a rill carrying water from a fountain near the house to the low end of the garden.

Surprisingly, it is the material's rusted patina that gives the garden warmth; without the rust, the steel might appear cold or industrial-looking. Drifts of graceful grasses, perennials, and silvery lamb's ears further soften the steel edges.

Chandler, who makes furniture and sculpture in addition to designing landscapes, had used scrap steel in his work for years, but this was his first attempt to use it in place of wood or other materials in the garden. In spite of the logistical challenges presented by such heavy materials, the steel was very successful and is likely to endure for many years.

ABOVE *Stone balls roll into place amid plantings of easy-to-care-for grasses and drought-tolerant herbs including lavender. The plantings stand up well to the hot Napa Valley sun.*

LEFT *Set atop a simple plinth, twisted metal sculptures glow in the setting sun, enhanced by the feathery sunlit grasses and sedges planted throughout the garden.*

Fantasy Island

HOME FOR THE HOLIDAYS

Before he ever set foot on an island, Greg Asbagh was smitten with the tropical landscaping he saw in the movies. A Caribbean honeymoon and other trips to the tropics set the hook deeper. So it was inevitable that when Greg and his wife, Maria, moved to the mild climate of coastal Southern California, he seized the opportunity to create his own private paradise.

A large pool with several waterfalls and a swim-through grotto went in first. The pool's bottom has a mix of aqua and black pebbles, which disguise its shallow depth. The sides are shaped with black artificial rock that simulates lava; the black Buckingham slate edging it looks like a natural continuation of the pool's basin.

The luxuriant greenery that surrounds the pool makes the garden feel like an authentic island retreat. First, Asbagh put in a canopy of palms and flowering trees; then he filled in an understory of ferns, philodendrons, and ti plants. The final touches are provided by low-growing bromeliads, New Guinea impatiens, and the traditional Hawaiian groundcover Moses-in-the-boat. "It's a true tropical garden," says Asbagh. "Not an inch of bare earth showing."

RIGHT *Tropical plants edge the lagoon-like pool, which has a shallow "beach" and a waterfall at opposite ends. Raised beds surrounding the pool are filled with flowers many gardeners grow as houseplants, including gingers, bougainvillea, plumeria, and bromeliads.*

FACING PAGE *A palm grows through the deck and rises above a table like a living umbrella.* "Blue Hawaii *was my favorite movie for the scenery alone,*" *says Asbagh.*

RIGHT *At pool's edge, palms wave above bromeliads and a potted pineapple. Giant flowering banana (*Musa ornata*) and ti plant (*Cordyline fruticosa*) are in the background.*

BELOW *Plenty of outdoor lighting keeps the garden feeling festive at night. This wooden lantern casts a glow on the surrounding tropical foliage; it sits atop a column of stone and slate. A topping of thatch echoes a palapa-style umbrella on a nearby patio.*

Cactus Checkerboard

A GARDEN WITH GEOMETRY

Escondido resident Peter Bailey doesn't own a lawn-mower and doesn't intend to. Instead of a thirsty, high-maintenance lawn, Bailey—an engineer—land-scaped 700 square feet behind his contemporary home in Escondido, California, with a grid of 2-foot concrete squares, crushed rock, and cactus. Outdoor living spaces flank other sides of the house, so the goal for this area was simply to make it look good both from eye level and from the house's second-story windows.

Before planting, Bailey leveled the soil, installed a weed barrier of black plastic, and outlined the grid using stakes and string. He arranged 25 precast con-crete squares in 5 rows, 2 feet apart. Crushed rock, chosen to harmonize with a backdrop of granite boul-ders, fills the rest of the grid and extends beyond it. Where the lines of crushed rock intersect, he cut 12-inch-diameter holes in the plastic, then planted a golden barrel cactus *(Echinocactus grusonii)* in each (16 total). He also installed drip irrigation, but he seldom uses it (only about twice a month in summer).

To add character to the checkerboard and visually tie it to its surroundings, Bailey removed one of the squares and replaced it with a tree aloe *(Aloe arborescens);* its leafy topknot echoes the silhouettes of palms and agaves on the rocky slope nearby.

ABOVE *Curvaceous and sculptural, agaves suit the architecture of the house.*

FACING PAGE *Golden barrel cacti* (Echinocactus) *surround a tall tree aloe. Each cactus gets an occasional sweeping with a broom to clear pebbles and leaf litter. Behind, a succulent mix grows among the boulders.*

BELOW *A planting of silvery blue agaves, red-tinged flapjack plant* (Kalanchoe thyrsiflora), *and blue* Senecio *resembles an underwater scene.*

ABOVE *Jutting off the house's great room, the reflecting pool stretches for over 100 feet. Neat rows of blue oat grass* (Helictotrichon sempervirens) *match the natural geometry of the many slender-trunked aspens* (Populus tremuloides) *on the property.*

Mountain Retreat

A FINE SENSE OF PLACE

The Grand Teton country in Wyoming is rugged and remote. This garden honors that native ecosystem. Sweeping views of meadows and mountains lend a peaceful quality to a property that was once a working ranch and cattle farm.

The garden's contemporary design, by Mark Hershberger, Bruce Greig, and Greg Stewart of Hershberger Design in Jackson, Wyoming, slips seamlessly into the surrounding countryside. This was achieved through the use of indigenous materials combined with plantings of native trees and shrubs. Local sandstone paves the terraces and patios around the house, as well as the paths that lead enticingly out into the meadows. Quaking aspens shelter the terraces, lending leafy shade on hot summer days. A long, narrow reflecting pool serves as a focal point, mirroring the drama of the changing sky and clouds.

ABOVE *Stands of native trees, sweeps of meadow grasses, and paths of warm-toned sandstone create a feeling of spacious tranquility in this Wyoming garden.*

LEFT *Cushioned outdoor furniture lends comfort and scale to the terraces and patios, built of native sandstone and detailed with strips of river rock.*

RIGHT *Are we indoors or out? Designer Steve Martino blurs the lines with a window cut into a stucco wall, encouraging breezes to blow through the outdoor rooms while framing a dramatic view of cactus.*

BELOW *Bold geometry suits the drama of the desert. Angled walls and contemporary water features shelter and cool the garden from the harshness of the desert just outside.*

FACING PAGE *The intense violet of the wall plays up the textural, curvy chairs and potted plant juxtaposed with smooth stone paving, tree branches, and a sleek fall of water. Crimson cactus blooms (inset) add spots of color.*

Desert Oasis
STYLED FOR OUTDOOR LIVING

Phoenix-based landscape architect Steve Martino is known for his designs that celebrate the Southwest desert in all its showy colors and austere beauty. When Andrea and Thomas Kotoske of Paradise Valley, Arizona, decided they wanted to remodel their older home to create more usable outdoor living space, they called on Martino to blend architecture with plants in patios that beckon and delight.

Now entire walls of the house slide open to terraces cooled by fans and falls of water. Cool gray stone walls retain a smooth-as-glass water feature. Cushioned, curvaceous chairs woven of water hyacinth invite repose. Boldly colored stucco walls spotlight the sculptural shapes of native desert plants, playing up the drama of spines and spikes. Mature palo verde trees cast shade to mitigate desert temperatures, making the outdoor rooms habitable year-round.

Slope Solution

CARVING OUT SPACE FOR A GARDEN

Usable outdoor space is a scarce commodity in steeply sloping gardens. But the Myers family was able to carve out enough room behind their turn-of-the-century home in Piedmont, California, for comfortable seating and a dining table as well as fragrant flowers and a fireplace. They hired landscape designers Richard Sullivan and Shari Bashin-Sullivan of Enchanting Planting in Orinda, California, to update the garden and find more level space for outdoor living. The designing duo began by ridding the property of a cramped concrete patio and unsightly old wooden retaining walls. They whittled out the bank behind the house to create sufficient level area for a spacious flagstone terrace, surrounded with angled stone and stucco walls. The wall's niches and corners house the wood-burning fireplace and provide planting pockets for a tumble of nasturtiums and scented heliotrope. Now the old house opens out to a paved, open-air room tucked snugly between slope and house, with plenty of space for plantings, entertaining, and eating outside.

FACING PAGE *The new flagstone terrace is large enough to serve as an outdoor living room for Zelie and Jack Myers and their four children. A sturdy trellis creates a shady grotto for the hot tub, while seating areas bask in sunshine and the fragrance of flowers.*

RIGHT *Raised planting beds and the outdoor fireplace are faced in stone, which contrasts with the smooth stucco of taller retaining walls. Tiered planters hold an inspired mix of flowering plants that soften the scene and perfume the air, including pale hydrangeas, dark purple heliotrope, angel's trumpet, and 'Peaches and Cream' nasturtiums.*

Floral Ribbons

COLOR WEAVES THROUGH THE GARDEN

The flower borders that wind through Betty Taylor's garden in Ketchum, Idaho, look so carefully planned you might assume that months of thought went into every subtle color nuance before the soil was ever turned. But that's not the case.

"I plunged right in and started to plant," Taylor says.

To give the planting some height, Taylor built a berm of soil down the center of the empty bed. Then she started designing by placing the plants—still in their nursery containers—on the soil, adjusting them until she liked the way they worked together. She placed tall plants in the back or clustered them atop the berm, then put the lower plants in front.

"As the border began to grow and fill in, I noticed flower colors that clashed," she says. "But I replaced them, and the border has continued to evolve."

What makes the flower show so striking every summer? For starters, the rich colors and textures that weave themselves together like a braid of pretty ribbons. Spikes of silvery lamb's ears create vertical brush strokes, while the same bright pinks, blues, and white repeat throughout the gently curving border. Large flowered plants like pale yellow daylilies and pink poppies add accents among a haze of smaller blooms.

ABOVE *Color echoes are found throughout the garden. Here, pale yellow yarrow picks up on the hue of butter-colored columbines; white Queen Anne's lace blooms between them.*

LEFT *White and peach lilies create cool contrasts for more richly hued annuals and perennials.*

FACING PAGE *Blue-green conifers create a striking backdrop for the gently curving border in Betty Taylor's garden. Deep-pink sweet William and poppies add punch to soft pastels found in the blooms of lavender ornamental allium, yellow daylilies, silvery lamb's ears, and tall, lavender-blue Salvia sclarea.*

Historic Hilltop
INTIMATE GARDEN ROOMS

This property sits at the crest of a hill on part of the historic Polmood Farm near Santa Fe, overlooking the Jemez and Sangre de Cristo mountains. Both the house and garden were designed to fit into this spectacular natural setting, as well as to enhance water conservation and fire prevention.

As the land slopes steeply down to the Tesuque Creek, it is crisscrossed by natural arroyos that feed storm waters into the creek. Above the house, trenches filled with straw bales help to capture some of the storm water and thus prevent erosion further down the hillside. Roof *canales*, or water spouts, divert water from the flat adobe roof down into the garden. Finally, in addition to providing spectacular views toward the mountains, the pool doubles as a water reservoir in case of fire.

The landscape architecture firm Design Workshop created a series of modest-size garden rooms around the house, including several courtyards and patios, a family dining and play area complete with sandbox, an herb garden, and the pool area. A guesthouse has its own garden space, where both people and plants (such as columbines, coral bells, and daylilies) find shelter under a grove of quaking aspens.

ABOVE *Uphill from the house, the slope is blanketed with blue grama grass* (Bouteloua gracilis) *and dotted with purple prairie clover* (Dalea purpurea). *The landscape beyond is covered with native piñon pine and juniper.*

FACING PAGE *Stepping-stones lead through a garden terrace to a set of sandstone steps softened with plantings of creeping thyme. The gate marks the entrance to the pool area.*

RIGHT AND BELOW *Heavy wooden gates and decorative fixtures are embellished with metal filigree in keeping with the Southwest style of the house.*

Structural Simplicity

CONTEMPORARY COURTYARD

ABOVE *Viewed from the entry courtyard, the poplar trees rustle in the breeze. Chandler chose them for their graceful, pyramidal shape and pale gold fall color.*

ABOVE RIGHT *Set into an alcove by the door, a slender wall sculpture shaped like a kayak suggests water and knife-edge simplicity.*

Outside the entrance to Jack Chandler's Napa Valley garden is an unusual parking area consisting of an even grid of poplar trees. Their slender trunks echo the simple lines of the long, low house set in a wooded canyon. Every flicker and sway of the poplars makes shadows that dance across the house's pale stucco walls. Another grid—a deep red metal gate—beckons visitors toward an entry courtyard, scented with citrus trees and enlivened by a trickle of water from a fountain. Inside the courtyard, paving and pebbles are dotted with fallen leaves that form an ever-changing mosaic on the floor.

The simple calm that pervades the courtyard is due to a limited number of carefully chosen elements. A steel sculpture of books set in a cabinet along with a card catalog—an homage to Chandler's wife, who is a librarian—rests against a vivid golden orange wall. An alcove beside the door holds a simple but elegant wall sculpture. This garden space demands little, yet it's soothing and powerful.

ABOVE *A sculpture by Jack Chandler matches the simple yet strong geometry of the courtyard's walls and floor.*

ABOVE *Combinations of drought-tolerant plantings line a gentle slope in Stacie Crooks's front yard. They include euphorbia, phormiums, yarrow, and sedums. Passersby can enjoy a sweeping view of the garden from the street below.*

FACING PAGE, ABOVE *A water basin filled with floating plants and a colorful ball accents a planting bed; the basin is surrounded with beach pebbles and fronted with pansies.*

FACING PAGE, BELOW *Lilies, coppery yarrow* (Achillea millefolium *'Terra Cotta'), and spiny, steel-blue sea holly* (Eryngium) *blend with blooming blue oat grass.*

Traffic-stopping Tapestry

PLENTIFUL PLANTINGS IN THE SUBURBS

Garden designer Stacie Crooks reshaped her garden to deal with changing weather patterns that have turned the Northwest climate more summer-dry Mediterranean than drizzly England. She tore out 2,700 square feet of hot, west-facing front lawn and replaced it with less-thirsty plants. The new garden serves as a living laboratory of drought-tolerance, as well as an attention-getting tapestry of flowers and foliage.

In just two years, Crooks's efforts resulted in abundant planting beds bisected by paths. Small shrubs, tall grasses, and perennials coexist happily, providing fragrance, textural interest, and seasonal color. Low maintenance is important for this busy mother of two, who practices what she calls "fusion gardening." "Plant everything closely and it fuses together so that you can't see the weeds," she explains.

The garden is hedged for privacy with a diverse tapestry of plants including rockrose, rugosa roses, *Elaeagnus,* evergreen *Ceanothus thyrsiflorus* 'Victoria', potentilla, and golden-leafed catalpas. The plants are cut back every winter; they grow large enough to obscure the road but not a water view. A backbone of evergreens carries the garden through the winter, such as *Viburnum tinus* 'Spring Bouquet', *Viburnum davidii,* lacy nandina, rosemary, and *Ilex crenata* 'Green Island', a Japanese holly Crooks describes as a "3 to 4 foot bump of texture."

The real glories of the drought-tolerant border are Crooks's grasses and perennials, planted in substantial swathes for real impact. Iris, wallflowers, alliums, and *Euphorbia characias wulfenii* and *E.* × *martinii* start the border out with a burst of springtime color. Silvery artemisia, *Senecio greyi* 'Sunshine', and Russian sage cool down red hot *Crocosmia* 'Lucifer' and bright ▶

ABOVE Aster × frikartii *and silvery* Senecio greyi *'Sunshine' are backed by the year-round structure of phormium and euphorbia.*

RIGHT *Crooks selected easy-care plants with a long season of interest such as succulents and little starry Mexican daisy* (Erigeron).

orange *Geum chiloense* 'Mrs. Bradshaw'. The flowers of coppery-toned yarrow (*Achillea millefolium* 'Terra Cotta') play off dark, purple-brown phormium. The narrow silvery leaves of the maiden grass *Miscanthus sinensis* 'Gracillimus' and the blades of blue oat grass *(Helictotrichon sempervirens)* fluff out the plantings. By late summer, willowy *Verbena bonariensis* and Joe Pye weed (*Eupatorium purpureum)* swamp the paths. The garden has a fresh flush of bloom in autumn with clumps of rudbeckia, sedums, and asters.

RIGHT *Nandinas,* Viburnum davidii, *and a host of heathers take center stage once the perennials have finished their summer show.*

BELOW *Fluid clumps of Japanese forest grass (*Hakonechloa macra *'Aureola') trim the paths and edges of the garden.*

Adobe Courtyard

SMALL AND STYLISH IN SANTA FE

This downtown refuge brings a refreshing new twist to traditional Southwest gardens. Using an earthy color scheme, Catherine Clemens and Elizabeth Robechek transformed a blank space into a contemporary retreat. All the elements are custom-built—from the black-bottom spa surrounded by stained concrete coping to the polished granite table with wood-and-metal stools.

The plantings are spare, in keeping with the area's minimal rainfall. A grove of aspens, set in "pools" of river rock, provides four seasons of interest as spring greens give way to glossy summer color, then turn to brilliant yellow before falling to highlight the tree's smooth, gray-green bark.

FACING PAGE *Understated lines prevail in the courtyard, including a long, narrow granite table and the single arc of a spa railing that is repeated in the metal legs of stools gathered around the table.*

ABOVE *A small grove of aspens fills a corner of the courtyard. The trees' flickering leaves are reflected in the lacquerlike surface of the table and the deep blue spa water.*

RIGHT *Adornment is often most striking in its simplicity. This sun-and-moon wall sculpture is framed with slender rays. Peeled logs line the walls as a reminder of Southwest style.*

Hollywood High

SLEEK AND STYLISH IN L.A.

Perched high in the Hollywood Hills with sweeping views of Los Angeles, this garden reflects the style of the midcentury modern house it surrounds. The home's simple and distinctive architecture sets the tone for the garden, creating a smooth transition from indoors to out. Owner Judy Kameon of Elysian Landscapes was inspired by L.A. designers from the forties and fifties, specifically by the work of landscape architect James Rose. Quintessentially Southern California, the garden is made for outdoor living, with a spacious patio and flexible furniture groupings. Oversized square pavers zigzag through the lawn in a bold, graphic pattern that visually widens the narrow lot. Masses of spiky phormiums and agaves add to the strong design while ornamental grasses round off its hard edges.

The warm-toned color palette of burgundy, gray, and green foliage plants plays up the Southern California climate. Pots and throw cushions provide colorful accents. Hoop chairs and other casual, retro furnishings are grouped and scattered about to invite relaxation and conversation. A cushioned bench long enough for two people to lie down fits in a sheltered spot that affords the best views of the city. While the symphony of ornamental grasses and bamboo clothes the garden in color and texture, the space is all about cool urban aesthetics and outdoor living.

ABOVE *Simplicity, line, and comfort, with cushioned bench and architectural plantings, rule in this sleek urban garden. The bed behind the bench is thickly planted to screen out the neighboring house.*

FACING PAGE *Elms provide some shade and shelter in this windy and mostly sunny hilltop garden. Artemisia, phormiums, and cordyline are grouped beneath the elms. Soft textural fountain grasses move with the wind and look good year-round.*

LEFT *The owners pulled a long table up to this built-in bench for the first Thanksgiving in their new garden, now two years old. Red cushions and glazed pots add further accents of color. A bowl fountain gently burbles.*

Native Pleasures

ON A WOODED ISLAND

When Deborah and Jim Heg moved from a 5,000-square-foot lot in Sausalito, California, to a waterfront lot on Whidbey Island, Washington, they were determined to capture the essence of their heavily treed property rather than transform it. They revel in the green and brown of native plants, the moss and shade, and their wide-open view of Puget Sound and snowcapped Olympic Mountains. Their lodgelike home settles into the curve of the land as if it had grown there.

Several mammoth Douglas firs fell during a windstorm, bisecting the lawns with their horizontal lines. The Hegs simply started with the fallen trees and landscaped outward, cutting into the lawn. Salal and ferns now partly cover the downed trees. Snags and broken stumps are treated as sculptural reminders of the property's history and left to sprout huckleberries and provide wildlife habitat. The Hegs have tamed five acres and left the other 17 acres as woodland and trails.

A curving, fern-lined driveway follows the route of an old logging road, winding past garages, a guesthouse, and a studio on its way to the main house. Even before the house was finished, they dug a round reflecting pond that forms the calm and secret heart of the property.

The Hegs found many native plants clustered beneath the firs and cedars. Rhodendrons, deciduous huckleberries, salal, sword ferns, foam flower, ocean spray, false lily-of-the-valley, and Oregon grape were thriving even on Whidbey's limited rainfall. Introduced plants include serviceberry, evergreen huckleberries, and more native rhododendrons.

Deer are as much a problem here as sun, wind, and drought, but the Hegs use no deer fences except in an enclosed garden, where Deborah grows plants the pests find especially tasty. Raised beds hold fruits and vegetables, as well as dahlias, roses, honeysuckle, and peonies.

On the water side of the house, granite terraces face southwest for a full dose of sunshine and sunsets. A totem pole carved by local artist Glen Russell is just shoreward from the view, at the site of the original cabin on the property. Native Americans placed such totems to welcome visitors, and the Hegs have placed theirs looking out to sea to greet guests arriving by boat.

FACING PAGE *The property is divided up by outbuildings and pathways as much as by trees and island plantings. Here* Clematis montana *smothers the studio with its fragrant flowers in spring.*

ABOVE *An old metal urn planted with plants that have variegated foliage provides a subtle focal point among the rhododendrons and fir trees. The plants add splashes of sunshiny color in the shade.*

Foreign Affair

CLASSIC BLUE ON BLUE

The West Hollywood garden of photographer Jeff Dunas and jewelry and garden designer Laura Morton reflects the couple's world travels and eclectic tastes. Morton designed the garden for outdoor living, with firepit, fountain, and lots of room for lounging. The warm Southern California climate is ideal for the mostly Mediterranean garden, which complements the style of the white concrete house. Cushioned benches,

a blue-and-white tiled patio, lanterns, and patterned pillows enliven spaces made for entertaining. A Moroccan-tiled water feature with bubbling fountain and jeweled edges, swimming pool, and octagonal gas firepit complete the scene of sumptuous comfort.

Citrus and banana trees emphasize the exotic feel of the garden, where guests can reach up to pluck figs, tangerines, limes, persimmons, or blood oranges.

"My husband and I wanted to add a sense of other-worldliness while keeping the overall feel relaxed," says designer Morton. "The architecture remains formal, and the plantings and pot groupings soften it and add a bit of wildness."

FACING PAGE *An Aegean blue wall, an explosion of fennel in a vase, and a custom-made tile table further the Mediterranean feel of the garden.*

ABOVE *Morton fitted an old Moroccan pot with a pump to create a bubbly fountain, and repeated the blue-and-white tile from the terrace on the raised pond.*

LEFT *The tiled terrace, centered with a gas-and-sand firepit and ringed with built-in banquettes, was designed to look out over a swimming pool. The little African stools add to the eclectic feel of this culturally diverse garden.*

Natural Elegance

PLANTING TO SUIT THE SITE

ABOVE *A simple arrangement of right-angled walls contains and separates the inner and outer landscapes, without visually blocking either completely. The wooden slatted fence warms up the cool combo of slate blue wall and 'Tuscan Blue' rosemary.*

FACING PAGE *The horizontal lines of the house extend out into the pool court-yard, the geometry playing off plantings of 'Tuscan Blue' rosemary,* Euphorbia rigida, *and* Olea europaea *'Little Ollie'.*

Marie and Jeff Moore had already remodeled and updated their ranch-style home in Los Altos Hills, opening the long, slender house to views of the outdoors. When they wanted to transform their windy hillside into a serene and livable garden, they hired Bernard Trainor to design around the challenges of harsh wind, clay soil, and browsing deer. To meld indoors and out, Trainor used landscaping materials similar to the house for a custom-designed glass-tile pool and hot tub. Steel fences and gates and slatted horizontal timber screens reflect the style of the modern home while serving as focal points in the garden.

Trainor selected tough plants that could tolerate both the warm and windy climate and the owners' desire to forgo deer fencing. Olive trees, sturdy ornamental grasses, drought-tolerant perennials, and a sedge lawn ▶

appear to blend the garden with the surrounding terrain. The rectangular pool, the horizontal lines of the slatted screens, and the curve of concrete walls visually tie the landscape back into the house. Trainor skillfully used stone and gravel to give the new garden a sense of age and permanence, and to create restful expanses of open space between the plantings. The smooth surfaces of the concrete water bowl and the pool further the sense of peaceful repose and serenity.

ABOVE *Alongside the pool, unthirsty plants create a tailored yet contemporary living fringe. A silvery hedge of dwarf olive (*Olea europaea *'Little Ollie') edges the concrete. Willowy tussocks of the restio* Thamnochortus insignis *rise behind. Simplicity of line and repetition of planting combine with the pool's reflective surface to create an atmosphere of serenity and contemplation.*

RIGHT *A concrete water bowl is a dramatic focal point in this quiet garden, its shape echoed by a curving concrete wall. In the background, drought-tolerant sturdy plantings include* Phormium *'Dusky Chief' and* Euphorbia amygdaloides robbiae.

ABOVE *The approach to the Moore property is casual and understated, with a stone and gravel walkway shaded by the gnarly, red-trunked* Arbutus *'Marina' trees and valley oak. The path is edged with the soft grasses* Carex tumulicola *and* Stipa arundinacea.

RIGHT *A casual tousle of native lawn softens the expanses of gravel and stone, surrounded by silvery olives, dark spikes of* Phormium *'Dusky Chief', and deer grass* (Muhlenbergia).

Tea and Tranquility

INSPIRED BY JAPAN

The inspiration for Richard Faylor's teahouse garden came from his seven-year stay in Osaka, Japan, where he worked as a writer. "The Japanese have figured out how to borrow a little piece of nature and immerse themselves in it," he says.

After a hectic workday in Boise, Faylor dons a pair of slippers, strolls into his backyard, and sits back in his teahouse. Reclining on the futon, he gazes upon goldfish and koi swirling in the nearby pond and listens to softly falling water.

Faylor built the teahouse himself in just a few days. The redwood-framed structure, which measures 7 feet wide, 6 feet long, and 4 feet, 4 inches tall, has a concrete-tile roof. In the evening, a lamp provides gentle reading light and illuminates a pattern in the wall.

The garden's lean planting scheme includes Hall's honeysuckle, a Japanese maple, and Oregon grape. The pond is fringed with sweet alyssum, *Vinca minor,* and woolly thyme.

ABOVE *A patio of pavers laid on sand links the teahouse with the pond. Faylor dug the pond two feet deep, lined it with rubber sheeting, built waterfalls at both ends, and installed a recirculating pump.*

INSET *A "moon window" shadow is cast on a wall.*

48

ABOVE *When evening falls, soft lights come on in the teahouse and the faux stone lantern beside the pond. A sense of enclosure gives the garden an air of tranquility. "The walls enclose the garden, and the teahouse encloses the viewer."*

Exotic Nights

MARRAKESH MEETS THE TROPICS

Eva Schwartz, trained in architecture but new to landscaping, capitalized on her Southern California climate to create a Moorish extravaganza of a garden. Colorful tiles, fringed parasols, and brightly embroidered and patterned fabrics set the mood along with tropical tree ferns and banana trees. From black bamboo chairs to Mexican tin lanterns, this retreat mixes ethnic influences freely to create a personal fantasyland.

Schwartz began her garden remodel by carving out four flat terraces from the steep, weedy hillside behind her contemporary Pasadena home. The sunny

BELOW *Underwater night lighting dramatically plays up the water features, and encourages lingering outdoors on balmy evenings. The tent furthers the casbah theme, with curtains that can be opened to the breezes or closed for warmth and privacy.*

site is ideal for growing large-leafed and bright-flowering tropicals like hibiscus, plumeria, bird of paradise, and cannas. Aiming for a junglelike effect, the designer planted showy red banana trees *(Ensete ventricosum),* giant timber bamboo *(Bambusa oldhamii),* palms, and philodendrons, then mulched around them, Hawaii-style, with dark lava rock.

A swimming pool lures visitors to the garden's lowest level. Influenced by the memory of fashion designer Yves St. Laurent's estate in Marrakesh, Schwartz painted the stucco wall next to the pool cobalt and installed wall fountains that spill into the pool. She outfitted a cushion-filled tent with diaphanous curtains. Guests can lounge here in draped splendor amidst Indian print cottons, or settle nearby on a curved and cushioned bench.

ABOVE *This suburban garden conjures memories of far-flung vacations that Schwartz took with her geologist father. Showy exotics, large-leafed foliage plants, and eye-catching decor create the feel of a tropical oasis.*

RIGHT *Orange cannas (inset), fragrant plumeria, bird of paradise, and red bananas spill over a walkway of black lava rock. A bevy of colorful Balinese baskets lines the path.*

ABOVE *A green glazed pot filled with tiki torches stands beside the garden doorway. Inside, a pathway winds through a small garden beside the guesthouse. The limestone pavers edged with ferns, bamboo, and bromeliads lead to a Buddha statue.*

ABOVE RIGHT *Crimson and scarlet bougainvillea drape themselves over the simple white walls of the garden as a climbing fig clambers upward. Rosemary and olive trees fringe the path.*

FACING PAGE *Large windows in the main house look out over the mature palms, giant banana, and bird-of-paradise plants below. More bougainvillea frames a wrought-iron balcony railing.*

Resort Living

BRINGING HOME THE HOTEL

Robert Glazier fell in love with hotels when working as a busboy at a Sheraton Hotel. "It was a place where the environment was relaxed and people came to have fun," he says. Thirty years later, Glazier is an architect who designs hotels and resorts all over the world. He brings the spirit of this work to the home he shares with his wife, Kelli, on a modest lot in Palo Alto, California.

The house is a contemporary take on Spanish colonial revival, inspired by local architecture. The white stucco walls, central entry courtyard, and tile roof are reminiscent of a traditional Mediterranean house. Kelli, an artist, chose colors and furnishings for the house—inside and out—that create an atmosphere of spalike serenity. Vivid splashes of color come from the tropical plants—palms, bougainvillea, and potted succulents among them. Special touches from the couple's travels add soul to the space and make it personal. It goes to show, Robert Glazier says, that "You can design something that is sympathetic to history, but totally new."

Indonesian Elegance

NORTHWEST WOODLAND ZEN

Faced with the challenge of a typically wooded hillside near Seattle, Ilga Jansons and Michael Dryfoos created a series of garden rooms connected by a network of pathways. These different areas reflect the couple's varied interests. Jansons refers to the garden as "pan-Asian fusion" for its mix of objects, including a Shinto shrine–like structure, various Buddhas, carved panels, bronze lions, and stone carvings.

The couple began the Ridge Garden in 1996 as a retreat and a setting for parties. Even though they were novice gardeners, they thought big, perhaps as a result of working at megacorporation Microsoft. When a nearby nursery went out of business, they bought 350 mature rhododendrons to make a near-instant garden beneath the canopy of big-leaf maples and Douglas

FACING PAGE, ABOVE *The centerpiece of the Asian garden is the hundred-year-old teak* joglo *(Javanese house) that is used as a moon-viewing pavilion. Other structures in the garden, including the tree house, were designed by Ilga Jansons.*

FACING PAGE, BELOW *The tree house high in the tree canopy contains a brightly dressed bed for summer sleep outs.*

LEFT *An elaborate system of streams, waterfalls, and ponds recirculates 350 gallons of water per minute. The koi are kept safe from predators thanks to the steep sides of the pond—which deter raccoons—and the trees overhead, which deter hawks and herons.*

BELOW *Two sets of steps lead to the tree house, which offers fine views of sunrises and glimpses of mountains over the treetops.*

firs. Underneath, astilbes, epimedium, ferns, foam-flower *(Tiarella),* hostas, primroses, pulmonaria, and trilliums pattern the ground.

Over the years the couple continued to buy property until the garden stretched over seven precipitously steep acres. Various landscape designers helped out with specific projects, but Jansons chose all the plants and put them into the ground herself. "I started out with hybrid rhododendrons, and have grown into species," she says.

Dryfoos has a love of high places, and his study of classical Indonesian music inspired the various structures set into the garden. A tree house furnished with a bed and decorated with carved Asian doors and prayer flags affords views out over the treetops to the mountains.

Modernist Vision

THE HOLLYWOOD JUNGLE

Jim Goldstein needed to travel far beyond familiar plantings to complement his ultracontemporary residence high above Benedict canyon. How can a garden compete with such architectural bravado? The fireworks start at the entrance, where more than 70 cycads decorate the front drive and slabs of stepping stones lead across a koi-filled pond to the front door.

Designed in 1963 by John Lautner and restored by Goldstein, the house is linked to the garden with vast expanses of glass and a viewing terrace overhanging the steep site. Designer Eric Nagelmann of Santa Barbara created a Bali-like fantasyland by planting

mature palms, hundreds of exotics, and 25 different kinds of banana trees between the existing pines and eucalyptus. Tons of good soil were hauled in, and an irrigation system was installed to dispense fertilizer and water to keep the jungly plants thriving. In the shade of the jungle, split-leaf philodendrons *(Monstera deliciosa),* Australian tree ferns, hibiscus, and protea form an otherwordly understory. To continue the angular architectural style of the house down the hillside, a zigzag path leads down several hundred steps into the garden. Along the way, the slope is interrupted with unexpected seating areas and garden sculpture.

FACING PAGE *Goldstein remodeled the house with expanses of glass to overlook his jungle paradise, which fills the canyon below. Mature palms provide privacy, but around the perimeter of the Hollywood Hills property he preserved spectacular views by planting low-growing zoysia grass, along with lantana, cannas, and kangaroo paws (Anigozanthos flavidus).*

RIGHT *The hard-edged architecture of Goldstein's futuristic house extends out into the garden, its edges softened by verdant foliage.*

BELOW *Concrete pavers traverse a lotus-filled koi pond to reach the front door. Clumps of taro rise from the water and capture sunlight in their leaves.*

ABOVE *An arbor fashioned of red alder leading to the back patio is covered with clematis and the climbing roses pale-yellow 'Malvern Hills' and salmon-pink 'Soaring Flight'. Stachys byzantina 'Big Ears' and Geranium × riversleaianum 'Russell Prichard' edge a perennial bed.*

Home Again
A GARDEN OF PLENTY

When Birgit Piskor moved back into her childhood home in Victoria, B.C., there weren't many plants but there were plenty of memories. She had grown up in the 1908 Edwardian home on a corner lot in one of the city's oldest neighborhoods. Trees that she had planted with her father now towered over the house, and an 80-year-old painted checkerboard patio that she had played on as a child was still there. But there was still much to do to make it a garden.

First, she removed the lawn in the narrow spaces on each side of the house and built fences and arbors of red alder to define a series of garden rooms. Piskor spent hours hauling pebbles from a nearby beach and set them into concrete to make pathways; similar pebble mosaics grace a fountain and edging strips for beds and borders. Finally, she started to plant.

It's hard to believe Piskor wasn't a gardener before she created this lush and colorful space. Every inch of sideyard, front yard, and back patio is filled with an exuberant mix of perennials, grasses, roses, and vines. Evergreen shrubs provide year-round structure. As a final touch, she crafted concrete columns and containers. Their earthy colors provide a contrast to the riot of colorful plants.

ABOVE LEFT *Piskor harvests red alder branches from clear-cut lumber sites on Vancouver Island and weaves them into wattle fences. This hot-colored fenceside combination includes the coneflower 'Mango Meadowbright', variegated* Heliopsis helianthoides *'Lorraine Sunshine', and* Coreopsis verticillata *'Moonbeam'.*

ABOVE *This narrow sideyard holds a mix of shade-loving shrubs and perennials on one side; to the right are plants that like a bit more sun. Purple-foliaged* Oxalis vulcanicola *'Zinfandel' spills from one of Piskor's handmade concrete containers.*

LEFT *The checkerboard patio dates from the 1920s; it is surrounded with packed-to-the-brim borders.*

59

Berkeley Blend

INDIA BY THE BAY

The VonHellen garden in the Berkeley Hills above San Francisco Bay is small and steep. Yet it lives large, thanks to subtle plantings and dramatic accents that blend East Indian and contemporary California sensibilities. The garden has two separate areas, one on each side of the house, each created by different designers. Yet it feels cohesive because both sections, while distinct in character, relate to the house. Both were planned for outdoor living many months of the year, and for enjoying the view year-round.

The first garden, designed by Lisa Ray of Berkeley, is more tropical in flavor. Seen from the living room, it blurs the line between indoors and out with luxuriant and colorful exotic plantings. The intimacy of a paved, enclosed courtyard emphasizes the tropical flair. Banana trees, datura, and papyrus create a bridge between dryland California and the home-owner's memories of flamboyant Indian flora. ▶

LEFT *The tropical side of the garden is shaded by a cobalt blue pergola and filled with exotic plants that thrive in the warm Berkeley Hills. Bold foliage plants like the Bengal Tiger canna* (Canna 'Striata'), *variegated bamboo* (Pleioblastus auricomus), *and ebony-tinged elephant ears* (Colocasia esculenta) *make an exotic picture year-round.*

The second space, a hot, southwest-facing garden designed by Josh Chandler, has as its focal point a cascade of three ponds and a sitting area. Drifts of ornamental grasses in frosted cream and soft green fill beds and edge the paths. They're low maintenance and drought-tolerant, while adding flow, texture, and movement with every breeze. Marigolds and candles often float in a water-filled traditional bronze vessel from Kerala, India, called an *urli*.

FACING PAGE *Sweeps of miscanthus, wild oat grass* (Chasmanthium latifolium), *and frosty curls* (Carex albula) *surround a statue carved from riverbed stone by a family friend.*

ABOVE *The hotter, drier side of the garden is carpeted in a simple palette of ornamental grasses for a lush texture beneath the native oaks. The seating and dining area at the far end of the walkway offers a restful roost in the midst of the garden.*

RIGHT *The use of an antique Indian urli basin personalizes the garden and brings another echo of the owner's homeland.*

Tough Beauties

HOT DESERT COLOR

Barbara Duno's garden in Santa Fe, New Mexico, overflows with so many colorful perennials that it looks as though it might be a grand mixed border at an English manse. And the flowers that fill beds beside her entry gate and around a pond are so lush and abundant that they recall hothouse prima donnas. The truth is, though, that despite their showy appearance, these rugged plants handle alkaline soil, dry weather, and quite a bit of frost. That's because Duno chose them carefully for her garden's site and conditions.

Many of the perennials are tough South African perennials such as hybrid torch lily *(Kniphofia)* — mostly in warmer shades of yellow and orange. She also grows 'Persian Yellow' rugosa roses, shrubby potentilla (in pots), California poppy, and Mexican hat. Violet *Penstemon stricta* provides a gentle contrast. To prevent crown rot caused by winter rains, Duno set plants such as *Kniphofia* higher than the soil line at planting time.

LEFT *Yellow and orange torch lilies and purple penstemons add splashes of color against the home's warm terracotta-colored walls.*

FACING PAGE *A beautiful jumble of plants surrounds a stone-rimmed pond, including lilies about to burst into bloom, roses, and penstemons. Southwest pottery enhances the colorful medley.*

Setting the Stage

A GARDEN OF EARTHLY DELIGHTS

Actor Peter Strauss's Ojai, California, garden is a stage set for his dramatic talents, with a bold array of his favorite thorny and spiny desert plants. It was Strauss's passion for succulents that turned him into a collector and then into a gardener. Although he grows acres of oranges and cultivates roses, he finds room for agaves and cacti and his beloved succulents, which flourish on the hot, dry site 80 miles north of Los Angeles. Rose and perennial beds trim the edge of the hilltop, adding a formal feel in contrast to a flurry of theatrical palms. ▶

FACING PAGE *A view toward the guesthouse, with plantings of cordylines, citrus,* Phlomis fruticosa, *and upright 'Tuscan Blue' rosemary.*

ABOVE *An orchard of mature Valencia orange trees creates a backdrop for the garden, separated from the ornamental plantings by* Elaeagnus pungens. *Spiky* Agave americana, *lime green* Euphorbia characias *in bloom, and bold* Agave salmiaina *'Salm-Dick' scatter the foreground. The apricot rose is 'Just Joey'; 'Mr Lincoln' is the vibrant red rose.*

INSET *Bird of paradise* (Strelitzia reginae) *in bloom. Strauss used to hate this plant, along with oleander and* Podocarpus, *which he referred to as "freeway plants." But he's come to admire its toughness and sculptural integrity in the garden. He says, "A clump in a bed in a lawn is a Southern California mainstay, and a mass of blooms in a tall glass vase ain't bad either!"*

Close to the 1925 restored Spanish colonial revival house, the gardens
are rectilinear and heavily planted with drought-tolerant plants. Decomposed granite paths lead to perennial, native, herb, and cactus gardens. As
the property sweeps away toward the citrus grove and distant views, the
garden curves along the hillside. The canopy of a venerable California live
oak shades the entry to Strauss's hacienda. He and his wife have created
a courtyard for outdoor dining here, with a café table and splashing fountain. In the adjacent garden, enclosed by stucco walls, Strauss grows his
favorite pink roses.

FACING PAGE *The bold, architecturally striking* Agave salmiana *is one of the succulents Strauss collects, despite its wicked spines. Next to it is* Opuntia robusta *('Silver Dollar Opuntia'), another monster of a plant well suited to extremes of temperature and drought.*

INSET *Gazanias from South Africa bloom consistently and dependably through the spring and summer.*

ABOVE *A circle of Adirondack chairs sits under a cluster of native coast live oaks* (Quercus agrifolia) *in the naturalistic part of the garden. While most of the garden is cultivated in orchards or ornamental plantings, Strauss says, "Nature herself can be an astounding landscape architect and sometimes should just be left alone."*

LEFT *A large coast live oak shades the courtyard, which also holds a crabapple tree against the wall, the yellow, tiered blooms of* Phlomis fruticosa, *and 'Tuscan Blue' rosemary, along with the yellow rose 'Lanvin'.*

ABOVE *In the back garden, concrete paving is punctuated by a variety of beds. Concrete cubes act either as planters or cushioned seats. An edible bed of 'Lollo Rosso' lettuce and artichoke is color-coordinated with bamboo, phormiums, cannas, and potted succulents.*

Small Wonder

FRESH IDEAS IN VENICE BEACH

Designer Stefan Hammerschmidt packed dramatic impact into this tiny Venice Beach garden, creating a world apart from the busy urban location for client Stefan Smith. The garden is as clean-lined and sleekly modern as Smith's remodeled 1920 bungalow, which has been transformed into a concrete, wood, and metal loftlike house. Due to the garden owner's hectic work and travel schedule, the garden was planned not only to play off the style of the house, but also to be a low-maintenance urban retreat. Hammerschmidt pushed the limits of the little lot (40 by 120 feet) to create a space that leaves the world behind at the front gate.

The drama begins at the property line, where a B-52 bomber wing forms part of the fencing. The home's entryway is a watery expanse studded with concrete pads for stepping-stones. The garden is serene and green with a miniature bamboo grove and tough ornamental grasses. Smooth concrete forms the hardscape, which includes pavers, steps, raised planters, and cushioned seats. The garden becomes more theatrical at night when the watery entry is lit up and the reflections from the horsetail hedge cast shadows on the airplane-wing fence.

RIGHT *More than a third of the front garden is a lily pond, crossed by concrete slabs that appear to float across the surface of the water. A B-52 bomber wing forms a shiny metal barrier behind a minimalist hedge of horsetail* (Equisetum hyemale).

Valley Sun

A CAREFREE VINEYARD GARDEN

It takes rugged ornamentals to flourish in the summer heat that is ideal for ripening grapes in the Napa Valley. To make a more hospitable environment for this garden, Freeland Tanner of Proscape Landscape Design first built stone walls around the perimeter, then filled the interior with heat-loving plants native to the Mediterranean. Brightly colored masses of sturdy daylilies, carpeting roses, small shrubs, and ornamental grasses create year-round texture and color. The rich mixture of plants softens the bold architecture of the walls and terraces.

BELOW *The fat stucco columns support sturdy rafters, which cast cooling shade on hot afternoons. Oversized pavers are surrounded by low-growing thyme and an inspired mix of barberry, phormiums, helichrysum, and potted rosemary.*

The style of the stucco house is echoed throughout the garden with touches such as classic columns, urns, and spires of rosemary in terra-cotta pots. This artfulness lends sophistication to the colorful, cottage garden–style plantings while defining open-air seating areas for sipping coffee on crisp mornings or dining on warm evenings. An arbor built with oversize columns defines the patio and provides shelter from summer's triple-digit temperatures.

RIGHT *Sweeps of pink 'Flower Carpet' roses, grasses, and long-blooming, drought-tolerant perennials like catmint (*Nepeta *'Six Hills Giant') lead the eye through the garden to the distant view.*

BELOW *Designer Freeland Tanner bermed planting beds for good drainage and laid out pathways between tough, drought-tolerant plantings of lamb's ears, daylilies, and Mexican feather grass (*Nassella tenuissima*).*

Simple Serenity

BORROWING DESERT VIEWS

Simplicity of design gives this Scottsdale, Arizona, garden a Zenlike atmosphere. The property enjoys views of Black Mountain and a desert panorama. To blur the boundaries between the garden and the surrounding desert, designer-builder Peter Magee used a few tricks. A giant "window" in a wall on one side of the patio frames views in that direction; the infinity-edge swimming pool, surfaced with black Pebble Tec (a nonslip, textured pool finish), drops off to meet the desert.

Sonoran Desert Designs planted the site lightly to enhance—not compete with—these backdrops. A gnarled 150-year-old ironwood tree was brought in with a crane. Agave in a large stone pot adds drama to the hardscape; beyond, mesquite and other native shrubs provide a subtle transition zone between garden and desert.

RIGHT *Water for the pool cascades from a cantera-stone scupper set in the side of a raised platform at one end of the pool. A solitary potted century plant* (Agave americana) *is an echo of the spiky desert plants found in the surrounding countryside.*

FACING PAGE *The infinity-edge pool seems to spill right out into the desert; comfortable seating reflects the spare and serene landscaping. An ironwood tree and the potted agave are silhouetted against the evening sky.*

BELOW *Like desert sentinels, four Argentine saguaros* (Trichocereus terscheckii) *congregate against a wall painted deep eggplant. At night, ground-level lights shining against the wall create dramatic shadows.*

Sleek and Simple

DRAMA DEFINES A GARDEN

John and Rita Emerson's two-year-old garden isn't like any other on the block—and they like it that way. There's no lawn to mow, no billowy shrubs to prune, and few flowers to fuss over, "My wife and I don't have green thumbs," John confesses, "so the garden is perfect for us." Yet ample greenery softens the edges of their contemporary house on a small lot in Los Angeles. Plants are mostly tough and unthirsty, and they are used with restraint to create simple drama.

Landscape architect R. Michael Schneider, who designed the garden, says "It's an architectural garden; materials are plants, stone, water, and the play of light on hard surfaces. Yet it's a garden with soul and spirit." ▶

ABOVE *Agave* 'Mediopicta Alba' *in a stone bowl provides a sculptural element near the entry. The charcoal color of the bowl matches the steel-clad wall panel behind, and contrasts with the deck of warm-toned, honey brown teak.*

RIGHT *"Eliminate clutter and highlight the most important ideas," Schneider says. In the back patio, three tree aloes (*Aloe thraskii*) cast silhouettes on house walls. Growing below them are phormium, kangaroo paws, variegated* Miscanthus sinensis condensatus, *Mexican feather grass, and* Yushania maling, *a delicate clumping bamboo.*

The appeal of the garden lies in its clean lines and contrasts of shapes, textures, and subtle colors. Planting pockets just outside the windows on the ground floor enhance the connection between indoors and outdoors. Container plants serve as bold accents to bring drama to corners and entryways. But this is no showcase. "This isn't just a garden to look at but to be in," says Schneider.

FACING PAGE, ABOVE *To slow the journey to the house and reveal the garden gradually, the entry steps lead to the first outdoor room, partially concealed by a horsetail hedge. You may hear bubbling water, but you don't spy the source until past the hedge where a reflecting pool comes into view.*

FACING PAGE, LEFT *Wood, pebbles, stone paving, water, and plants blend together to create a multi-textural passage. A planting of blue fescue is edged with rosemary, while the lower pavers are laced together with strips of gray-green Dymondia.*

FACING PAGE, RIGHT *A zigzag wall is capped with teak for backyard seating. Japanese blood grass fringes the back edge of the seat, while blue oat grass surrounds the shapely trunks of mature 'Manzanillo' olive trees, found at an old grove and hoisted into position by crane.*

RIGHT *In raised planters above the driveway, two large blue-green century plants* (Agave americana), *a sticklike ocotillo* (Fouquieria splendens), *and a tall tree aloe are sculptural focal points among smaller soft green agaves and low-growing cool blue Senecio mandraliscae. Rosemary 'Severn Sea' trails over the walls.*

Growing Room

A SMALL GARDEN LIVES LARGE

Robyn and Dana Hogan wanted to create an Italian-style garden around their new home in Monarch Beach, California. The warm, dry climate was right for an echo of southern Europe, as was the Mediterranean-style stucco home. But the tall house's footprint took up most of the property, leaving a problem of proportion and lack of space for outdoor living. The Hogans worked with landscape architect Theresa Clark to squeeze as much garden as possible out of every outdoor inch.

RIGHT *A front entry gains more presence when the walk to the door feels like a stroll along a garden path. This is done by tucking thyme between paving stones and layering plants to create interest. Even the cobblestone driveway is inter-planted with zoysia grass.*

BELOW *Olive trees, bright red 'Simplicity' roses, and silvery ground covers carry the Mediterranean theme right out to the street.*

They started out with several sizable plants, to give the house some scale. Multitrunked olive trees are tall and substantial enough to link house and garden. An illusion of spaciousness was created by growing vines up arbors and fences, and layering plants to create fullness and seasonal interest. Behind the house, a flagstone terrace serves as an outdoor dining room, with pavers set far enough apart so that swathes of sedum and thyme can grow between, softening and greening up the back garden. The home's façade is laced with jasmine, a little rosemary hedge can be clipped for cooking, and the garden feels spacious despite its relatively small size.

RIGHT *A small garden appears larger when materials and colors are repeated. Creamy stone paving is used in the front and back garden, with gravel in the same warm tones. An iron pergola draped in vines softens the imposing façade of the house.*

LEFT *Shapely olive trees, a vase of sunflowers, red geraniums, and yellow roses set the tone for outdoor dining.*

BELOW *With little planting space, the Hogans made use of every possible scrap of soil. Vines climb walls and cascade from balconies, while verdant ribbons of thyme and dwarf succulents grow between paving slabs.*

FACING PAGE *A circular pool, benches, wrought iron, and the twisted trunks of silvery olive trees lend Old World charm to the garden.*

Walled Wonder

GARDENING IN DEER COUNTRY

ABOVE *Within the south- and west-facing walls, Macdonald grows a colorful array of her favorite plants, which include delphiniums, peonies, and roses. To squeeze abundance out of the average 75-day growing season, she grows heat-loving edibles, such as basil and artichokes, in the greenhouse.*

INSET *Macdonald favors hardy shrub roses such as 'What a Peach'.*

LEFT *Pots of bright annuals dot the steps. Strawberries grow through string netting in the foreground. The metal trellis holds pots of geraniums and honeysuckle.*

On the west side of Alex and Gina Macdonald's contemporary log home in Ketchum, Idaho, a dry-stacked stone wall encloses a garden. This barrier is both picturesque and utilitarian, allowing the Macdonalds to grow a bountiful array of flowers and vegetables that would otherwise be devoured by passing deer and elk. By capturing the sun's heat and radiating it inward, the wall also creates a warmer microclimate for the garden, extending the too-short growing season here at an elevation of 6,500 feet.

Gina Macdonald worked with Webb Landscape to design walls that would be sturdy enough to withstand both powerful elk and heavy snow loads. The buff-colored Utah sandstone slabs were artfully arranged into 7-foot-tall walls that taper from 4 feet wide at the base to 2 feet wide at the top. Tender climbing vines such as sweet peas cling to the warm walls.

ABOVE *A bevy of exotic flowers, punctuated by scarlet and sunshine-yellow kangaroo paws* (Anigozanthos), *tumbles together in a casual cottage style in the front garden. Peeled logs frame a cool entry porch.*

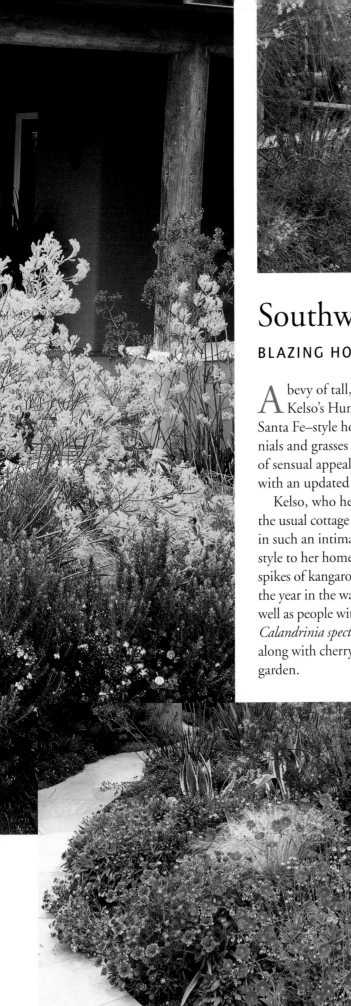

Southwest Style

BLAZING HOT COLOR

A bevy of tall, spiky, and bold flowers plays off the pale stucco of Cory Kelso's Huntington Beach home. The sturdy, horizontal lines of her Santa Fe–style house are enlivened by a casual, colorful tumble of perennials and grasses that comprise her southwest-style cottage garden. A mix of sensual appeal and old-fashioned design combines traditional charm with an updated and unusual plant palette.

Kelso, who helped design the garden and now maintains it, passed up the usual cottage mix of roses, phlox, and columbine that might be expected in such an intimate and profuse planting. Instead, she adapted her garden's style to her home's architecture and the region's climate. The tall flower spikes of kangaroo paws *(Anigozanthos)* add sunny color for ten months of the year in the warm Southern California climate. They attract birds as well as people with their appealingly fuzzy texture. A lively mix of magenta *Calandrinia spectabilis,* various perennials, and small ornamental grasses, along with cherry red Meidiland shrub roses finish off this blaze-of-color garden.

ABOVE *A yellow-flowered palo verde tree arches over a colorful display of silvery lavender, kangaroo paws, and accents of Mexican feather grass.*

LEFT *'Bush Sunset' kangaroo paws and magenta* Calandrinia *mingle with blanket flower (*Gaillardia × grandiflora *'Goblin') beside the walkway to the Kelso home.*

Cozy and Colorful

VIVID HUES HEAT UP A HILLSIDE

This hillside garden retreat is where Diana Stratton seeks refuge and respite. Only a third of an acre, the site's steep topography makes it feel much larger. The walls, steps, and six terraces that traverse and retain the slopes afford various perspectives of plantings and art in a highly personalized and ornamented space.

Stratton takes full advantage of her garden's microclimate. Although this Northern California location, near the town of Healdsburg, experiences freezes,

BELOW *A café table echoes the warm hues of cannas and roses behind. Indigo colors recall the exotic feel of Stratton's Moroccan childhood.*

LEFT *Potted grasses provide soft contrast to slick glazed balls.*

BELOW *Pale lime green chairs add bright contrast to the house's blue walls. Blue cushions tie the color scheme together.*

BOTTOM *The garden's architectural elements are made mostly from recycled materials. The greenhouse that Stratton calls the "jewel of the garden" was crafted with old windows salvaged from her home's remodel.*

Stratton's garden is tucked into a protected pocket of Fitch Mountain warmed by the nearby Russian River. Even more warmth is added by the lively color palette of indigo and sunny yellow inspired by Stratton's childhood in Morocco. A brilliant blue greenhouse and colored walls and furnishings are focal points. Stratton, a garden designer, echoes the greenhouse blue in ceramic spheres and pots of lobelia, and plays off it with lush plantings in chartreuse, burgundy, coral, and hot pink. Cannas, variegated gingers, taro, datura, and other exotics grown in pots (and overwintered in the greenhouse) evoke a tropical feeling on this hillside of native oak and madrone.

European Enchantment

MAKING FORMAL FUN

Garden designer Carole McElwee lives in a tiny 1929 cottage and works in a Gothic-style folly (a fanciful garden structure), both of which were on the property in Capistrano Beach, California, when she bought it a decade ago. Here she fashioned an enchanted, Old World garden. Inspired visually by the eccentricity of the buildings and horticulturally by the frost-free climate, McElwee divided the garden in the English manner into several intimate spaces. She then filled the "rooms" with abundant Mediterranean plantings. Roses, vines, and perennials tangle in a riot of color, contained by gates, hedges, and clipped boxwood. McElwee took out all the lawn except for a small green oval of grass. Gravel and bark paths lead past fountains and a swimming pool, and beneath arbors. Glimpses of the garden are revealed around corners and through gaps in the thick hedges of *Pittosporum undulatum*. Some garden rooms are cozy places for sitting or dining. But because the folly, which serves as her office and as a guesthouse, is such a fun and frivolous place, McElwee planted the garden near it in a wild flowery style. An exuberant mix of Peruvian lilies *(Alstroemeria),* old-fashioned roses, and flowering shrubs adds to the Alice-in-Wonderland feel of the garden.

RIGHT *A quiet seating area outside the folly is adorned with cool white roses and a cushioned bent-willow chair.*

BELOW *McElwee turned the old chicken house into a tool shed, complete with a lacy curtain on the paned windows. To the left of the door is a pot holding a lemon-scented variegated geranium. A tangle of rose and morning glory vines frames the door.*

INSET *'Polka' climbing rose, which has a light, fruity fragrance.*

Generous Grasses

A GARDEN OF COLOR AND MOVEMENT

San Francisco landscape architect Topher Delaney began her renovation of the Gennet family's Napa Valley landscape by injecting it with color. An old concrete block wall, which Delaney describes as "really grim," ran the length of the garden. She plastered the concrete with an acrylic stucco coating in a vivid violet blue, which set the color scheme for the entire garden.

Then she took advantage of the blustery site by planting drifts of fluffy, bleached-blond Mexican feather grass *(Nassella tenuissima)* to ripple in the wind. This grass softens the hard edges of paving and swimming pool. New paths of decomposed granite meander through the garden. To complement the violet wall, Delaney chose Russian sage, yellow yarrow, and sedums, which thrive in dry, hot weather. A mass planting of multistemmed fruitless olive trees offers a layer of foliage to tie house and garden together. The celadon haze of the olive trees creates a pleasant umbrella of leaves through the heat of summer.

LEFT *Silky blond Mexican feather grass creates a meadow effect that mimics the rolling Napa Valley landscape.*

FACING PAGE *A multistemmed olive tree (Olea europaea 'Majestic Beauty') is a shapely accent.*

BELOW *The swimming pool is the center-piece of the garden, especially dramatic at night when the house reflects in its watery surface. At night, uplights enhance the pool's beauty.*

Foliage Extravaganza

A LUXURIANT ISLAND GARDEN

ABOVE *Paths wind through the foliage in shades of green, yellow, and plum. Ti plants rise like a forest of tiny palms on the left while angel's trumpet dangles its blooms in the center.*

INSET *Brightly patterned foliage plants like croton and coleus mingle together.*

It's a gardener's fantasy to grow lush-leafed houseplants outdoors, specimens so large that you can walk beneath and look up into their flowers. Larry and Fern Kane's tropical paradise garden near Kailua-Kona, Hawaii, carved out of a steep slope above the Pacific Ocean, fulfills such a fantasy. Think of strolling along paths mulched with crunchy macadamia nut husks beneath the huge dangling bells of angel's trumpet. The scents of plumeria, gardenia, and tuberose fill the warm air. Designer Julie Ellison took full advantage of the spectacular setting and tropical weather to design a garden of exotic foliage interwoven in green, purple, and red.

The garden measures 165 by 60 feet, part of the four-acre property. Paths wind through borders so luxuriantly planted that corners and boundaries are obscured, making the space seem much larger.

RIGHT *A focal point planting rising out of a shapely urn stands out against a backdrop of red ti plants, philodendrons, and other foliage plants.*

BELOW *Immature pineapple, perhaps the best-known member of the bromeliad clan, blushes amid variegated foliage.*

More than 150 different kinds of exotic plants—including dracaena, dumb cane, bromeliads, palms, and philodendrons—are combined in a heady mélange of color, bloom, texture, and scent. The bold combinations of foliage colors won this garden a *Sunset* Western Garden Design Award, prompting one juror to say it was "like a Hawaiian English garden."

structures

ARBORS & TRELLISES | DECKS |

FENCES & GATES | FIREPLACES |

GARDEN PAVILIONS |

KITCHENS | PATHS | PATIOS |

PLAY AREAS | PONDS |

POOLS | RAISED BEDS |

SHEDS | SHOWERS |

SPAS | STEPS | WALLS

Arbors & Trellises

An arbor is an all-in-one outdoor structure. It offers shade from hot sun, coverage from rain, and shelter during cool evenings. Yet it allows in the breeze, the sounds of nature, and the fragrance of flowers. An arbor has a magnetic effect in the garden; people tend to congregate underneath it, whether mingling at a garden party or just relaxing with a good book. It's also a major structure that can dramatically reconfigure your outdoor space, tying together different areas or architectural elements of the garden, directing foot traffic, and providing privacy or screening.

Typical sites for an arbor include over a patio, around a pool or spa, or as a bridge or transition between different sections of the garden. In a larger garden you are more likely to have enough room for a freestanding arbor, but the structure is easily attached to a house or garage wall. In a small backyard, an arbor is likely to become the major focal point of the space. Whatever the size of your garden, if you plan to do a lot of entertaining under the arbor, it should be easily accessed from the kitchen. If you would prefer your arbor to be a destination point in a far corner of the garden, be sure there is a pathway to entice people toward it.

Dressing Up

The most natural adornment for an arbor is a climbing vine—favorites include clematis, grapes, honeysuckle, jasmine, kiwi, roses, trumpet vine, and wisteria (see page 202). Many of these are hefty, long-lived plants—easily weighing hundreds of pounds—so be sure that your arbor is strong enough to support the weight of foliage and fruit. The other significant consideration is whether to plant an evergreen or deciduous vine. When deciduous leaves drop in winter, an arbor allows the sun to shine through and warm the interior, a basic means of seasonal climate modification. An evergreen vine will keep the arbor well-shaded year-round.

ABOVE *The voluptuous growth of grapevines makes a shady roof above a simple cedar arbor placed poolside. The arbor measures just 12 feet wide, 8 feet deep, and 8 feet high, yet is strong enough to support four of the vigorous vines. Flagstone covers the floor beneath.*

LEFT *Rising high over a passageway, this stately arbor frames a vista of the countryside beyond the garden. Dramatic clusters of show-stopping wisteria hang from the rafters.*

FACING PAGE *The bold lines of this arbor suit the contemporary landscaping that surrounds it. Substantial square columns support beefy, rough-hewn rafters. Water courses down a rill under the structure, culminating in the center of a circle of inlaid pebbles.*

Rafters sit atop beams and are spaced for plant support or shade.

For spans up to 6 feet, use 2-by-6-in. **beams**; for longer spans, use 2-by-8s.

Columns or **posts** should be at least 4-by-4 inches; columns may be wood or composite material.

Footings must be strong enough to secure weight of structure and extend below the frost line.

Arbor Construction

The key to arbor construction is to think of a crisscross or stacking principle, with each new layer placed perpendicular to the one below it: first posts, then beams, and finally rafters. If you are building an arbor over a deck, lengthen the deck's posts to make them tall enough to support the arbor, or bolt the arbor's posts to the deck's substructure. For an arbor set in the ground, set the posts in postholes (see page 113) or attach them to post anchors sunk into a concrete patio or footings.

When the arbor is attached to a building, a ledger takes the place of an end beam. You can connect the ledger to wall studs, to second-story floor framing, or to the roof. If your house wall is brick or stone, drill holes and install expanding anchors to bolt the ledger in place. Then set the rafters on top of the ledger or hang them from it with anchors or joist hangers.

Generally, the lowest beam should not be less than 6 feet 8 inches above the outdoor floor surface. A taller arbor gives vines room to grow and feels more spacious. Leave at least 4½ feet of floor space for a dining table.

Shade Strategies

You can control the degree of shade cast by your arbor by the way in which you position the rafters. Rafters that run east–west provide the most shade, especially at midday; those running north–south cast less shade. 1-by-2s or 1-by-3s set on edge provide more shade when the sun is at an angle in the morning and late afternoon. Set with their longest width flat, they provide more midday shade when the sun is directly overhead. Again, depending how much shade you want, you can leave the rafters bare or cover them with vines or a material such as bamboo or lattice. The arbor shown below is left uncovered, with widely spaced rafters, to provide just enough—but not too much—shade.

Trellis Treatments

A smaller version of the arbor, a trellis is generally a more delicate structure whose primary purpose is to support plants. But they can also add screening and vertical interest, and serve as dividers in the garden. Most trellises are ready-made, which means you must carefully select models that suit your house architecture and garden style. Keep the following in mind.

Get your style straight. A bent-twig trellis will look out of place against the wall of a Victorian house, whereas a cedar or painted lattice suits a wide variety of house styles.

Keep it in proportion. The trellis's scale should suit its setting. A 2-foot-high grid can overpower a small container, but even a 7-foot tower can look puny in a large open space.

Match the plant. A lightweight trellis may back a modest container plant, while a large, sturdy frame can dress up a garage wall or form a backdrop for an entire garden. Vines are deceptively vigorous, even annual types, so be sure your trellis is large enough to support the plant rather than being overwhelmed by it.

Focus on fasteners. Most trellises consist of vertical and horizontal pieces secured together with nails, screws, or wire. Reinforcing these can add years to the life of your trellis. If attaching the trellis to a wall or fence, use wooden spacers to improve air circulation and allow easy removal of the trellis for repairs or painting to the surface behind. Use galvanized hardware, and install anchors on plaster or brick walls.

FACING PAGE *An arrangement of lattice trellises turns this outdoor patio into a tropicalesque retreat. Solid wooden 4-by-4-inch posts and beams support arched lattice panels. The structure is painted a crisp white and hung with golden-orange fabric panels.*

RIGHT *This tentlike awning supported by a simple metal frame casts shade without taking up a lot of visual space in a small courtyard garden. A lantern hangs from the center of the structure.*

Fabricating Shade

Sleek shapes and taut surfaces give shade sails a dynamic presence that belies their practical mission. The idea for these tensioned fabric canopies comes to the West from Australia, where, years ago, canopies were made of sailcloth. Now, architectural sails are made of high-tech synthetic knits that wear better and block out UV rays—up to 95 percent with some fabrics and colors.

The sails need to be attached to heavy-duty stainless-steel anchors—either on separate posts, between trees, or on an existing structure. Because the fabric is under such tension, installing the sails is a two-person job; as municipal building departments become familiar with the sails, they are adding building codes, so check with your local building inspector regarding applicable codes in your area. To create architectural interest, you can install the sails with bold changes in height and direction from one corner of a sail to another, overlapping panels, and mixing different colors or shapes.

Decks

Simply put, a deck serves the same purpose as a patio; it's an extension of your house that offers space for dining, entertaining, and relaxing. But a deck has a number of advantages over a patio. It often creates new space rather than using existing space in the garden. And it can easily overcome the challenge of a sloping, bumpy, or poorly drained site. The lumber used in its construction is durable and resilient underfoot, and it won't store heat the way stone, brick, or concrete does. And a new deck can substantially alter the way people move in and through your house.

Determining the Style

There are few home styles that a deck doesn't suit, although the casual nature of a wooden deck can look out of place with a formal garden or house. Matching deck details—including overheads, benches, railing, and steps—to the house will make the deck seem like part of the structure rather than an addition to it.

A well-designed deck is sized to fit both the house and the yard comfortably. As a rule of thumb, you'll need at least 20 square feet of decking to accommodate one person comfortably, so a 12-by-20-foot deck (240 square feet) can handle up to 12 people at once, although you'll need additional space for furniture, plants, grills, and other items.

Decks can abut the house or tuck into a remote corner of the garden, but the classic attached deck is accessed from a living room, kitchen, or master bedroom—or all three. A low-level deck can link house and garden, offering a new perspective on garden beds or distant views. A low-level wraparound deck links interior spaces with a series of boardwalks or landings. You can follow the shape of your house, or play off it with angular or curved extensions.

Detached decks form quiet retreats, whether tucked underneath trees or elevated to catch afternoon sun or shade. The route to such a deck can be direct or circuitous. You can enhance the sense of a hideaway with the addition of an overhead arbor, water feature, or spa.

FACING PAGE *This platform, which faces east over Washington's Puget Sound, resembles the bow of a boat skimming smoothly across the water. The rounded portion of trimmed cedar decking measures about 24 feet across. Long panels of ¼-inch-thick transparent acrylic plastic, set into grooves in the rails, keep the view unobstructed.*

BELOW *A pool deck that extends over the water is covered with a high, sloping overhead, offset from its posts for striking effect. The section overhanging the pool makes it easy to dive into the water; comfortable seating is set out for lounging.*

Electrical lighting and outlets are either 120 volt or 12 volt and may require a permit to install.

Plan for built-in **details** such as benches and storage when designing the deck.

Use quality 2-by-4 or 2-by-6 lumber or wood composite for **floor decking**; these resist warping and splinters.

Precast concrete piers are embedded in poured concrete **footings**; these must extend below the frost line.

Fascia conceals joist ends; bendable composite fascia boards are best for curved edges.

Stair construction is regulated by codes; stairs and landing must be illuminated.

Local codes set minimum **post** sizes and spacing; those taller than 3 feet may require bracing.

Electroplated, galvanized, or stainless-steel metal **framing connectors** join various components of the deck.

Deck Construction

A low-level deck can be set either on posts sunk into concrete footings or on beams attached directly to the concrete piers using post bases sized for the beams. A ledger joins the deck to the house framing. Joists attach to the ledger and beams, providing the underlying frame for the surface layer of decking.

If the deck is over 2 feet above ground, it should be surrounded by a railing, which typically consists of posts, rails, and balusters. Stair risers are optional, but railings attached to stringers are a good idea on even low-level decks.

A deck must be built to support certain minimum loads; local building codes will specify how much weight a deck can support per square foot, as well as requirements for footings, railings, stairs, and deck height. The strength of the deck is determined by the size of the beams and joists, and the distance they must span. Lumberyards and home-building centers generally have standard span tables for each dimension of common lumber species. Although a low-level or raised deck can be constructed by a homeowner with a basic knowledge of construction, a deck that is cantilevered out from an upper story, or over water—or one that is on a hillside or unstable soil—must be designed by a qualified structural engineer and installed by a professional.

Secure deck to house framing with a **ledger**; flashing protects wall from moisture.

Beams bridge posts or piers; they may be single timbers or multiple 2-by members.

Joists are typically spaced 16 or 24 inches center to center and secured to ledger and beam with hangers.

Prevent water from collecting around door sills, behind the ledger, and between decking by allowing for adequate **drainage.**

Eco-smart Wood

Shrinking forests and dwindling supplies of quality lumber have encouraged the development of both environmentally sensible wood products and engineered materials suitable for decks and other garden structures. To protect Western forests, consider woods other than the best grades of redwood and cedar, which generally come from the oldest trees. Instead, seek out plantation-grown woods or those from certified forests or look for suppliers of salvaged lumber from demolished buildings.

Some manufacturers combine landfill-bound wood with waste plastic to make wood-polymer composites. These weatherproof products can be used for decking and railings—but not for structural members. Available in several colors, they can also be painted or stained and cut, drilled, and shaped the way standard lumber can. For families with young children, these synthetic boards have the additional advantage of being splinter-free.

Deck Details

Some clever carpentry and a few extra touches can turn a simple wooden platform into an outdoor room—and integrate a deck into the landscape.

- Decking patterns can be as elaborate as you wish. Vary the direction of decking to signal transition zones such as stairs and platforms.

- Built-ins can include seating, storage, a firepit, or even a water feature.

- Railings may be wood or a complementary material such as metal, cable, or glass, and can vary in height to provide privacy as well as safety.

ABOVE *Overlapping angles and changes in decking direction emphasize steps, highlight benches and planters, and turn a potentially plain deck into an architectural statement.*

ABOVE, RIGHT *Seating benches built into this deck in the woods frame the arching branches of an ancient oak tree.*

RIGHT *Steps lead to different levels in a wraparound deck. Tensioned steel cable that runs through posts makes a safe but visually airy railing that complements the contemporary house.*

Build It: A Low Deck

1. Waxed cardboard tubes are convenient for pouring piers onto footings. While footing is still wet, set tube in hole and push several inches into footing. Fill tube with concrete, tamping down with a 2-by-4 to remove air pockets. Smooth and level the surface. With concrete still wet, insert an anchor bolt into each pier (shown) or alternatively insert one-piece post base.

2. When concrete is fully cured, remove cardboard tubing and attach post base. Set a post in each post base, securing it temporarily. Plumb the post by checking it on adjacent sides with a carpenter's level. Attach temporary braces to two adjacent sides. Drive nails through the post bases into the posts.

3. Procedures for attaching a ledger vary depending on the type of siding on your house. Most important is to connect the ledger to the house framing or foundation—never just the sheathing. The size and spacing of bolts should be spelled out in your building code. Installations against wood siding will require a drainage gap and flashing for moisture protection.

4. To determine post height, set a straight 2-by-4 atop the ledger and put a carpenter's level on top of the 2-by-4. Hold the other end of the 2-by-4 against each post, adjusting until it is level. Mark the post at the bottom of the 2-by-4. Mark the cut line, then use a circular saw (shown) or handsaw to cut the post. Add post caps to the top of each post.

5. If possible, position string lines representing the sides of the deck and use the string to align the beam at each end. Lifting a typical deck beam (such as this double beam) may require two or more people (shown). Check that the beam is parallel to the ledger using the string lines; secure the post caps to the posts and beam.

6. Begin installing joists with an end joist. Set the joist against the end of the ledger and fasten with nails or deck screws. Attach reinforcing angle brackets to the inside corners (shown, top). Then use joist hangers to secure joists along the length of the ledger (shown, bottom), ensuring they are square. The other end of each joist will sit atop the beam; you can secure it with metal ties.

7. Trim the joists to length, allowing them to extend beyond the beam. Align decking boards atop the joists, spacing them about $3/16$ inch apart for drainage. Use a chisel or pry bar to keep deck boards straight as you install the fasteners (shown). As you approach the last several rows, plan to rip small amounts off the length of each board rather than leave yourself a single, narrow row at the edge of the deck.

Fences & Gates

One of the things we value most in our gardens is a sense of seclusion, and a good-looking fence helps foster that sense of a secure, private retreat from the outside world. A well-designed fence or outdoor screen can do much more than mark out a property line. It can filter the sun or moderate strong winds and mute the cacophony of street traffic, noisy neighbors, and barking dogs. As partitions, fences divide the yard into separate areas for recreation, relaxation, gardening, and storage. And they provide vertical surfaces for decoration and support for plants.

Although they serve many of the same purposes, the differences between fences and walls are based on construction. Walls are masonry, whereas most fences are built partly or entirely of wood. The versatility of wood is reflected in the wide variety of its forms—split rails, bent twig, grape stakes, dimension lumber, poles, plywood, bamboo, and more. The inclusion of louvers, slats, lattice, or see-through trellises can edit or create views. The materials and design you choose for your fences will probably depend on price and the function the fence is to serve. A board fence may be the best choice for a full privacy screen; a trellis panel may work better to divide the garden into separate rooms.

Alternative materials to wood run from inexpensive galvanized wire (chain-link) or vinyl to ornamental iron or custom metalwork panels that become works of garden art. Whatever your choice of fencing, coordinate the fence with the style and materials of your house. Louvered or board fences are the most versatile, complementing a variety of western house styles.

Most communities have regulations restricting fence height—generally 4 feet high in front yards and 6 to 8 feet in the backyard. But these restrictions can vary considerably even from one neighborhood to another, so check with a local building department or community planning office (a landscape professional also should be able to provide this information).

Fences along boundary lines are commonly owned and maintained by both neighbors. Make every effort to come to a friendly agreement with your neighbor on the location, design, and construction of the fence. If you can't come to an agreement, you can circumvent the problem by building the fence entirely on your land, just a few inches inside your boundary.

ABOVE *Translucent fence panels create a visual barrier that seems not quite solid and lends an air of mystery. Such panels, usually made of fiberglass, are especially valuable around pools and spas, where privacy—but not complete screening—is desired.*

FACING PAGE *Staggered fences in contrasting wood tones add a sense of concealment while leading the eye around corners. A narrow wooden walkway leads through the fences.*

LEFT *Modeled on a traditional Japanese* sukashi-gaki *fence, this simple bamboo fence marks the boundary between a shrub border and a stepping-stone path. The vertical and horizontal pieces of bamboo are lashed together with special twine.*

Fence Construction

Most wooden fences have three parts: vertical posts, horizontal rails or stringers, and siding. Generally, fence posts are 4-by-4s and rails are 2-by-4s, but fence siding varies enormously.

Few lots are perfectly smooth, flat, and obstruction-free. If your fence line runs up a hill, build the fence so that it follows the contours of the land, or construct stepped panels to maintain horizontal lines.

Posts may be capped with decorative tops; they are usually 4-by-4s.

Boards or **pickets** may alternate sides and may butt against each other or be spaced apart.

Swing clearance between fence and posts is usually $1/2$ in.

Top and bottom **rails** may be joined to posts with a butt joint, notched joint, or lap joint.

Kickboard adds finished look.

Allow adequate **hinge clearance** for sturdy hinges.

Footing is poured concrete; gravel base adds drainage and rock helps keep posts from rotting.

Build It: A Board Fence

1. Lay out the fence run, driving wooden stakes into the ground to mark each end post. Then run string between the stakes, drawing it tight (left). Use tape to mark the center position of intermediate posts along the string. Dangle a plumb bob between each post, then mark the corresponding post center on the ground (right). Using a posthole digger or auger, dig holes 6 inches deeper than the posts will be set, and three times wider. Place a flat stone in the bottom of each hole, then add 6 inches of gravel.

2. Center the post in the hole and surround it with concrete, tamping it down to remove air pockets. Check that the post is level (shown). Fill to 1 to 2 inches above ground level, then slope the concrete away from the post to divert water.

3. After setting posts in concrete, you have about 20 minutes to align them before concrete hardens. Install end posts first, bracing them with 1-by-4-inch stakes while the concrete cures. To align posts between the ends, use spacer blocks and string to locate the posts, spacing each a block's thickness from the line (shown). Cut posts to height after they are set.

4. Brush on wood preservative where rails and posts will meet. For a simple butt joint to join rails to posts, have a helper hold the rail level and use a square to make sure each rail is perpendicular to the post (shown). Toenail the rail to the posts or use metal brackets.

5. Stretch a level line from post to post to mark the bottom of the siding. Use a carpenter's level to check the first board for plumb, then secure it to the end post with screws roughly three times as long as the board's thickness. Secure additional boards one by one, checking alignment as you go (shown).

Gate Basics

- Deciding where to locate your gate is usually pretty simple, as most gates are placed for convenience—where fences and walls intersect walkways or driveways.

- Walk-through gates must provide clearance for equipment such as wheelbarrows and tractors, furniture, and other large items that are periodically moved in and out—36 inches wide is the minimum.

- A common solution for a wide entry is a gate opening from the middle, or a gate on rollers for a driveway.

- Entry and boundary gates usually swing in toward the house or garden, but a gate within the property can swing in the direction of greater traffic flow.

- On sloped ground, the gate should swing toward the downhill side so it can easily clear the ground.

- For safety, a gate that opens onto stairs should ideally be placed at the top of the stairs rather than the bottom, and should swing away from the steps.

RIGHT *This tall, arched entry gate is inset with sinuous curves of wrought iron topped with a welcoming rising sun pattern.*

BELOW *Simple rust-red pickets are topped with decorative finials for a modest entryway that lets a grapevine steal the show.*

RIGHT *Sturdy double wooden gates are characteristic of Southwest gardens. These weathered panels are set off by the pale color of the adjacent adobe walls.*

BELOW *A fanciful arrangement of found objects—including croquet mallets and old tools—has been fashioned into this wood-framed entry gate.*

115

Fireplaces

An outdoor fireplace can transform a patio into a true open-air room—one that is warm, welcoming, and comfortable in all but the most wintry weather.

You can install a fireplace in a sheltered entry court-yard, along the rear wall of a home, at the boundary between paved and planted areas, even in a wooden deck—anywhere you want to create a gathering spot. But before you get too caught up in planning, consult with your local building inspector to find out code requirements for both setback and chimney height. In most municipalities, a freestanding fireplace is considered a separate structure that requires a building permit.

Choosing a Fireplace

Outdoor fireplaces have the same basic elements as indoor ones, namely a footing, a center firebox that surrounds the actual fireplace, and a chimney for venting the exhaust. Noncombustible fireboxes are made of metal or constructed of masonry and lined with fireproof bricks. Metal units are often known as "zero clearance" because their double- or triple-wall chimney sections can be installed in contact with combustible framing material. Masonry fireboxes use

either prefabricated or custom-built chimney sections or more traditional stone, tile, or brick interiors. Another option is a natural-gas–fueled model that contains a log set made of a cementlike, heat-resistant ceramic material molded to look like real logs; these don't require a chimney because the exhaust is released through slots in the frame.

Chimneys should include a spark arrester—a screen that prevents large embers from escaping. You'll reduce fire hazards further by always using a fireplace screen, keeping any combustible materials away from the hearth, burning only dry, well-seasoned firewood, or switching to wood substitutes when fire danger is high in your area.

Beyond these basic elements, an outdoor fireplace can fit into almost any landscape design, with chimneys and hearth surrounds of stone, stucco, slate, or tile, elaborate mantels and hearths, and built-in seating.

A fireplace can form part of an outdoor entertainment area that includes a cooktop, barbecue, refrigerator, and plenty of comfortable seating. Just don't forget to set aside a convenient spot nearby for firewood.

FACING PAGE, ABOVE *A low concrete wall reflects firelight and warmth toward a backyard gathering place in Yakima, Washington. Tom Berger designed the firepit to underscore the mountain view, while large boulders flanking the hearth connect visually with the rocky terrain.*

FACING PAGE, BELOW *Southwest style and building materials join forces in this elevated patio made for evening entertainment. Native stones face the fireplace and an arc-shaped* banco *(bench) curves around the warmth.*

LEFT *Spending an evening around an aboveground firepit is like camping out without leaving home. This gas-fueled flagstone model warms Juan and Ann Castro in San Mateo, California.*

BELOW *Freestanding and graphic, this concrete fireplace rises from a patio of square pavers. Leafy ferns and shrubs behind soften the bold structure.*

LEFT *An imposing chimney of staked terra-cotta tiles seems to be built right into a steep hillside. A spacious hearth and overstuffed furniture add impressive scale.*

FACING PAGE *This cozy scene is the perfect setting for telling tall tales; the firepot is portable, which means you can easily put together an inviting conversation group.*

BELOW *A metal firepit glows softly in the center of a bluestone patio, a safe distance from colorful foliage and flowers.*

Fireplace Basics

You don't need a building permit for a simple firepit or chiminea (a pot-bellied, freestanding fireplace). But common sense dictates that you take extra care when buying or building a place to burn wood outdoors.

- Never leave a fire unattended.

- Situate fireplaces and firepits away from combustible materials, such as dry grasses and other highly flammable plants (see page 301).

- Use a chimney to elevate the release point of smoke.

- If using a firepit, make sure it is completely level and stable.

- Burn dry, well-seasoned firewood. Generally, hardwoods (oak, madrone, maple, hickory, and ash) burn cleaner than softwoods (fir, pine, and cedar).

- For smoke-free burning, use a gas fireplace fueled by natural gas and fitted with a log set made of a cementlike, heat-resistant ceramic material molded to resemble real logs.

- Observe fire ordinances and don't use your fireplace on no-burn days or when it's smoggy or windy.

- Have your fireplace cleaned regularly by a professional.

- Add a spark arrester. Chimneytop units trap and break up embers.

- Keep a fire extinguisher or a garden hose with a sprayer nearby.

- To reduce pollution and minimize the chance of sparks escaping, choose wood substitutes, such as wax-based logs or those made of "densified wood"—compressed sawdust. Compressed logs made from recycled coffee grounds, molasses, and a bit of wax burn cleaner, emit a taller, more natural flame through their burn cycle, and have a mildly sweet scent rather than a chemical smell.

- Don't overfill a fireplace or firepit.

Garden Pavilions

A covered garden structure is a refuge away from household bustle, a place to sit quietly or even spend the night during warm summer weather. Whether your structure takes the form of a traditional gazebo, a rustic ramada, or an enclosed open-air bedroom, there's something unique about a pavilion that is placed away from the house. The building changes how you perceive and use your outdoor space, creating different focal points, and affecting the way people walk around the property.

To find the best site for your property, walk around and view the entire garden from different angles. Do you want a long view over the surrounding countryside, or would you prefer a secluded niche? Consider the kind of sun exposure you want—if your main deck or patio is in full sun, you may prefer to find a shady corner. Is the site practical—level, with good drainage—or will it require additional preparation? Finally, does it contravene any setback or zoning requirements? Once you have identified the best site for your pavilion, it's time to think about the structure itself.

A Question of Style

As with any large garden structure, there should be a relationship between your pavilion and your house architecture as well as any other garden structures such as fences, arbors, and decks. This doesn't mean you are restricted to the same siding and roofing materials as your home, but it does mean you should give some thought to how the building complements its surroundings.

In the West, gazebos often differ from old-fashioned Victorian-style versions, even when they retain a traditional six- or eight-sided peaked roof. The construction can be substantial, as in a Northwest timber-framed structure, or light, with little more than four peeled posts connected by pairs of 2-by-6-inch posts. You can enhance the design with features such as path lighting or down-lights, built-in benches, window boxes, water features, or even a spa.

In the Southwest, ramadas evolved from the buildings that sheltered workers from the sun during harvest time. Originally built of mesquite or cottonwood poles, they were usually open on three sides to take advantage of breezes. The concept translates well to many other parts of the West. The traditional building materials—adobe, plaster, and tile—withstand intense sunlight, and a fan can increase air circulation and cool the structure.

Another imported structure that has made itself at home in Western gardens is the teahouse, a building that straddles the form and functions of a gazebo and an outdoor retreat. Originally conceived as a site for the ritual of the tea ceremony, a tea-house may be nothing more than a raised platform covered on three sides, or it may be a more complex structure with several rooms divided by sliding *shoji* screens. All teahouses, though, have a simple, almost rustic, quality.

ABOVE *A teahouse appears to float on water, but it's actually set on a deck in a shallow pool. In the Japanese style, the roof extends beyond the walls to create a surrounding veranda.*

LEFT *Twin structures continue the symmetrical motif in this water garden. The exaggerated arching rooflines recall Asian architecture and are topped with decorative balls that echo the stone orbs below.*

FACING PAGE *This classic eight-sided gazebo looks at home in its lush green setting. Open, airy framing forms a seating area beneath a shingled roof.*

ABOVE *Inspired by the Hawaiian lagoons she loves to visit each year, Ruth Hunter decided to re-create an island paradise in her Los Angeles garden. The tin-roofed shelter has a floor of redwood, supporting poles of galvanized steel covered with split bamboo, and a back wall of reed matting.*

LEFT *Palapas call to mind swim-up bars and sun-kissed beaches. You, too, can bring home a taste of the tropics with a similar open-sided thatched garden structure. The thatching may be reeds or palm fronds and should be treated for water resistance.*

ABOVE *An intricately carved Chinese opium bed, decked out in fabrics from India, Italy, and France, becomes a multicultural garden retreat.*

LEFT *Ramadas are a regional tradition in the Southwest. This one has posts and crossbeams of mesquite and a roof of ocotillo canes. Colorful accessories enhance its Southwest simplicity.*

Hub is eight-sided; secures rafters.

Roofing may be siding, shakes, or shingles.

Post bracing is mainly decorative.

Knee walls or railings enclose sides.

Raised wooden deck on concrete slab supports ground-level gazebo.

Building a Gazebo

Despite the many differences in designs, most gazebos need certain components: a foundation, posts or walls, beams, rafters, and roofing material. The support usually comes from a simple post-and-beam frame that is well within the abilities of a do-it-yourselfer. A six- or eight-sided gazebo roof hub is a bit trickier to lay out and assemble. If you have chosen a fairly traditional gazebo design, chances are there's a kit on the market that would make the job of cutting and assembling easier. Just be sure to research any company before you buy; the best manufacturers will offer not only detailed assembly instructions, but also follow-up support via phone or e-mail.

Remember that if the roof is solid, it must be sufficiently pitched to allow water to run off. To permit easy clearance and avoid a cramped feeling, make the overhead at least 8 feet high. Your local building inspector can answer any questions you have about footing or slab dimensions, or about the sizes of posts and roof components you'll need if building the structure from scratch. If you plan to run electricity to the structure, you'll need a permit for the work.

Green Roofs

A green roof is more than just the equivalent of a patio garden with potted plants; it's an ecological system that can limit energy costs, improve the air, and provide a habitat for wildlife. Although most green roofs in the West have been installed on large commercial or public buildings, the same technology can be used to design green roofs for residential structures. Garden outbuildings such as sheds, gazebos, and garages make good candidates for green roofs.

Green-roof construction is based on layers; these provide structural reinforcement, moisture control, insulation, and a special growing medium. The type of plants you can grow depends on the slope of the roof and the degree of sun and wind to which the roof is exposed. Some favorites include grasses, succulents, and low-growing ground covers.

This green roof in a foggy neighborhood of San Francisco was designed by architect Karin Payson with the help of Paul Kephart of Rana Creek Habitat Restoration. The roof is planted with natives that can both tolerate salt-laden fogs and attract birds and butterflies. Shown here are common yarrow (in bloom), beach strawberry and *Sedum spathifolium*.

Kitchens

Cooking and dining outside for much of the year is one of the great traditions of living in the West. The centerpiece of family cookouts and entertaining has long been the barbecue, and its familiar kettle shape still graces many patios and decks. But you can also customize your outdoor kitchen to suit pretty much any kind of cuisine and your own entertainment site.

As with an indoor kitchen remodel, an outdoor kitchen project can quickly grow in size and scope, so do a little research before you call in the contractor. If you live in a cold-winter area and cook outside for only part of the year, a simple grill and some counter space may be enough. More elaborate facilities around the barbecue may include food preparation and serving areas, storage cabinets, an under-the-counter

refrigerator, a vent hood, a sink with a garbage disposal, a dishwasher, and a place to eat. L- or U-shaped layouts allow for buffet counters and dining islands with ample storage shelves and cupboards. Depending on what you like to cook, you can install pizza ovens, griddles, infrared rotisseries, built-in woks, deep-fryers, and much more. Built-in entertainment centers with TV or stereo systems are other possible additions.

The best place for an outdoor kitchen is almost always adjacent to the house, so that you can tap into plumbing and electrical lines. Another favorite spot is near the swimming pool. You must route water supply pipes, drainpipes, gas line, and electrical cable or conduit to the kitchen either beneath a concrete slab or—if the kitchen is next to the house—by means

of an exterior wall or overhead. In cold climates, pipes should be insulated or equipped with valves at low points to facilitate drainage in winter. Drainpipes must slope toward the main house drain, which can affect the location of your sink.

An area used for cooking and eating outdoors should be at least partially sheltered by a simple overhead or housed in an arbor. Depending on the site's exposure and microclimate, you may need to add screens, trellises, or even heavy-duty sliding doors to moderate wind, rain, or hot sun. Also be sure to place your grill or cooktop in a location where smoke and cooking odors will not drift toward the seating area.

Maintaining and cleaning outdoor cooking facilities can be a challenge. Use protective grill covers and rugged materials such as concrete and tile so that you can clean the kitchen area simply by hosing it down.

An outdoor kitchen is subject to local building, electrical, and plumbing codes and will require permits from the appropriate inspectors. If you're planning an extensive kitchen addition outside, it's best to consult a landscape architect or contractor familiar with such additions.

ABOVE AND LEFT *Italy was the inspiration for this kitchen in Healdsburg, California. The look is defined by the materials: stone columns, flagstone pavers, hand-hewn wood beams, terracotta roof tiles, and warm-toned plaster walls. The focal point is an elevated wide-mouthed pizza oven that also warms the patio.*

FACING PAGE *Outfitted for serious cooking, this kitchen houses slate-covered counters, a sink, a built-in barbecue, a mini-refrigerator, and a hearth.*

Kitchen Basics

Lighting Downlighting illuminates preparation areas; more diffuse fixtures, perhaps dimmer-controlled, can create ambience.

Electricity Outdoor electrical outlets, light fixtures, and switches must be protected by watertight boxes; all outdoor outlets must also be protected by a ground fault circuit interrupter (GFCI).

Grill The area around the grill should be "zero clearance," meaning the grill touches no combustible surface. Connect a built-in grill to a permanent gas line, making sure you can access the regulator and shut-off valve. Leave 36 inches of counter space on either side of the grill.

Ventilation If a grill is under an overhead or roof, you may need to provide a ventilation hood.

Sink May have hot and cold water, or just cold. Stainless steel is weatherproof; stone or ceramic are more expensive. Plumbing is subject to local codes.

Flooring Should be durable and easy to sweep or hose down. A drain aids cleanup.

Refrigerator Most often placed under the counter; buy a model specified for outdoor use.

Design Select materials that will complement the colors and materials used on your house and on other garden structures.

Counters Counters should be at least 30 inches deep and 36 inches high and made of a durable, noncombustible material such as granite, tile, slate, or fabricated stone.

Design Strategies

*There are many ways to arrange an outdoor kitchen, but here
are three approaches to help you imagine the possibilities.*

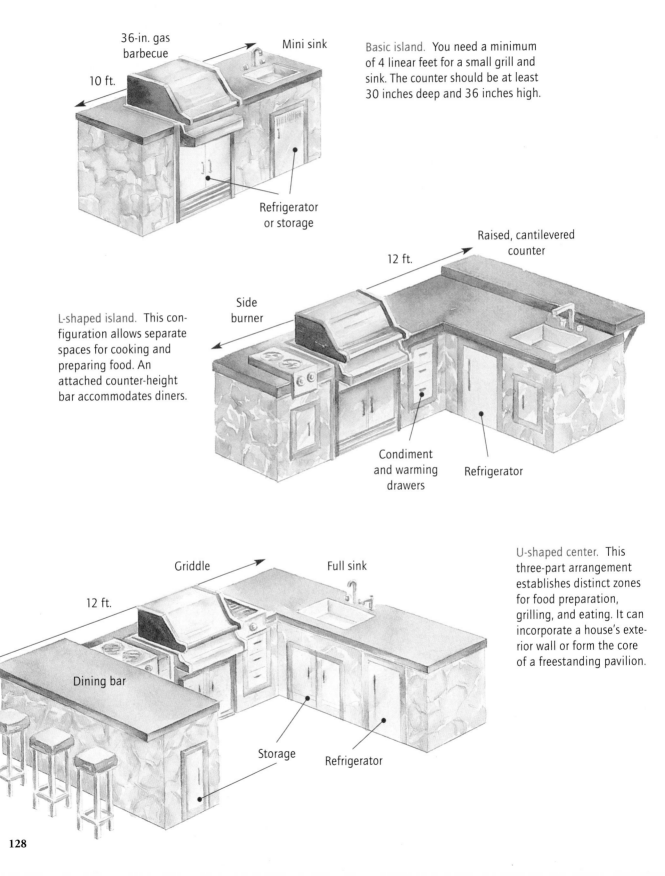

36-in. gas
barbecue

Mini sink

10 ft.

Basic island. You need a minimum
of 4 linear feet for a small grill and
sink. The counter should be at least
30 inches deep and 36 inches high.

Refrigerator
or storage

Raised, cantilevered
counter

12 ft.

Side
burner

L-shaped island. This con-
figuration allows separate
spaces for cooking and
preparing food. An
attached counter-height
bar accommodates diners.

Condiment
and warming
drawers

Refrigerator

Griddle

Full sink

12 ft.

Dining bar

U-shaped center. This
three-part arrangement
establishes distinct zones
for food preparation,
grilling, and eating. It can
incorporate a house's exterior wall or form the core
of a freestanding pavilion.

Storage

Refrigerator

Carol and Lynne Stephens loved spending time in their Northern California backyard, so the desire for a built-in barbecue was natural. They couldn't find a premade model to meet their needs, though, so they built an outdoor kitchen themselves. They had a perfect place to install the kitchen: up against the house on their rear patio, where there was ample room for a simple L-shaped counter. A trellis provides partial shade.

The project took two months of mostly weekend and evening work. It includes a barbecue, sink, bar, and storage space along with gas, electricity, and plumbing lines. The area shares a wall with the kitchen, making it easy to talk and pass food and dishes through a connecting window.

Build It: A Family Kitchen

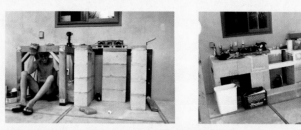

1. Once plumbing, gas, and electrical outlets are in place, you can construct a basic framework for the cooking center—where the grill or oven will be—out of fire-safe concrete blocks. Form a support for the base of the sink and bar from wood framing. Cover the grilling counter and buffet area with cement backerboard (a strong, water-resistant base for tile).

2. Around the sink counter and the buffet surface, use water-proof tile backing to underlay the tile.

3. Set the tiles (slate is shown here) in place with tile mortar and fill in spaces with a grout specified for exterior use. You can also cover the backerboard with a light coat of stucco painted to match house walls.

4. Once the framework is completed, install and hook up the sink and barbecue. In this kitchen, plumbing and gas lines, as well as under-counter storage, are fronted with weatherproof stainless steel doors.

LEFT *Sioux and Terry Elledge love to entertain outdoors, so they organized their Napa, California, garden around a covered pavilion featuring a cooking center, wine-tasting bar, and dining area. A post-and-beam overhead supports a gabled roof of bamboo fencing covered with panels of corrugated fiberglass; the combination protects the bamboo from rain but allows sunlight to filter through.*

ABOVE LEFT *A carved granite farmhouse-style sink lends rustic character to the Elledge kitchen. The counter and backsplash are covered with slate tile.*

ABOVE RIGHT *This outdoor living and kitchen patio features a pizza oven set into a low seating wall; freeform paving on the patio echoes the stout dome of the oven.*

BELOW *This timeless patio designed by Nick Williams has all the comforts of home: a state-of-the-art barbecue with tile counter and sink, a firepit for toasting marsh-mallows, and an outdoor hearth to gather around on chilly evenings. The fireplace, counter base, and wall are formed with Rastra blocks made of recycled plastic foam and cement.*

RIGHT *Pavers seem to float in a sea of succulents, including 'Sticks on Fire' euphorbia and blue* Senecio mandraliscae *in Suzy Schaefer's garden in Rancho Santa Fe. The tough sedum ground cover thrives even with the foot traffic along the path.*

BELOW *Raised stepping pads of dark cobblestone rise above the ground as they weave their way through a grove of bamboo.*

Paths

A path does a lot more than get you from A to B. It defines the way your garden is viewed. It calls attention to lush plantings, offers surprises, and creates destinations. Paths are ideal for creating visual garden trickery—making a small space seem larger by concealing the pathway's end, for instance. Likewise, you can use "forced perspective" to gradually diminish the width of the path to make it appear longer.

Paths also affect the garden experience. In a larger garden, you can allow room to meander, passing through open ground as well as shaded spots. In a smaller space, you can alternately reveal and conceal special plantings, a piece of sculpture, a small bench, or a mountain view. A path can even become an experience in itself—arranged in a spiral to form a labyrinth, or widening to allow for seating before narrowing to invite further strolling.

The width of your path depends on how you'll use it. If the path will wind discreetly through a garden and serve only as a walking surface, 2 feet is adequate. To allow room for lawn mowers and other equipment, make it 3 feet wide. For two people to walk abreast, as in an entry path, it should be 5 feet wide.

Tailor your choice of material to the task at hand. Major access walks should provide easy traffic flow and an even, nonstick surface such as brick, pavers, concrete, unglazed tile, or uniform stone slabs. Well-defined edgings keep plantings at bay. If you are unlikely to be pushing a wheelbarrow or wheeling a bicycle along the path on a regular basis, a rustic path of gravel or bark chips blends into the surrounds with its uneven texture and natural colors.

Adobe blocks, rough cobbles, stone mosaics, and other casual materials can be embedded in concrete to make an artistic statement. For a concrete path, or any other nonporous material, plan to pitch the path slightly to one side for drainage, or build it with a slight crown in the center. Runoff needs about ¼ inch of slope per foot.

At night, low-voltage path lights provide plenty of illumination but little disorienting glare. If your terrain is steep, plan for one or two broadly spaced steps for safety and comfort.

ABOVE *Designed for accessibility, Elizabeth Twaddell's landscape works well for someone in, or out of, a wheelchair. A gently sloping pathway leads through the garden; it is both wheelchair ramp and tricycle path.*

RIGHT *To brighten up this pathway with quick and easy color, the designers at Sisters Specialty Gardens filled in around buff pavers with white, pink, and blue annual nemesias. Low, mounding chamomile and thyme grow between the annuals.*

ABOVE *Pavers are arranged like dominoes on a surface of crushed gravel; the joints between the stone are filled with greenery, but the edges are left bare. The pale stone pavers echo the color of the roses behind.*

LEFT *An elevated, weather-bleached wooden boardwalk lets you admire your garden from a new perspective. The foliage of grasses, agapanthus, and daylilies spills over the sides.*

BELOW *Exuberant gardens call for paths with originality. This one features a mix of stone pavers and bricks interspersed with sweet alyssum.*

LEFT *Wide, smooth flagstone slabs lead from front gate to doorway. The pale sandstone color of the pavers harmonizes with the butter-colored house walls.*

Build It: A Flagstone Path

1. Mark the edges of the path with string and stakes (shown). A straight line is rarely the most interesting; even a small path becomes more intriguing with a slight bend or two.

2. Dig out the soil to a depth of 4 inches. If you like, you can use the excavated soil to make a berm. Tamp down the soil firmly, then recheck the depth (shown). Spread 2 inches of base rock or crushed gravel over the soil and tamp down. Use a carpenter's level placed along a board to check that the base is level.

3. Spread about 1 inch of builder's sand over the path to accept the flagstones (don't tamp it down). The flagstones should be about ¹/₂ inch above ground level once set in place.

4. Set the stones in place (shown), moving them around until you find a pleasing arrangement that requires a minimum of cutting. Tap each stone down firmly with a rubber mallet. Check for level, adding or taking away sand as needed. Finally, sweep damp sand into the cracks.

The slopes surrounding this sunken terrace resemble an undersea garden with spiky agaves and aloes, stacked rock walls, and sculptural olive trees that cast shadows on the patio floor.

Patios

Whether covered by an arbor or open to the sun, the patio is likely to be one of the best-used parts of the garden. Its essential ingredients include comfortable furniture, shelter, privacy, and a surround of favorite plants. Patio enhancements take many forms—water features, overheads, cooking facilities, or fireplaces.

The most common spot for a patio tends to be immediately outside the house, accessed by French or sliding doors, but if room allows, don't limit yourself to a single space. Consider a series of interrelated spaces connected by steps, or a detached, protected patio in the corner of your lot. Even a neglected sideyard may be the spot for a private, screened sitting area. Or an existing driveway could be converted. Enclosed by a wall, and accented with plantings, a small front lawn could be transformed into an entry courtyard.

A comfortable dining area includes the table, plus 36 to 48 inches for chair space on all sides. A typical round or square table requires an area 10 to 12 feet square. For a barbecue area, allow space for at least one small preparation table. A space 6 by 8 feet will fit a cook and a couple of supervisors.

ABOVE *A simple gravel clearing becomes a Mediterranean-style patio with the addition of a few bistro chairs and a round table. A substantial olive jar reinforces the theme.*

LEFT *Blending indoors and out, this jungly patio is filled with palms and big-leafed tropical plants, including a pair of banana trees in matching urns. Wicker furniture and a patterned floor rug add to the exotic mood.*

Masonry Materials

The material you choose for your patio must meet several criteria. It should harmonize with the other landscaping materials in your garden. It must be weatherproof, able to tolerate the amount of rain or frost that you have in your area. Finally, it should provide a surface that is appropriate to the demands you will place on it.

A durable, stable outdoor floor can be made without concrete or mortar, by laying brick, pavers, or flagstones on a firmly tamped bed of gravel and sand; other materials are more finicky and call for a firmer subsurface.

Brick. Although they are not as strong and weather resistant as other paving materials, brick adds rustic charm to almost any landscape. Bricks may be a single color, speckled, or composed of several slightly different hues. Used common bricks are often partially covered with white efflorescence. Consult with a local dealer to make sure that the brick you buy will last as a paving material in your area.

Stone. *Flagstone* is a general term referring to large, flat stones that are 1 to 4 inches thick. Common types

Build It: A Brick or Paver Patio

1. String mason's lines from stakes to mark the edges of the patio. Excavate the patio area to an even depth and fill with 2 inches of gravel. Dig a 5-inch wide and deep trench around the edge of the patio and fill it with 2 inches of gravel. Install 2-by-4-inch wood edging, driving stakes every few feet (above) to hold them in place.

2. Spread landscaping fabric over the gravel. Cut the pieces carefully and butt them tightly against the edging. Overlap each strip by 6 to 8 inches. Spread sand over the fabric, and use a rake to make it as level as possible. The sand should be a little damp; if it dries out, spray it with a hose nozzle set on mist.

used in the West are limestone, sandstone, or slate. The rough, bumpy surface of most flagstone offers excellent traction in wet conditions but makes it somewhat difficult to scoot a chair away from a table. *Cobblestones* are roughly cut into squares or rectangles with rounded edges, usually from 6 to 12 inches square. Granite cobblestones are expensive but stunning and are often used for borders, accents, or small walks.

Pavers. Concrete pavers are usually less expensive than brick or stone, which makes them the obvious choice for many people. However, the faux appearance of many types makes it a challenge to blend them into a landscape. Newer types come closer to the look of weathered natural stone. Pavers may be square, round, rectangular, or hexagonal; "interlocking" pavers are designed to fit together like a jigsaw puzzle.

Tile. Natural *stone* cut into square or rectangular tiles creates a formal-looking surface. Many stone tiles must be laid in a bed of mortar atop a solid concrete slab or they will crack; thicker and stronger types can be set in sand like bricks or pavers. For splashes of color, *ceramic* tile is a good choice. *Mexican Saltillo* and *terra-cotta* tiles have a soft reddish glow that lends warmth to a patio, but most types are suitable for warm climates only.

ABOVE *Square stone pavers interplanted with grass provide a geometric contrast to a riot of tropical foliage in the background. Clean stone planters and a fireplace carry the look to an upper patio.*

FACING PAGE *A hillside aerie has both floor and walls faced in simple flagstone that don't call attention away from the cityscape. Lights set into the walls provide low-level illumination for evenings out; the furniture is clean and simple.*

3. Level the sand with a bladed screed. (If the patio is over 7 feet wide, you will need a helper to hold one end of the screed.) Start at one end, moving the screed across the patio to smooth the sand to the thickness of a single brick.

4. Start laying out the bricks in one corner, abutting the edging. Lay the bricks tightly against one another, tapping each into place with a hand sledge or mallet. Check level frequently. If you have a lot of angled cuts to make for the patio edges, consider renting a masonry saw.

5. Scatter fine sand over the pavers and use a soft bristled broom to sweep the sand into the joints. Tamp down on the bricks to settle the sand down into the joints. Sweep more sand into the joints and tamp again until the joints stay full.

ABOVE *Two paths intersect to create a sitting area; chunks of honey-colored cobblestone mark the boundaries and flank beds of clipped boxwood.*

RIGHT *A knee wall of terra-cotta red bisects this cozy sideyard. Although much of the floor is decomposed granite, blue-stone pavers create interest at the edges of the space. Creeping thyme and silvery lamb's ears add color to the floorscape.*

FACING PAGE, ABOVE *Mixed concrete, inset pebbles, and rough boulders create interest in this natural-looking patio, which calls to mind a mountain stream bed. Teak furnishings add warmth.*

Loose Materials

For economy and good drainage, both gravel and crushed rock can provide material for patios. Gravel is collected or mined from natural deposits, crushed rock is mechanically fractured and graded to a uniform size. Frequently, gravel is named after the region where it was quarried. Gravel surfaces tend to shift when walked on, but the movement will be minimized if you use a compacted base of crushed rock or sand. Edgings of wood, stone, concrete, or benderboard will help to keep loose materials out of beds and lawns.

When choosing gravel, consider color, sheen, texture, and size. Take home samples as you would paint chips. Keep in mind that gravel color, like paint color, looks more intense when spread over a large area. And if you live in a region with regular rainfall or fog, remember that moisture can also significantly darken its hue.

Concrete

Though sometimes disparaged as cold and forbidding, poured—or, more accurately, cast—concrete is even more variable in appearance than brick. Used with well-made forms, it can conform to almost any shape. Furthermore, it can be lightly smoothed or heavily brushed, surfaced with handsome pebbles, swirled or scored, patterned, or molded to resemble another material. Other ways to modify a standard concrete surface include color dusting, staining, masking, acid washing, and tinting. And if you eventually get tired of the concrete surface you have chosen, you can use it as a foundation for a new pavement of brick, stone, or tile set in mortar.

The standard slab for pathways and patios should be 4 inches thick. In addition, you will have to allow for at least a 2-inch gravel base in areas where frost and drainage are not problems, and a 4- to 8-inch base where they are likely to be cause for concern. Wooden forms are usually 2-by-4s set on edge; for curved forms, choose either tempered hardboard, plywood, or redwood benderboard.

Mosaics in Concrete

Mosaics range from formal geometric patterns to eclectic designs that combine stones, broken pottery, glass beads, and shells. The most successful installations are set on a level, prepared surface and have edgings to hold the mosaic in place. The finished mosaic should slope slightly to either side for runoff; see page 283 for further details.

Play Areas

Kids love to have a place they can call their own in the backyard. It can be something as simple as a sandbox or slide, or an elaborate climbing structure or even a tree house. Whatever your child's play setting, the first requirement is that it should be safe, which means that it must be suited to the age and skill level of the children who will be using it.

The first decision to make when planning a play yard is where to place it. Preschoolers may feel safe—and can be more easily supervised—if the area is close to the house. Also take into account sun, wind, and shade. Hot sun increases the risk of sunburn and can make metals or concrete burning hot, so install such surfaces in the shade or facing north. In most parts of the West, dappled shade is ideal for a children's play area; if you have no spreading foliage, choose the north side of the house or construct a canopy of lath or canvas to provide relief from direct sun. In very damp areas, however, such a site can encourage the growth of slippery moss or mold, and a more sunny spot may be more suitable.

There are many ways to make your garden child-friendly. Gravel paths, for instance, are frustrating for kids on wheels; a smooth concrete surface at least 24 inches wide is best for bikes, roller skates, and scooters. Along boundaries, the need for fencing is obvious. Also securely enclose the play area from the driveway, as well as the pool, a spa, or any other body of water. Finally, have a secure place to keep sharp or heavy tools, garden supplies, and equipment.

RIGHT *This stucco wall was transformed into a children's outdoor art studio with a coat of blackboard paint.*

BELOW *A pint-size playhouse is accessorized with clapboard siding, shingled roof, dormer windows (complete with window boxes), and a little front porch.*

FACING PAGE *Tucked into a corner in this Beaverton, Oregon, garden, a colorful 16-square-foot playhouse is furnished with a child-size table and chairs.*

FACING PAGE, INSET *Keeping curious cats out of the sandbox when it's not in use, this spider-web cover is lightweight enough for kids to handle themselves.*

RIGHT *This back-yard is set up like a city park, with an open grassy area for playing, hanging sling chairs, and colorful steel sculptures made by owner Ginny Davis.*

BELOW, LEFT *Bright primary colors appeal to kids of all ages, as do exotic plants such as these tall bamboos that rustle at tree-house height.*

BELOW, RIGHT *A stage? A playhouse? This play center will be up to whatever task a child can imagine. Four plat-forms of varying heights, each roughly 5 feet square, form decks and a sandbox. A 3-foot-tall panel of outdoor fabric wraps around the outer sides of one of the decks.*

Play It Safe

- The lumber used for play equipment must be rot-resistant—especially the members that are in contact with the ground—and splinter-free. Nontreated redwood and cedar are the best choices.

- A general rule for any play structure is that no opening—railings, monkey bars, ladders, and windows—be between 3½ and 9 inches wide, because these spaces can trap a small child. Ladders should have uniformly spaced rungs and be placed at a 75° angle from the ground. Any elevated surface—such as a platform or a ramp—should have a guardrail.

- Allow at least 6 feet of "fall zone" around all sides of swings, slides, and climbing structures, then cushion it well with 6 to 12 inches of wood chips, mulch, sand, or pea gravel, or with mats made of safety-tested rubber or rubber-like materials. A low wall or edging around a play yard will contain loose materials.

- If you are buying a play structure as a kit, how hefty are the pieces? Minimums are 4-by-4-inch posts, 4-by-6-inch swing beams, and ¾-inch-thick deck boards. Edges should be smooth and corners rounded.

- Hardware for a play structure should be sturdy and rust-resistant. Key joints should be fortified with bolts and metal braces.

- Finally, be sure that all equipment is age appropriate.

Polyester **rope** is best.

Guardrails for older children should start at 30 in. above ground.

Soft, flexible **swing seats** are safest.

Fall zone should be at least 6 ft.

Slides must have raised sides; double wall types are safest.

Ladder angle should be 75°.

Ponds

It doesn't take a lot of water to soothe the soul. Even a small pond can have a cooling effect—both physically and psychologically. The size of your pond will be restricted by the space available, but you can make a pond almost any shape and style you wish. If you want to start small, consider the decorative pools and water features shown on pages 288–291.

Placing the Pond

The obvious spot for a pond is where everyone can enjoy it. But because children find ponds irresistible, check with your local building department about any requirements for barriers, as well as for setbacks from property lines, electrical circuits for pumps and lights, and pond depth. Generally, ponds less than 24 inches deep do not need a building permit.

If you are planning to add plants or fish to the pond, consider the climate in your garden. The pond must be protected from strong winds and sited away from messy trees. *Don't* choose a low-lying (or "bottom") area that will constantly overflow in wet weather. The backyard is only one place to build a pond. The addition of moving water to a front patio or a sideyard can add interest and block the noise of passing traffic.

There are plenty of ways to harmonize the pond with its surroundings. A rock garden filled with native stones may suit a natural looking landscape. Adjacent to a lawn, a wide concrete or stone lip overhanging the pond edge can be especially useful as a mowing strip. Near a wooden deck or arbor, an edging of redwood or other rot-resistant wood can link the structures together. Borders can look especially lush pondside, and will help to attract wildlife such as birds and butterflies.

Stocking the Pond

A filter is not always necessary to keep the pond clear. A well-balanced pond contains a healthy balance of fish and oxygenating plants. Fish feed on algae, as do water snails, which are a valuable addition to any pond. Algae thrive on sunlight; surface plants such as water lilies, lotus, and water hawthorn provide coverage to minimize algae growth. Koi require a pond at least 2 feet deep, a pump for aeration, and a filtering system.

ABOVE *Part of a garden devoted to attracting wildlife, this pond is not only well-stocked with fish, but is also a water source for birds, dragonflies, and butterflies. To make the pond even more enticing to winged creatures, owner Barbara Thuro surrounded it with nectar-rich Jupiter's beard and sweet alyssum.*

FACING PAGE *The centerpiece of this Taos garden is a free-form natural-looking pond. Stones outline its perimeter, while water-thrifty perennials, including Russian sage and white-flowered* Datura inoxia, *crowd around in a colorful jumble. Two biofilters keep the water sparkling.*

LEFT *A giant gunnera leaf sheds water into the smooth surface of a brick-lined pond in the Waterman garden on Bainbridge Island, Washington. "Floating" across the pond are a series of stepping stones.*

Pond Construction

Garden pools range from for-mal reflecting pools and deep, plant-filled koi ponds with sophis-ticated pump-and-filter systems to simple naturalistic types that house a few plants and some goldfish. A do-it-yourselfer can easily build a pond such as the one shown here. The hard work lies in digging the hole and installing the liner, which can be quite heavy.

A flexible liner can take on almost any shape, accommodating curves and undulations, as well as the "shelves" that will hold mar-ginal aquatic plants. Home and garden centers stock liners ranging from less-expensive PVC (poly-vinyl chloride) to higher-grade EPDM (ethylene propylene diene monomer, a roofing material), a durable rubber that you can expect to last for 20 years.

Another option is preformed rigid fiberglass or polyethylene pool shells, which come in a variety of shapes and configurations, some with built-in waterfalls and small streams. These simplify the design process and can be expected to last 30 years or more. Preformed shells are easy to install but require more precision in excavation than flexible liners, and the hard "lip" around the edge can be difficult to conceal.

Choose a border that harmonizes the pond with the surrounding landscaping. Boulders and flag-stones are popular choices, but options range from mortared tile, brick, or pavers to a simple lawn edging or wood timbers—stick with a material that you have elsewhere in the garden.

Anatomy of a Pond

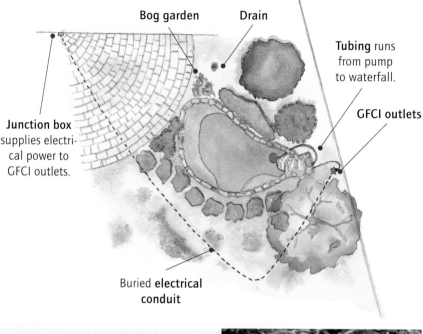

Bog garden **Drain**

Tubing runs from pump to waterfall.

GFCI outlets

Junction box supplies electri-cal power to GFCI outlets.

Buried **electrical conduit**

Build It: A Garden Pool

1. Install a GFCI outlet to power the pond pump and any lighting. Use a garden hose or a long rope to outline the edges of the pool in a shape that is pleasing to you. When you are satisfied with the size and shape, use spray paint or colored sand to mark the perimeter of the pond.

2. It's best to put off purchasing the liner until after the hole is dug and you can calculate the size that you need. As you dig, snip off stray roots and remove stones. If you find a sig-nificant number of roots, reshape or shift the pool outline to avoid dam-aging a desirable plant. First, dig the entire pool down to the height of the marginal shelves. Mark the edges of the shelves as you did the perimeter, then dig out the rest of the pond.

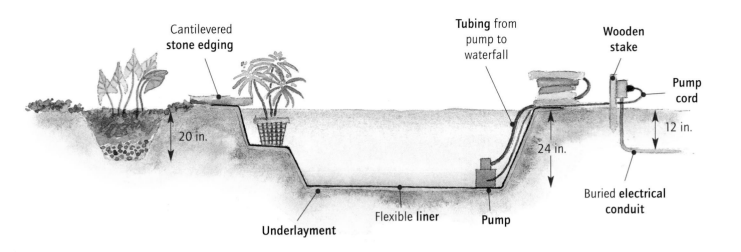

Cantilevered **stone edging**

Tubing from pump to waterfall

Wooden stake

Pump cord

20 in.

24 in.

12 in.

Underlayment

Flexible **liner**

Pump

Buried **electrical conduit**

3. Set a long 2-by-4 across the hole and use a carpenter's level to check that the sides are of equal height; if they are uneven, use some of the excavated soil to build a berm around the low side. Leave the 2-by-4 in place and use it as a guide to check the depth of the hole and of the marginal shelves, digging or filling as needed.

4. Underlayment protects the pool liner from being damaged by sharp rocks or other objects in the soil. Use stones to hold the underlayment in place until the liner is added. An alternative to a liner is to install 2 inches of sand on the bottom and sides of the hole.

5. Shift the liner into position, draping it to follow the contours of the hole as closely as possible. Weigh down the edges of the liner, then start to fill it with water, tucking in wrinkles at the edges as required. When the pond is full, install the edging as soon as possible, then add plants, fish, and accessories.

Falling Water

Waterfalls and spill fountains bring to the garden the sound of splashing water, adding a whole new sensory experience to a pool. A well-designed waterfall resembles a never-ending flow of water; in fact, there is really only a limited amount of water circulated by a pump and tubing. The water features can be as large or small as you please; just be sure to install a recirculating pump and tubing large enough to handle the volume of water.

Cascading water calls for a watertight liner—either a flexible one that you can trim to fit your water channel, or a prefabricated unit similar to a rigid pool liner. Both are available at pool supply and home improvement stores. The placement of rocks and boulders around a waterfall determines the character of the falls. Irregularly shaped rocks in the center of the channel create miniature rapids; narrowing the sides of the waterfall compresses the waterfall into a thicker curtain. Gaps, grooves, and other irregularities in the lip create unique patterns.

Spill fountains have long streams of water coming from a source above or adjacent to a pool. Such fountains can be simple tiers of pans, with the water flowing from one level down to the next, or wall fountains, where the water rises up through a tube and then pours back into a container or pool. The water can pour directly into the pool from a pipe, exit the mouth of a lion or gargoyle, or overflow from a basin.

ABOVE *A divided curtain of water spills from the stacked-stone center of this fountain into a basin filled with arching water plants. A surround of vivid scarlet-orange walls and a rustic stone orb add sculptural touches.*

INSET *A koi nudges up to a water lily.*

FACING PAGE *Steep slopes naturally lend themselves to tiered waterfalls. Here, a stream falls over a series of spillways into a pool, then recirculates back up. Pink-blooming rockrose adds color streamside.*

RIGHT *Sheets of water fall around massive slabs of stone set upright in a shallow pool.*

Pools

Swimming pools no longer occupy center stage in Western gardens—they've slimmed down to fit into landscapes rather than overpower them. Still, you'll want to be sure you have enough pool for the kind of aquatic fun you enjoy. Children, for instance, need a wide, shallow area. Lap swimmers require a long, straight section—up to 40 feet will allow you to execute several swift strokes before having to reverse direction. Unless you like to practice dives, a pool need not be deeper than 4 or 5 feet.

The sun patterns in your garden will help determine the pool's location. Wind is the next important factor—it can greatly affect the perceived warmth of a pool as it ripples across the water. If prevailing winds blow across your property, you may need to install windblocks. Few yards are perfectly flat and, in fact, some of the most spectacular pool settings are hillsides, but building a pool into a steep slope calls for additional engineering.

Because of its size, you may not be able to make your pool completely private, but you'll probably want it secluded from passersby and neighbors. Although the pool needn't be immediately adjacent to your house, there should be clear access from the pool to a changing room and bathroom. You'll also want it convenient to reach—and well lit in the evening.

Even with a modest-size pool, there are many shapes other than rectangular, circular, and kidney-shaped. Consider an alternative outline if your yard is small or awkwardly shaped, or if you want to preserve a large tree, rocky outcropping, or other landscape feature.

Plan for a paved area or deck surrounding or adjoining the pool. The surface should be nonskid and slightly sloped to drain away from the pool. It's best to isolate lawns and planting beds from the pool; otherwise, swimmers will drag plants and soil into the pool with each entry.

Building a Pool

Pools can be built above ground, in-ground, or partially in-ground and integrated into your garden's design. For pool construction, concrete (either poured or sprayed-on) is the most durable. Interior finishes

RIGHT *Stone decking is a perfect choice to unify a long, narrow pool and spa with the clean-lined modern architecture of this home.*

FACING PAGE *A lavender color theme links the pool chairs, blossoms, and ball around the pool in the garden of Ginny Davis. A new "ruin wall" divides the pool from the rest of the garden.*

BELOW *A deep swimming hole built by Mark David Levine and Don Goldstone matches the scale of background trees and the large boulders that surround the pool. Plants as well as water drape and spill over the sides.*

include paint, plaster, and tile, in ascending order of cost. To keep the cost down, save tile for details—edgings, step markers, and around the water line.

Vinyl-lined pools are usually much less expensive than concrete, because the liner is prefabricated and the pool can be installed in as little as a few days. The liner generally rests on a bed of sand and is supported by walls made of aluminum, steel, plaster, concrete block, or wood. These walls can extend above grade, making them especially economical for sloping sites. One-piece fiberglass shells are also fairly quick to install; the shell is supported by a bed of sand.

No matter what type of in-ground pool you choose, the construction begins with excavation. The process is similar to the construction of a house's foundation; to lessen the impact on your landscape, make decisions with the contractor in advance, including exactly where the access route will be, the location for storing excavated soil, and which portions of the yard will be disturbed by heavy equipment.

153

Pool Details

Once you've defined the broad goals for your pool, take a good look at the elements within it:

Wiring. Nothing adds to the allure of a pool more than good lighting. Fountains and other water features also demand wiring for electric pumps. Needless to say, water and electricity call for the services of a professional.

Plantings. The area around a swimming pool is a harsh environment for plants, thanks to the combination of pool chemicals, strong sunlight, hot concrete, and humidity. To make wise choices, take note of the plants that grow well for your pool-owning neighbors and consult with a knowledgeable nurseryman in your area.

Stairs and pathways. How will you and your guests move from house to pool to the broader landscape? Your options for surfacing paths and steps are even

LEFT *Water spouts set into a background of mottled blue tile spill small cascades of water into this swimming pool. Tiled steps lead to a brick firepit in a sitting area.*

Safe Swimming

According to the U.S. Consumer Product Safety Commission, the vast majority of people drowned or injured in a swimming pool are children under the age of five. Most municipalities have laws requiring some kind of protective barriers for a swimming pool. Familiarize yourself with these local guidelines when designing your pool.

- A barrier—either a fence or a wall—at least 4 feet high should completely surround the pool. A fence should have slats less than 4 inches apart, and the bottom should be no more than 4 inches above the ground (right above).

- Gates should be self-closing and self-latching; they should close in the direction of the pool. The latch-release mechanism should be at least 3 inches below the top of the gate and no opening near the latch should exceed

$1/2$ inch to keep little fingers from reaching through to release the latch (right, below).

- Safety covers for both swimming pools and spas should meet the weight-bearing standards of the American Society for Testing and Materials (ASTM), and have no gaps along the perimeter through which a small child could crawl.

- Equip the pool with basic rescue equipment, including ring buoys, rescue tubes, and a shepherd's crook (a long hooked pole).

- If a pool is part of your landscaping plan, make sure your kids learn to swim. Do your part by learning water rescue techniques, artificial respiration, and cardiopulmonary resuscitation (CPR).

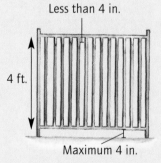

Less than 4 in.

4 ft.

Maximum 4 in.

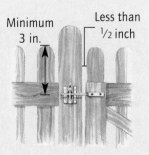

Minimum 3 in.

Less than $1/2$ inch

Steely blue-gray agaves and low-growing Senecio mandraliscae *make long-lived poolside sculpture against a background of bamboo. Both plants and glazed urns reflect beautifully in the water.*

BELOW *Sleek curtains of falling water splash over a ledge into the pool in Bob and Linda Shelby's backyard. A coping of stone is wide enough for seating at the pool's edge.*

wider than for patios and decks—but keep loose materials such as gravel or wood chips well away from the pool surround; these can make pool maintenance a never-ending task.

Water features. A water slide, waterfall, or fountain can add drama, elegance, or just plain fun to your pool. To add a fountain that connects to the pool's plumbing, you'll need the help of a professional pool technician.

Furnishings. As with plants, poolside furniture must take a lot of abuse, so choose materials that can tolerate the exposure to water. Keep comfort in mind, too; to accommodate everyone who will use the pool, you may want to buy chairs or benches in several different sizes and styles.

Shade. Plants, arbors, shade sails, and cabanas all provide essential sun protection around the pool. In addition, an overhead structure can screen your site from above—to block views from neighboring homes or apartments.

Raised Beds

There are many advantages to raised beds. Filled with organically rich soil, they warm up quickly in spring, provide perfect drainage, and often yield heavier crops of vegetables and blooming flowers. They make it possible to garden over heavy clay soil or rock-solid caliche. They can be underlined with hardware cloth to foil gophers and moles. On sloping terrain, they can create level terraces to extend the cultivated area.

In most cases, you can turn any plot of ground into a fairly substantial raised-bed garden—in little time and for a modest cost.

Because you reach in to plant and maintain most raised beds, the center of each bed should be no more than an arm's length from the edge, making the width around 4 feet. Eight to 10 feet is a good length. The height should be at least 10 inches; for wheelchair gardening, which is facilitated by raised beds, make the height about 24 inches.

Framing and Filling Beds

Wood is used to frame most raised beds. Because untreated wood rots fairly quickly where it contacts soil, most people use rot-resistant cedar or redwood, pressure-treated lumber (see page 158), or composite lumber. Large timbers are often used to frame many raised beds, but you can build smaller-scale beds with sides made from two 2-by-5s or 2-by-6s stacked on top of each other. (Don't try to make sides out of single 2-by-10s or 2-by-12s; such extrawide boards will warp and pull apart at the corners.)

Interlocking concrete blocks and dry-stacked rocks and flagstones are also commonly used to form beds. If you use stones, place the largest ones at the bottom.

You can fill a bed with amended native soil or imported topsoil. In most instances, you can improve native soil by digging in a 4- to 6-inch layer of compost, well-aged manure, or other organic material before planting. If your native soil is too hard or rocky to amend easily, bring in topsoil that contains at least one-third organic matter by volume. Since soil settles over time and organic matter decomposes, you'll need to replenish the soil every spring before planting.

ABOVE *Raised planting beds beside a staircase are filled with yellow-flowered* Anigozanthos *and burgundy New Zealand flax. A tracery of espaliered honeysuckle is set against a burnt-orange wall.*

FACING PAGE *You don't need lots of space to grow herbs and vegetables. This quartet of 4-foot-square raised beds is packed with home-grown produce, including beans, tomatoes, lettuce, peppers, and herbs. The beds are edged with durable 2-by-6-inch Trex composite lumber.*

LEFT *Cobalt-blue painted walls and a pair of sculptural inhabitants set the stage for a mix of butter-yellow flowers and foliage.*

Pressure-treated Wood

Traditionally, pressure-treated lumber has been used to build garden structures that come into contact with soil or water—including raised beds used to grow edible plants. For years this lumber has been treated with a chemical containing chromated copper arsenate (CCA), which has been banned by the Environmental Protection Agency (EPA) as a preservative for wood intended for residential use. New compounds—including alkaline copper quat (ACQ) and copper azole (CBA-A, CA-B) are approved by the EPA as low-toxic wood preservatives. Although the toxicity of these products is less than that of CCA, you should still wear gloves and a dust mask when working with treated wood. And because the copper content of these woods is corrosive to aluminum and regular steel, be sure to use corrosion-resistant fasteners such as stainless steel or galvanized metal.

Redwood and cedar heartwoods have a natural resistance to decay and termites. You can opt for these woods in potential contact areas, such as raised beds, or you can line planters with impermeable plastic or sheet metal. Another alternative to lumber is wood-polymer composites such as ChoiceDek, Trex, and TimberTech (see page 107).

Some salvaged wood, such as railway ties, has been treated with creosote, a toxic chemical that should not be used for any garden construction.

ABOVE *A parterre of stone-edged raised beds filled with clipped evergreens presents a formal appearance.*

BELOW *Raised beds filled with richly amended soil produce picture-perfect vegetables at Chalk Hill Clematis Farm in Healdsburg, California. Metal topiary frames in the beds hold tomatoes; gourd and hop vines conceal utilitarian metal poles. Polyethylene drip tubing runs along the tops of the boards; ¼-inch microtubing extends into the bed to water lush stands of basil.*

Build It: A Raised Bed

Inspired by stone walls she saw displayed at England's famous Chelsea Flower Show, Marilyn Herlihy Dronenburg of Fallbrook, California, dry-stacked flagstones to frame raised beds in her vegetable garden. She used "patio-cut" flagstone (1½-inch-thick slabs roughly 8 to 18 inches wide and long), which stacks easily, making it ideal for these mortarless walls. The beds measure 5½ by 11 feet and are about 2 feet tall.

1. Use a string to outline the bed's footprint, then measure and record its dimensions, including the wall's proposed height. Take the measurements to a flagstone supplier, who will determine how much you need. Define the bed's perimeter with powdered limestone or gypsum. Excavate or add soil as needed to create a level foundation for the bottom layer of stones.

2. Use the largest and most irregular slabs to build the bottom layer. Place stones with straight edges facing away from the bed and jagged edges facing in. To break oversize slabs into smaller pieces, first score a line on both sides of the stone with a chisel. Wearing gloves and protective goggles, place the stone's scoring line over a piece of scrap wood and hit the stone on the unwanted side with a sledgehammer.

3. As you stack each subsequent layer, check for level. Overlap slabs to avoid vertical seams. Fill in gaps with smaller pieces. For stability, angle each wall inside toward the bed 1 inch for every 1 foot of height. Use the most uniform pieces for the top layer. Backfill the walls with soil and tamp to settle it; then you are ready to plant.

Sheds

Every garden can benefit from a spacious, well-organized, safe place in which to store garden tools, supplies, and equipment. But a garden shed can be a much more valuable garden structure. With a few modifications, even a simple outbuilding can become a garden getaway—a potting shed, a craft studio, a playhouse, or just a place to read, tinker, and relax away from the hustle and bustle of the main house.

A building this size is a prominent feature in almost any garden, so it's worth integrating your shed into your landscape design. If you choose a prefabricated model from the local home and garden center, look for one that is similar in style to other structures in your garden. Keep in mind that you can dress it up with siding, shutters, or decorative woodwork to mirror your house architecture.

It's a common mistake to underestimate the amount of room you'll need for storage and workspace. When planning the shed, draw a simple floor plan that includes all the items you'd like to keep in the shed, such as lawn equipment, bicycles, and any seasonal items like furniture. To maximize the amount of storage space, consider where you could hang tools on the wall, or if there is any extra headroom that you could use to stow objects overhead.

It's worth making sure that the structure you want for your garden is in compliance with local regulations before you build it. Most small garden sheds can be built without a permit, but there are exceptions. In most municipalities, size matters; any shed larger than about 120 square feet requires a building permit. In some places, the issue is whether the structure is considered permanent—that is, does it have a poured

RIGHT *A cupola and French doors hung with curtains make this little building a backyard retreat.*

FACING PAGE *This country charmer has an air of rusticity, with board-and-batten siding, a shingled roof, and salvaged windows and door.*

LEFT *Looking like a fairy-tale cottage, this shed is tucked into a corner of Sharon Brasher's Reno garden. Pink 'Ballerina' roses scramble over the shingled roof.*

FACING PAGE *The eye-pleasing appeal of this shed belies its practicality. Designers Nan Reid and Steve Reid, Jr., gathered salvaged components for the construction, including multipaned windows and French doors.*

BELOW LEFT *A peaked roof with finial tops off this unconventional outbuilding in a Los Angeles garden.*

BELOW *This cozy little clapboard building with scalloped shingles is surrounded by hostas; honeysuckle scrambles over the roof.*

162

foundation? Certainly if you are planning to bring electricity to the shed from your house panel, you'll need an electrical permit. Finally, don't get too attached to a particular spot in the garden before checking on any zoning restrictions, setback requirements, or easements—a quick call to the zoning department can usually answer these questions.

Building a Shed

Even if you aren't a master builder, you can probably tackle the assembly needed to put together a shed kit from a mail-order company. Such kits run the gamut from simple lean-tos to elaborate cottages, and many offer custom options such as porches, reproduction hardware, and various siding and roofing options.

For those with more building expertise, consider purchasing an architect-designed shed plan. The best companies provide not only the plan itself, but drawings you can submit for permits, complete material and cut lists, and back-up help if you run into difficulties when building the shed.

Your building inspector can tell you if you need a frost-proof foundation—usually concrete piers that extend below the frost line. For most smaller sheds, or those that will be used for simple storage, a poured foundation isn't necessary—you can site the building on 6-by-6-foot timber "skids" or precast concrete piers. Whichever method you choose, set the foundation members on several inches of gravel, and be sure that they are completely level before you begin construction.

Showers

Outdoor showers are a practical necessity at beach homes, making it easy to rinse salt and sand off feet before they are tracked all over the house. But you can enjoy the pleasures of bathing out of doors wherever you can create a bit of privacy and run some plumbing lines.

To supply the shower head, you typically extend both hot and cold water lines through the wall of your house or an outbuilding. Components made specifically for outdoor showers are more expensive than for indoor types, but they prohibit rust, which is a problem for both fixtures and faucets.

In addition to plumbing water into the shower, you'll need a way for it to drain away. Keep in mind that if you plan to regularly use soap, shampoo, and cleaning products in the shower, the runoff from the shower is considered waste water. Some plumbing codes require that any waste water should be connected to your home's main drainage system; check with your local plumbing department. If your shower is connected to the

main drain, further building requirements may call for a roof over the shower, to prevent rainwater from entering the system. A drain shut-off might also be an acceptable solution.

Screening Strategies

To keep a shower open to the landscape yet maintain some privacy, you can employ a number of strategies. You can incorporate one or more walls of an existing structure, or install a surround of any waterproof material—treated wood, fiberglass, stone, or even plants. One contemporary option is lightscreen panels, a modern take on traditional stained-glass windows; they contain transluscent marbles suspended in an aluminum grid to block views but not light.

Don't underestimate how much space is needed to make a shower comfortable. You'll want towel racks or hooks beyond the reach of shower spray, and ledges for soap and shampoo. Finally, be sure the floor surface is nonskid and that the area around the shower is provided with adequate lighting for late-night hose-downs.

ABOVE RIGHT *A tall curving wall of lava rock makes a suitably exotic screen for the bathing enclosure, which is filled with water-loving tropical plants and ferns.*

RIGHT *Capistrano Beach landscape architect Theresa Clark managed to fit a shower into this narrow sideyard. Stone tile facing matches an antique limestone sink just beyond the doors.*

FACING PAGE *This shower, designed by Jim Matsuo, is adjacent to a swimming pool in a terraced garden in Topanga Canyon, California.*

FACING PAGE INSET *A stone ledge holds soap and a candle.*

Spas

Whether the focal point of a garden or a private retreat, a spa or hot tub has understandable appeal: an invigorating bath alfresco, enlivened with jets of water, in a tub large enough to accommodate both social and solitary soaks. Spas also double as decorative water features. Waterfalls, fountain jets, formal tile or natural stone borders, and exit streams that meander to a swimming pool all link the spa with its surroundings.

Spa siting is to some extent governed by plumbing and the spa's support equipment, which must stand a short distance away. Heaters, pumps, and filters are compact, but they must be connected to electrical and gas lines. You'll feel more comfortable if your spa is hidden from passersby; build an arbor or a gazebo around the spa, or screen it with live plantings or an arrangement of fences and walls.

For safety, spas should be inaccessible to young children and should be covered with a safety cover approved by the American Society for Testing and Materials (ASTM). Be sure to light steps, deck edges, and other potentially hazardous places. See page 154 for more information on poolside safety.

ABOVE *Mark David Levine designed this therapeutic spa for his parents' garden. The wide steps provide gentle access into the water; natural-looking boulders blend the spa into the garden.*

FACING PAGE, ABOVE *Surrounded by a stacked-stone wall, this sunken terrace in an Aspen garden provides privacy for the Zenlike spa within. Carefully placed accent boulders, a curved stone retaining wall, and native shrubs link the patio to the background of montane forest.*

FACING PAGE, BELOW *In the backyard of their Tucson home, Mohit and Sherry Modi can enjoy the view toward the Santa Catalina Mountains from their spa. Linked to the rest of the garden with a series of low walls and surrounded with native plants, the spa is integrated with the landscapes both in and outside the garden.*

Portable Spas

A portable, or self-contained, spa is more like a home appliance: it doesn't have to be permanently installed and comes as a complete unit, ready to be plugged into a 120-volt outlet (or wired to a 240-volt circuit). Its support equipment, or "skid pack," is part of the package. A "skirt," typically of redwood, surrounds the spa's inner shell. No building permit is required; the unit can sit on a concrete slab or a sturdy deck. You may surround the spa with benches, screens, or other amenities to create an integrated outdoor environment.

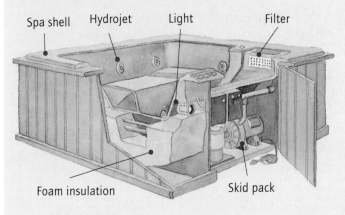

Spa shell   Hydrojet   Light   Filter

Foam insulation   Skid pack

RIGHT *Rough-hewn boulders lead up a steep embankment in the garden of Marta Kramptiz in Oakland, California. Landscape designers Shari Bashin-Sullivan and Richard Sullivan surrounded the steps with ribbons of pink and bronze plants that lead the eye up the slope.*

Steps

In addition to their obvious practical function—as transitions between different levels or from one part of the garden to another—steps can be accents that set the mood for an entire landscaping scheme.

Scale is important. Principal entries require steps that are inviting and that allow several people to climb them at once. Service-yard steps, on the other hand, can be scaled down to fit their more limited use. Most dramatic are wide, deep steps that lead the eye to a focal point. Stairs can also double as a retaining wall, a base for raised planters, or garden seating.

Poured concrete and masonry block usually present a formal, substantial look. Unglazed tiles, concrete pavers, and adobe fit into Mediterranean or Moorish gardens. Natural materials such as stone and wood add an informal touch and fit into less structured landscapes. Such informal steps are also easier to construct. Matching the building material used in a patio, paths, or walls helps unite the garden's overall landscaping. On the other hand, contrasting materials draw attention to the steps and the areas of the garden they serve. Combining materials can create a transition between unlike surfaces.

Regardless of the material you use, put safety first: treads should give safe footing in wet weather. And steps should be adequately lit at night with unobtrusive, nonglare path lights or fixtures built into risers or adjacent walls.

Soften the edges of a series of steps, and help walkers find them without difficulty, by placing containers or open beds along their borders. You can add planting pockets within a wide series of tiers.

Size Matters

Your garden layout and the steps' function will influence your decision about width. Simple utility steps can be as narrow as two feet, but 4 feet is more typical. To allow two people to walk side by side, steps should be at least 5 feet wide. To design your steps, work out a plan on graph paper. To calculate the rise and run on a sloped area, hold a long, straight board with a level on top and measure down from it to find the stairway's total rise. Divide the total rise by the desired rise height for each step to find out how many steps you need. Then multiply the number of steps by the run for each step to estimate the total length of the stairway. Rarely will the steps fit exactly into a slope as it is; you may need to cut and fill the slope to accommodate the steps.

If your slope is too steep for even 8-inch risers, remember that steps needn't attack a slope head-on: sometimes the most appealing solution is an L- or even a U-shaped series of multiple flights. Break the runs with a wide landing between, using the transition to house a seating nook or a wall fountain.

BELOW *Mortared brick steps have a formal look, but these are softened by a curved edging at the base and plants that spill over the top and cover the stairs' sides.*

Safe Stepping

- Ideally, the depth of the tread plus twice the riser height should equal 25 to 27 inches. For both safety and ease of walking, the ideal dimensions are a 6-inch riser with a 14-inch tread.

- Though riser and tread dimensions can vary, their relationship should remain the same.

- Risers should be no lower than 5 inches and no higher than 8 inches.

- Treads should never be smaller than 11 inches.

- All the risers in any one flight of steps should be uniform in size; treads may have to vary to accommodate a curve.

- Timber or masonry steps should have treads that are sloped at a rate of 1/8 inch to 1/4 inch per foot, so rainwater can easily flow down the stairs.

- If stairs will be used by children, they should have railings to prevent falls.

Step Dimensions

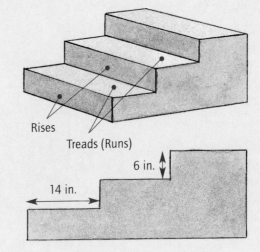

Rises

Treads (Runs)

6 in.

14 in.

ABOVE *These wide, curving steps covered with flowering thyme look soft enough to serve as a slide rather than a stairway.*

RIGHT *Sturdy timbers—either 4-by-4s or 6-by-6s—are good heights for step risers. Here they are set into ledges cut into a slope; level treads are covered with turfgrass.*

LEFT *A contemporary entry stairwell mixes concrete and wood; lighting is built into the wall for safety.*

BELOW *In the lush Eugene, Oregon, garden of Joan Kroft, a set of stone steps is covered with the luxuriant growth of baby's tears.*

Dressing Up Steps

Small plants that grow in joints soften the appearance of steps and offer even more opportunities to add greenery to the garden. Larger plants are best for light-traffic areas; use smaller plants if they will be walked on often. A spreading or creeping plant adds more greenery but may be trampled; some quick-growing types may grab too much territory.

Tuck succulents—such as sempervivums, echeveria, and little sedums—into the seams between stone steps. They'll quickly reproduce and form interesting patterns. Plants for shady stairs include baby's tears, black mondo grass (*Ophiopogon planiscapus* 'Nigrescens'), and some dwarf sedges. Thyme is the classic plant for tucking into nooks and crannies; it releases a delightful scent when stepped on. Also good for sunny spots are chamomile, Corsican mint, *Dymondia margaretae*, Scotch moss (*Sagina subulata*), and blue star creeper (*Pratia pedunculata*).

Don't forget that stairs can be used to display some favored pieces of garden décor. Wide landings and treads provide the ideal perches for colorful containers, urns, and sculpture.

Walls

They define space, provide privacy and security, edit views, screen out wind and noise, and hold the earth at bay. Walls bring an unmatched sense of solidity and permanence to a garden. Once you've determined a wall's function, you can choose its location, height, width, and degree of visual permeability. You'll also need to select materials that coordinate with the style and design of your house and existing garden structures.

Among the most typical materials for garden walls are masonry units: brick, concrete block, or adobe. Although their uniform size lets you assemble them piece by piece without worrying about matching shapes and sizes, it does take experience to quickly lay a brick or block wall that is straight and level.

Poured concrete walls offer more design possibilities because the surface texture and shape are established by wooden forms. Most of the construction work goes into building and stabilizing these forms; the actual "pour" is usually accomplished fairly quickly.

ABOVE *A curving retaining wall showcases the beauty of stone in hues that range from honey to aqua.*

LEFT *Wall or planting bed? Rock-garden greenery spills from planting pockets in a stacked-stone wall.*

In the hands of a mason, stone forms walls that seem integral to their landscapes. Stone that is prominent in your region will look the most natural in your garden. Visit a stoneyard or building materials supplier to check your options. Stone colors range from nearly pure white to shades of gray, brown, yellow, and red. Don't be afraid to mix hues in a single project; it's almost impossible to make a bad color choice when it comes to stone.

Building Walls

Whatever material your wall will be, it must be supported with a solid foundation, or footing. Poured concrete is the best footing you can provide because it can be smoothed and leveled. Usually, footings are at least as deep as the width of the wall and twice as wide. But consult local codes for exceptions.

For very low walls—those under 1 foot high—you can lay the base of the wall directly on tamped soil or in a leveled trench.

RIGHT *Classic Southwest gardens are all about thick, earthen walls that appear to grow from the surrounding soil. Age and abundant desert plants lend this one an air of stability, security, and a bit of mystery.*

LEFT *Dry-stacked stone retaining walls do double duty on this Ketchum, Idaho, hillside. The mortarless walls of Oregon argillite stabilize the slope while creating planting terraces for perennials, shrubs, and small trees.*

Windows & Doors

Whether earth-toned adobe or contemporary poured concrete, the blank façade of a wall invites ornamentation with openings, niches, and decorative insets. Strategically placed windows break the sense of enclosure to offer tantalizing glimpses of the natural landscape beyond or of another garden room. Wall portals become temptations, luring visitors to investigate what lies on the other side.

FACING PAGE, ABOVE *Light and shadow passing through a circular opening illuminate different hues of these stone- and sand-colored walls.*

FACING PAGE, BELOW LEFT *A Southwest entryway reveals a view of the garden within; the sturdy wooden gates contain diamond-shaped openings and a long, narrow window to one side.*

FACING PAGE, BELOW RIGHT *A filigree wrought-iron grill has been set into a dressed-stone wall.*

RIGHT *Pink Japanese anemones peek through a paneless cobalt-blue window.*

BELOW *A blank wall perforated by a moon window frames a portrait of blooming flowers.*

Wall Coverings

Although a concrete-block or poured concrete wall is relatively easy to build and fairly inexpensive, the finished product can look utilitarian. You can dress up a wall with brick or stone veneer that gives the appearance of solid masonry. You can paint a poured concrete wall any color you like, even create a mural or a trompe l'oeil effect. Or you can cover the wall with stucco colored to complement your landscaping.

Stucco (sometimes called plastering stucco) covers imperfections in a wall, creating a blank slate that you can paint or decorate at will. It also softens the look of a wall, rounding edges and creating a smooth appearance.

The best place to find God is in a garden.

You can dig for Him there.

-George Bernard Sha

Plastering a wall is a two-part operation. The first layer—called a "scratch coat"—should be about ⅜ inch thick and must be applied over a latex bonding agent. This layer is then scarified—roughed up with a commercial tool to help the finish coat's "bite"—before the finish coat is applied.

It can take practice to get the hang of stuccoing, and the finished texture reflects the artistry and experience of the worker. Many different effects can be achieved, from smooth to travertine; the important thing is for the pattern to be consistent. For a long-lasting color that doesn't need to be painted, mix the plaster with dry colorant.

ABOVE *Tucson barrio homes painted different earthy shades crowd a sidewalk. Hanging vines add a tracery of green.*

LEFT *The walls of Thomas Hobbs's Mission Revival house in Vancouver are painted a peachy terra-cotta. Here, the wall picks up tones in a slate patio and steps; a wrought-iron grill set into the wall covers a mirror.*

FACING PAGE *A compelling color somewhere between coral and cherry defines the boundary of this contemporary garden. Stenciled on the wall is a traditional gardening motto.*

FACING PAGE, INSET *Color-washed walls of different hues grace Linda Cochran's garden. This one is a rosy tan color and houses a small built-in bench.*

plants

TREES | PALMS | SHRUBS |

ROSES | VINES |

LAWNS & ALTERNATIVES |

PERENNIALS | ANNUALS |

BULBS | EDIBLES |

TROPICALS | GRASSES |

BAMBOO | NATIVE PLANTS |

PLANTS FOR POTS |

EASY PLANTS

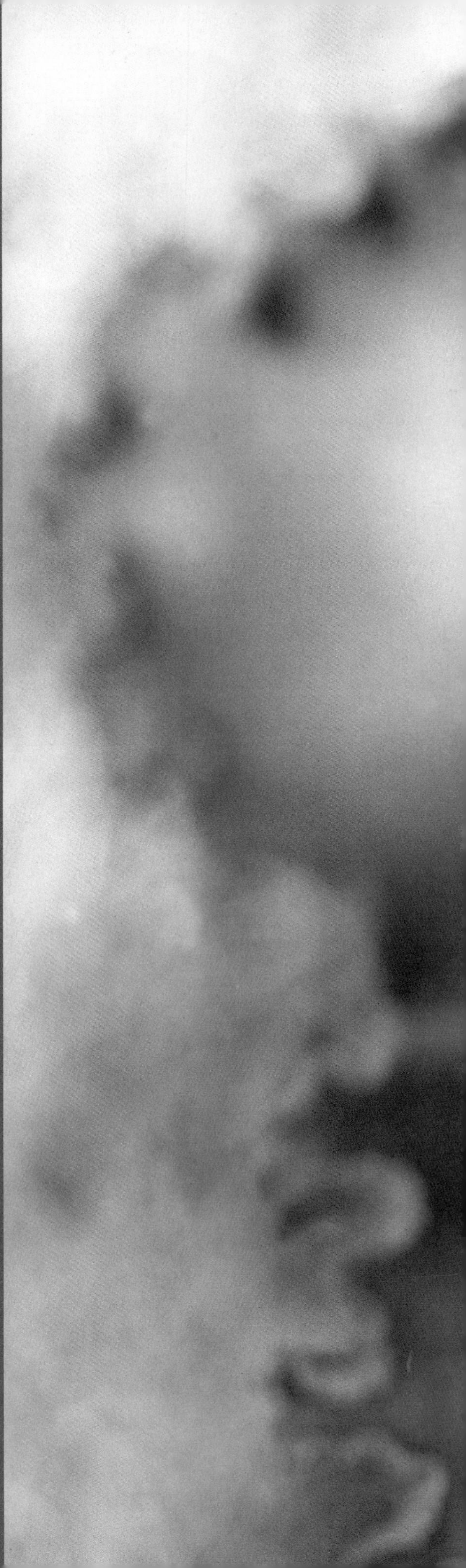

LEFT *Venerable European hornbeam* (Carpinus betulus) *spreads its picturesquely twisted branches from a stout (often characterized as "muscular") trunk covered in ridged bark. The tree's spreading canopy offers filtered shade in summer, then leaves turn rusty gold in fall before dropping.*

INSET *Available in a variety of named selections, Japanese maple* (Acer palmatum) *reliably puts on a show of fall foliage color, from yellow through orange to shades of red.*

FACING PAGE *Weeping blue Atlas cedar* (Cedrus atlantica 'Glauca Pendula') *spreads gracefully drooping branches over a stone water basin.*

Trees

Trees set the tone of a landscape, whether they are palms rustling near a Southern California beach or aspens shimmering on a Northwest mountainside. In the garden, trees do even more. They provide shade and shelter, frame vistas, and block eyesores. They establish perspective, make dramatic sculptural statements, or form focal points. A tree can be a haven for birds, a support for a clambering vine, or a place to hang a simple swing.

One quality shared by all landscape trees is their relative permanence—a very valuable quality in new housing developments. It also means that you should choose carefully; it's a big job to remove a mature but unsuitable tree.

Tree Characteristics

Each year new growth springs from a tree's basic framework, gradually enlarging the structure. Because the growth habit of a mature tree is not always evident in a young sapling, be sure to find out what shape the tree will ultimately develop. Some have a fast-growing central trunk; others send out branches in a more lateral fashion to create a rounded crown.

All trees are either *deciduous* or *evergreen*. There may be no more reliable guide to the passing of the seasons than a *deciduous* tree, which produces new leaves in spring and retains them through the summer. In fall, the leaves may change colors and then drop off. *Evergreen* trees retain their foliage year-round, although they regularly shed individual leaves. *Broadleaf evergreen* trees have wide leaves; *needle-leafed evergreens* have needlelike foliage or narrow leaves composed of tiny scales. Most *conifers* are needle-leafed evergreens, although a few are deciduous.

Selecting Trees

Choose trees based first on your needs. To block the sun, for example, select a species with a sizable canopy. For screening, look for trees that produce branches on their lower trunks. For a focal point, choose a tree with flowers, fruits, attractive foliage, interesting bark, or a striking silhouette.

Trees bring many colors to the garden. Flowers run from sunshine-yellow laburnum to purple jacaranda. Foliage colors may be purple (plum), steel blue (eucalyptus), golden (ginkgo), or sport unusual variegations and even multiple hues (such as tricolor beech). Bark can range from a creamy grey to almost midnight black. Finally, don't forget about trees as a source of edibles for the garden, whether apples or avocadoes.

To avoid disappointment, choose trees that will flourish in your garden's conditions. Some can withstand howling winds and freezing temperatures; others can survive in the scathing heat of the desert. Most of the pests and diseases that plague trees are specific to particular species (see page 332).

A desire for shade or privacy may tempt you to purchase a fast-growing plant, but such a tree can soon overpower its space. Some trees need plenty of underground space for aggressive root systems—which are strong enough to infiltrate drainage pipes and lift paving. And those that drop masses of leaves or fruits are best sited far from pools and patios.

Large Trees

Sometimes, only *big* will do. In a sizable garden, large trees can mark the garden's boundary or act as an "eraser" for an off-site eyesore. Where the house is tall or massive, larger trees provide the appropriate scale to the structure. And, of course, most large trees cast large pools of shade.

Ask yourself whether you need an evergreen, one that will be a presence throughout the year? Or is a deciduous one better—perhaps one that bears lovely flowers, colorful fruits, or a blaze of autumn color before leaves drop? Remember that winter-bare trees can be objects of sculptural beauty, their trunks and limbwork varied by the color and character of their bark. Finally, structural integrity—how strongly the limbs are attached—is especially critical in windy locations and in regions where snow and ice are the norm. Broken limbs disfigure a tree; and the larger the tree, the greater the damage (and the more difficult it is to remove).

BEST SMALL TREES

Deciduous

Acer circinatum Vine maple

Acer palmatum
  Japanese maple

Amelanchier Serviceberry

Bauhinia variegata
  Purple orchid tree

Cercidium Palo verde

Cercis canadensis
  Eastern redbud

× *Chitalpa tashkentensis*

Cornus florida Flowering
  dogwood

Crataegus phaenopyrum
  Washington thorn

Erythrina crista-galli
  Cockspur coral tree

Lagerstroemia indica
  Crape myrtle

Prunus Flowering cherry

P. cerasifera Cherry plum

Evergreen

Arbutus 'Marina'

Callistemon citrinus
  Lemon bottlebrush

Citrus Orange, lemon

Eucalyptus torquata
  Coral gum

Magnolia grandiflora
  'St. Mary', 'Victoria'
  Southern magnolia

Olneya tesota Desert
  ironwood

Rhaphiolepis
  'Majestic Beauty'

Compact Trees

A good tree for patios, decks, or containers minds its manners. It has roots that remain underground rather than prying up paving or invading nearby flower beds. It produces no sneeze-making pollen, nor does it drop excessive leaves or messy fruit. Even when fully grown, a small tree should not be too tall, and should have a canopy with a pleasing shape.

Some deciduous trees work well, even though you must sweep up in fall—Japanese maples, with their lightly crumpled leaves, are a good choice. In mild-winter areas, broad-leafed evergreens such as citrus provide fine, deep shade year-round, along with tasty fruits. Conifers are rarely recommended for patios, but they make wonderful container subjects, especially the dwarf forms.

ABOVE *An artful front garden in Paradise Valley, Arizona, features a handsome palo verde tree* (Cercidium). *The tree contributes height to a mixed planting of agaves, cactus, and desert marigold.*

Planting and Caring for Trees

A healthy tree is no accident. To guarantee that your new tree develops into the robust specimen you envision, you need to pay attention to three points.

First, buy a sturdy plant. In bare-root trees, look for a well-balanced root system that is substantial enough for the trunk and branches it supports. With container-grown stock, you can't assess roots directly. Instead, check to see if the tree's size seems too small or too large for the container. If too small, the plant probably was recently moved to the container; the root system may not fill out the soil. If too large, chances are the root system is congested from having grown too long in the pot; check drainage holes and soil surface for matted roots, the telltale signs of overcrowding. For both bare-root and container-grown specimens, inspect the bark to be sure it's not damaged in any way; wounds (including sunscald) are potential entry points for disease. Also look at the trunk: if it tapers gradually and evenly, the plant has had optimum growing conditions and should make the transition to your garden easily. But if the trunk tapers markedly from base to top, the plant has been stressed in the growing ground or in the nursery; such a plant will be slower to establish.

Second, take time to plant the tree well. Proper planting depth and good root distribution are critical to good growth in the years to come.

Finally, attend to watering and early training while the tree is becoming established. Periodic deep watering will encourage rapid establishment. Proper staking (see middle right) and selective pruning (see bottom right) of trunk branches will speed development of a husky, self-supporting trunk. (In later years, after they're well established, most trees will need pruning at some time, especially if they're growing in windy areas. For more on tree care, see pages 351 and 357.)

Proper watering Use a sampling tube to check the soil around the tree's drip line (which corresponds to the perimeter of the tree's branch canopy, see page 184). Water should be penetrating at least 12 inches below ground to ensure that it reaches the root zone. A deep-root irrigator helps moisture soak below the surface of the soil to the tree's roots.

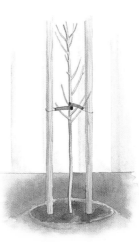

Proper staking Careful staking of a young tree is important in windy areas. Position the tree between two sturdy stakes at least as tall as the tree's lowest branches. Secure the trunk to the stakes with flexible ties.

Selective pruning Young trees become established faster if their lower branches are left to develop along the trunk for the first few years after planting. Once the trunk is at least 2 inches thick, begin removing the lower branches gradually, over a period of several years.

Tree-friendly Remodeling

A tree's canopy is easy to see, but, as the drawing at right shows, half of the tree—its root system—is out of sight. Because it lies unseen, the root system is especially vulnerable to damage during construction and garden remodels. Injured roots are hindered in their ability to take up water, air, and nutrients. The damage won't show up immediately, but the result will gradually manifest in the decline and eventual death of the tree.

To ensure a tree comes through a remodel project intact and healthy, you need to protect its roots, trunk, and canopy. Clearly mark trees to be saved; if possible, cordon off each tree with bright tape on stakes surrounding the tree at its drip line. Before construction begins, make sure your contractor knows your wishes about your trees and will convey them to workers; spelling this out in the remodeling contract is good insurance.

The best route to success is to avoid *any* building within the tree's root zone; this minimizes or eliminates the risk of soil compaction. Try to keep any new structure from being built too close to a mature tree; allow at least 1 foot of space between the trunk and any new structure for every inch of trunk diameter (measured at 54 inches above soil level.) Learn where new underground lines will go; if they're slated to cut through the root zone, try to get them rerouted. Also check plans for new paving; solid pavement over an established root zone is a recipe for trouble down the road.

If it's not possible for contractors to work outside the tree's root zone, you can remove up to one-third of a healthy tree's roots without severely harming the tree (though the tree may take several years to adjust to the change with normally robust growth). Should it be necessary for heavy equipment to move over the root zone, you can take advance steps to minimize soil compaction. First, cover the area from the trunk to the drip line with a 12-inch-thick layer of wood chips; top this mulch with interlocking sheet-metal plates or plywood sheets, either of which will distribute the equipment weight beyond the point of direct impact.

Calling a Pro

Arborists do more than prune trees. These professionals, certified by the International Society of Arboriculture (ISA), can evaluate a tree's health, age, present and future size, and any hazards it may pose. He or she can tell you if a mature tree is worth saving, based on its health, or if the effort would be a waste of time and money. If you have a tree that is totally in the line of construction, an arborist can advise if it could be successfully moved. When a tree is to remain, it's a good idea to have an arborist consult with the contractor to learn the exact location of construction work and to coordinate the building process with the tree's preservation. If necessary, the arborist can do any pruning needed to allow clearance for moving heavy equipment onto the site. In a garden with large trees, an annual checkup by an arborist can spot potential problems before they develop into structural failure and property damage.

Trouble Spots

The Canopy

Broken branches. Large branch stubs, left by breakage or careless pruning, seldom heal over.

Topping. Pruning back to topmost, terminal branches to make way for roof overhangs cuts back a tree's food-making potential (see page 186).

The Trunk

Injuries. Heavy equipment and machinery can gouge the trunk, exposing the tree to disease and insect pests.

The Roots

Most roots are within the top 24 inches of soil, and they can extend far beyond the drip line. They're susceptible to damage from the causes shown below.

drip line

Leading Causes of Root Damage

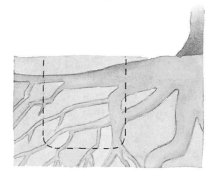

Trenching. Digging trenches for utilities too close to the trunk can seriously injure or sever tree roots.

Protective Measures

The Canopy

If low branches need removal to make way for heavy equipment, hire an arborist to do it.

Instead of topping, cut selected branches back to lower laterals.

The Trunk and Branches

If you work close to the trunk, prop hay bales against it to protect the bark.

Use rope to tie thinner, flexible branches up and out of the way of trucks and machinery.

The Roots

Put a temporary fence around the tree as far outside the drip line as possible.

Lay plastic tarps over the ground out to the drip line to keep out soil contaminants.

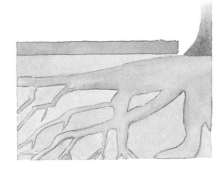

Solid paving. Nonporous paving under the canopy can prevent water and air from reaching roots.

Grade change. As little as a couple of inches of fill dirt, if it does not have good drainage, can smother roots.

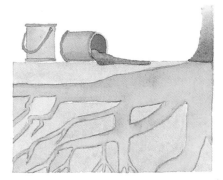

Soil contamination. Spilling wet concrete, paint, or solvents within the root zone can poison the tree.

Framing a View

Trees make wonderful views themselves, but they can also be used to enhance—or creatively conceal—the areas surrounding your property. For instance, if a tree interrupts a favorite perspective, you can selectively prune it to restore your view of water, mountains, or cityscape. Depending on how you wish to frame the view, choose the technique shown here that will accomplish your goal.

If the tree is large or difficult to access, you may need to call in a professional to do the job (see page 184). If you are skillful enough to remove a good-size tree limb, first look for its branch collar—a raised lip or wrinkle at the junction of the trunk and limb. Make a preliminary cut on the underside of the branch just beyond the collar to prevent the falling limb from tearing bark on the trunk. Then cut through the branch from the upper side.

LEFT *This* Juniperus chinensis *has been carefully pruned to maintain views of Vancouver's north shore mountains beyond.*

Do Not Top

One of the most common pruning errors is topping—reducing the height of a mature tree by sawing back its top limbs. Rather than accomplishing the goal of shortening the tree, this practice is the quickest way to ruin its appearance forever. In fact, such pruning stimulates the tree to send out scores of weak shoots from the cutoff points; often these shoots are taller, coarser, and denser than the tree's natural crown. A topped conifer can develop patchy tufts of needles along its trunk, making the tree look rangy and off-kilter. If you have a tree that has outgrown its spot, consult an arborist about an alternate way of scaling it back.

Windowing

If a tree grows so densely that it blocks views of the surrounding landscape, selectively remove some of the lateral branches to open up the view. Window a tree equally on both sides, even if both sides are not obstructing the view.

Thinning

This technique not only opens up views, but it gives a tree better resistance to the wind. Don't prune main limbs, but clear out bunches of foliage and the smaller branches that grow between them. First remove weak branches and vertical water spouts, along with any branches that rub or cross each other. Then selectively prune along the main limbs, leaving more branches toward the end of each main limb to leave a natural-looking bushy canopy.

Skirting Up

Removing the lower limbs (also known as limbing up) of a midrange tree can reveal a view without ruining the shape of the tree. Don't skirt up more than half of the tree's height. In addition, if the tree is top-heavy, thin it so that it doesn't look like a lollipop.

Crown Reduction

To lower a tree's canopy, prune the tallest branches as far down to the trunk as possible, but near small side branches that point in the same upward direction. If there are no such branches, track a tall limb down to one of its own upward-pointing, robust secondary branches. Cut just above this branch.

Flowering Trees

All trees are not created equal. Many of the West's favorite trees are those that reward the gardener with an annual bonus of colorful blossoms. These floral cloud-bearers come in all sizes, from patio to skyline, in all shapes, and some are suited to the entire range of Western climates. In addition, you can choose among trees that flower in each of the four seasons (see sidebar). Some of them display their colorful bounty on bare limbs, giving you a moment of total color; others offer their display as spangles on a leafy canopy.

Before buying a flowering tree, determine that the one you want will thrive in your climate. Even though they may *grow* well enough, some types require a guaranteed amount of winter chill to blossom, and some need a particular amount of maritime influence or inland heat. A bit of advance planning can prevent future disappointment.

FACING PAGE *Flowering dogwood* (Cornus florida) *lives up to its name each spring when trees become clouds of pink (or white, in some varieties) before leaves emerge. The opposite-season bonus is bright red fall foliage.*

ABOVE LEFT *Callery pear* (Pyrus calleryana).

ABOVE RIGHT *Flowering cherry* (Prunus serrulata *'Kwanzan').*

FOUR SEASONS OF FLOWERS

Arranged by season of bloom, here are the West's favorite flowering trees—guaranteed performers within their adapted areas and widely available in nurseries. Some flower exclusively in the season where listed, but many (identified by an asterisk) achieve peak bloom in the listed season with flowers beginning in the preceding one or extending into the one that follows.

Spring flowers

Amelanchier Serviceberry
Catalpa
Cercidium Palo verde
Cercis canadensis Eastern redbud
Cornus florida Flowering dogwood
Jacaranda mimosifolia Jacaranda*
Malus Flowering crabapple
Prunus Flowering cherry
Pyrus calleryana Callery pear
Tabebuia chrysotricha Golden trumpet tree

Summer flowers

Albizia julibrissin Silk tree
Chilopsis linearis Desert willow*
× *Chitalpa tashkentensis* *
Erythrina Coral trees*
Lagerstroemia indica Crape myrtle*
Magnolia grandiflora Southern magnolia*
Robinia × ambigua Locust*
Sophora japonica Japanese pagoda tree

Fall flowers

Bauhinia × blakeana Hong Kong orchid tree*
Chorisia Floss silk tree*
Erythrina humeana Natal coral tree

Winter flowers

Acacia baileyana Bailey acacia
Bauhinia variegata Purple orchid tree
Erythrina caffra Coral tree
Callistemon citrinus Lemon bottlebrush*
Magnolia × soulangeana Saucer magnolia
Prunus Flowering plum*
Pyrus kawakamii Evergreen pear

Palms

Palms are synonymous with the sun-kissed beaches of California and Hawaii. Yet even though many of the palms in our gardens hail from tropical South America, Asia, and the South Pacific, only a few are native to the West. Still, from San Diego to Vancouver, B.C., palms line our streets, punctuate our skylines, and bring jungle effects to our gardens.

Palms are inherently exotic looking, but they are also eminently practical. These trees have compact root systems, and many are easy to transplant even when mature, which can result in instant landscaping. Palms can be squeezed into narrow parkways or planted close to swimming pools, as their roots won't break up sidewalks or foundations, and they produce minimal litter. As if that weren't enough, palms are generally low-maintenance and pest free.

Night lighting shows off the stateliness and spectacular fronds of palms. You can backlight them, shine spotlights up on them from below, or direct lights to silhouette them against a pale wall.

FACING PAGE *What says "tropics" better than palms? This Southern California backyard replicates a South Pacific lagoon, the mood set by luxuriant king palms (Archontophoenix cunninghamiana).*

Archontophoenix cunninghamiana *King palm*
A regal palm that grows quickly to 60 ft. Eight- to ten-foot dark green leaves; purple flowers. Takes some frost when established. Grows best out of wind; needs abundant water.

Howea forsteriana *Paradise palm*
The classic hotel-lobby palm. Grows slowly to 30 ft. Dark green leaves require occasional trimming. Wind tolerant; needs abundant water and partial shade on the coast, full shade inland.

Syagrus romanzoffianum *Queen palm*
Fast-growing to 50 ft. tall. Also needs abundant water, fertilizer, and shelter from winds. Lush, plumelike leaves grow to 15 ft. long. Suffers in 25°F/–4°C frost.

Rhapis *Lady palm*
Multiple stems grow slowly to 12 to 18 ft. Dense growth, dark green, glossy leaves. Prefers rich, moist soil and protection from sun and winds; hardy to 22°F/–5°C.

Trachycarpus fortunei *Windmill palm*
Stiff, upright shape can reach to 30 ft. Trunk is hairy and brown; fronds can be trimmed. Looks best in groups, Hardy to 10°F/–12°C.

Chamaedorea *Bamboo palm*
Clumping, bamboolike growth to 5 to 10 ft., Frost tender; needs ample water and some shade.

Brahea armata *Mexican blue palm*
Pretty desert palm that grows slowly to 40 ft. Spiny, silvery blue leaves and striking white blossom stalks need a yearly trim. Heat and wind tolerant; thrives with regular watering.

Phoenix roebelenii *Pygmy date palm*
Grows slowly to 6 ft., with soft, feathery leaves. Wind resistant but suffers below 28°F/–2°C. Grows only in mild climates with some shade and watering.

King palm   Paradise palm   Queen palm   Lady palm   Windmill palm   Bamboo palm   Mexican blue palm   Pygmy date palm

ABOVE *Arching beautifully at the back of a tropical border, the coconut palm* (Cocos nucifera) *is, of course, best suited to gardens in zone H2—the coconut palm belt in Hawaii. Dwarf forms are best for most gardens.*

LEFT *A row of mixed Mexican fan and queen palms add height and drama against a bold terracotta wall outside the Ritenour residence in Los Angeles.*

FACING PAGE *The palms in this desert-like garden can tolerate dips in temperature to 20°F/–7°C. Nearest the house are Mexican fan palms; in the center is gray-green pindo palm* (Butia capitata). *The low-growing plant in the foreground is sago palm* (Cycas revoluta), *a cycad that adds variety to the theme.*

Hardy Palms

Palms in Pocatello? As improbable as the question seems, the answer is "yes." Needle palm, *Rhapido-phyllum hystrix,* reliably takes 0°F/−17°C and has survived temperatures even lower. It's not your tropical-lagoon palm—plants are trunkless, making a 6- to 8-foot foliage mound—but the 3-foot, deeply cut fanlike leaves provide a dramatic and distinctly exotic touch to cold-country gardens.

Two other familiar palms are nearly as cold-hardy. Mediterranean fan palm, *Chamaerops humilis,* endures temperatures as low as 6°F/−14°C; it's another clump-forming type, although over time it gradually elevates its tufts of fan-shaped leaves on short trunks. For a hardy, single-trunk type, windmill palm *(Trachycarpus fortunei)* lifts a crown of fanlike leaves on an upright, shaggy trunk eventually to 30 feet; plants survive winter lows to about 10°F/−12°C. Even the classic desert-oasis date palm, *Phoenix dactylifera,* has endured tempera-tures as low as 4°F/−15°C, though foliage is severely damaged when the thermometer hits 20°F/−7°C.

In regions where winter lows typically are below freezing but not truly frigid, the following palms will persist as long as temperatures fall no lower than about 20°F/−7°C: Mexican blue palm *(Brahea armata),* Guadalupe palm *(Brahea edulis),* Canary Island date palm *(Phoenix canariensis),* palmettos *(Sabal* species), California fan palm *(Washingtonia filifera),* and Mexican fan palm *(Washingtonia robusta).*

Shrubs

Take away the shrubs from your property and you'll remove much of what makes the garden comfortable, safe, and inviting. Without shrubs, there would be no hedges to keep children and pets safely in bounds and no lilacs or roses to gather for bouquets. House lines would seem stark without the softening effect of feathery evergreens or flowery rhododendrons. Shrubs become permanent fixtures, altering traffic flow and defining the shape and limits of the garden, dividing various areas of large gardens into more intimate spaces.

Just as a large sofa can help fill a room, shrubs add weight and substance to a landscape. And just as furniture defines a room's character, shrubs define a garden's style. Closely clipped hedges lend formality; those with dramatic natural shapes set a contemporary tone. Those with cascading branches make a border look naturalistic, while those with loose, flowering branches can form the basis for an overall color palette.

Shrubs are generally used as either hedges, focal points, or as members of mixed borders. They also create smooth transitions from ground level to surrounding tree canopies. Like trees, these plants are either *deciduous* or *evergreen*. They grow—or can be clipped into—a variety of rounded, tapered, or fountainlike shapes. With showy flowers, fruits, or fall color, they also offer seasonal appeal. Some serve as a foil for more colorful foreground plants; others have variegated, showy foliage year-round. Finally,

some of the garden's most divine fragrances come from flowering shrubs.

For the lowest maintenance, choose shrubs with cultural needs that your garden can meet—these vary enormously for different shrubs. Rhododendrons and azaleas, for instance, thrive in the semishade of overhead trees and acid soil that is moisture-retentive but not soggy. Shrubs from southern climates, however, such as grevillea or protea, need plenty of sun and little water.

FACING PAGE *Flowering shrubs are a number-one choice for permanent garden decoration. Few can surpass the beauty and elegance of rhododendrons, available in a rainbow of colors. The fragrant flowers of 'Loderi King George' emerge pink and then fade to white.*

ABOVE *Left to its own devices, firethorn (Pyracantha) grows as a rangy, irregular shrub. But with careful pruning and training, you can coax it into a free-form espalier to decorate a wall or fence.*

Shaping Shrubs

Most shrubs need some regular pruning to keep their shape, to reduce diseases, and to produce healthy flowers and fruit. Correct pruning at the proper time of year will lead to bushier plants with more flowers—which may or may not be the look you desire. Most flowering shrubs are pruned after their blossoms fade; other deciduous shrubs bring forth long stems each year from the base and benefit from an early-spring removal of some older stems. Evergreens (such as boxwood and many conifers) can be pruned at any time of year; exceptions are bloomers such as camellias.

Some of the best flowering shrubs are medium- to large-size plants that have been trained to a treelike form with a single, upright trunk. These are known as *standards*. Others are multitrunked shrubs that have been pruned up to reveal sculptural trunks and to form a treelike canopy. For more advice on pruning and caring for shrubs, consult a gardening professional or the *Sunset Western Garden Book*.

Shrubs in Mixed Plantings

All shrubs, especially evergreens, lend permanence to flowering borders that change with the seasons; in cold climates, those shrubs may be a valuable source of winter interest. Flowering shrubs can be showy members of the mixed border, reflecting the color of nearby trees or blending into the color scheme of surrounding perennials, annuals, and grasses. An advantage of incorporating shrubs into borders is that they needn't be staked, deadheaded, cleared away, or lifted for winter storage.

ABOVE *A mixed border curves about a cozy corner in Terry LeBlanc's Victoria, B.C., garden. Featured in the bed are burgundy-colored smoke tree, dahlias with dark foliage, and pink-blooming tree mallow (Lavatera).*

RIGHT *With plenty of tropical flair, this sizzling border in Linda Cochran's garden is filled with a bold mix of shapes and textures. It includes hardy banana,* Catalpa bignonioides *'Aurea', and blue-leafed* Melianthus major.

196

Plant It:
Shrubby Centerpiece

Annuals and perennials *are joined by flowering shrubs in a stunning display of spring and summer color. Dominating the planting is a purple butterfly bush* (Buddleia davidii) *which lures butterflies to a host of additional nectar-bearing flowers.*

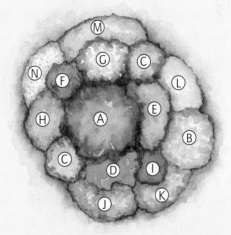

A *Buddleia davidii* 'Empire blue' Butterfly bush *(1)*
B *Lantana* 'Irene' *(1)*
C *Agapanthus orientalis* Lily-of-the-Nile *(2)*
D *Penstemon × gloxinioides* 'Garnet' Border penstemon *(3)*
E *Centranthus ruber* Jupiter's beard *(4)*
F *Lavandula × intermedia* 'Provence' Lavandin *(1)*
G *Chrysanthemum × superbum* 'Alaska' Shasta daisy *(6)*
H *Salvia coccinea (5)*
I *Verbena bonariensis (1)*
J *Dianthus gratianopolitanus* 'Bath's Pink' Cheddar pink *(5)*
K *Scabiosa columbaria* Pincushion flower *(3)*

L *Iberis sempervirens* 'Snowflake' Evergreen candytuft *(2)*
M *Coreopsis grandiflora* 'Early Sunrise' *(4)*
N *Lobularia maritima* Sweet alyssum *(5)*

Roses

Roses have fortunately broken out of the stiff constraints of formal beds to become components of the contemporary garden. The twentieth-century love affair with plants such as hybrid teas—producers of show-quality flowers on so-so plants—waned as breeders developed landscape roses with attractive blossoms on well-foliaged, disease-resistant plants. At the same time, renewed enthusiasm for roses of bygone eras have brought back into cultivation countless charming antiquities. The result is a cornucopia of flower shapes, sizes, and colors on plants that flower repeatedly.

Ground covers. Plants that spread widely but grow no taller than 2 feet are perfect for covering sunny slopes and for filling parking strips and raised beds. Flower Carpet is a series of such plants.

Borders and hedges. *Floribundas* and the larger-growing *miniature* roses are the premier plants for grouping *en masse*. The floribundas offer large clusters of generally medium-size blossoms on compact plants 2 to 5 feet tall. Spaced 18 to 24 inches apart (the closer spacing in colder regions), they make excellent hedges of pathway borders. Many miniature roses fill the same niches but with smaller flowers and leaves. Among floribundas, white 'Iceberg', pink 'Simplicity', red 'Europeana', and yellow 'Sun Flare' are classics; good miniatures include white 'Gourmet Popcorn', pink 'Jean Kenneally', and red-and-white 'Magic Carrousel'.

FACING PAGE *Sun-loving roses thrive in Barbara Duno's Santa Fe garden. In the foreground are Pink Meidiland ground cover roses; the coral-colored floribundas are 'Marmalade Skies' and 'Saraband'. Beside the seating area is the fragrant miniature yellow rose 'Sun Sprinkles'.*

FACING PAGE, INSET *The shrub rose 'Crown Princess Margareta'.*

BELOW *'Polka' clambers over a metal arbor in Helen Henderson's Los Angeles garden. This climbing rose has apricot and peach tones, and thrives in mild climates.*

In rose circles, old garden roses are those varieties belonging to classes that existed before 1867—the likely date in which the first hybrid tea rose was introduced. Through diligent collection and identification, a striking assortment of old roses is now available from specialists; some have even made their ways into mainstream catalogs. These historic varieties fall into two broad classifications. The old European roses—*albas, centifolias, damasks, gallicas,* and *moss* roses flower only in spring. The other classes—chiefly *bourbon, china, damask perpetual, hybrid perpetual, noisette,* and *tea*—flower repeatedly through the season.

Uses for these venerable beauties are the same as suggested for modern types. Choose according to plant size and shape, flower color and style, and whether you demand flowers from spring to fall or are content with one lavish spring display.

If you fancy the style of the old roses but aren't concerned about planting living history, some contemporary shrub types are good substitutes. Some shrub roses embody the floral styles of old roses, yet are overall more disease resistant and offer flowers in warm tones not found among the antique types.

Cottage garden and mixed border plantings. The bulk of modern *shrub* roses fits perfectly into landscapes featuring a variety of other shrubs, perennials, and annuals. Choose the roses according to the colors you need and plant sizes appropriate for the planting. Modern shrubs encompass plants from 2 to 8 feet tall, in shapes from rounded to upright to vase-shaped, and in the full range of flower styles and colors. Some are cataloged simply as shrub roses, others are found among the various trademark-identified groups such as the David Austin English roses, and the French Romantica, Generosa, and Meidiland roses. Gardeners in the coldest-winter regions should look for hybrids of *Rosa rugosa,* which survive sub-freezing winter temperatures.

Fences, arbors, and trellises. A great array of *climbing* and *semi-climbing* roses are tailor-made for decorating vertical surfaces. Choose carefully, matching the plant's vigor to the space you want adorned. Look to the more modest growers for trellis display—smaller climbers like 'Altissimo' and 'Abraham Darby'. To cover an arbor, seek out the most vigorous types like 'Climbing Cécile Brunner', 'Awakening', and 'Climbing Iceberg'. 'Blaze' is a classic for enlivening split rail fences.

ABOVE *Grafted onto an upright trunk, a bushy floribunda rose becomes a standard or "tree" rose. To prune standards, follow the guidelines for the particular rose type but aim to create a symmetrically rounded head.*

Pruning

Rose pruning is not an annual exercise designed to punish gardeners! Yearly pruning removes less-productive growth, which can sap energy from more vigorous stems, and helps keep plants healthy by removing dead and twiggy material that congests a bush and offers safe haven for insects and disease.

For repeat-flowering roses, the best pruning moment is toward the end of the dormant season, just when growth buds begin to swell. In mildest-winter areas, this will be January; in coldest-winter regions, April may present the first opportunity (around the same time you see bloom on *Forsythia*). For shrub and old garden roses that flower only in spring, traditional pruning time is right after flowering has finished; strong new growth made after bloom will bear the next spring's blossoms. However, it's easier to see what you're doing during the leafless dormant season; at that time, you can prune out all dead, old, and unproductive stems, then give bushes a subsequent touch-up pruning after spring bloom ends.

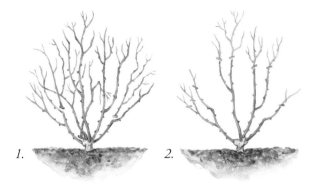

1.   2.

Hybrid Teas, Grandifloras, Floribundas, and Polyanthas *(left)*

1. *First, thin the bush, removing old canes and weak, twiggy branches. Then, open up the bush and create a vase-shaped plant by removing branches that cross through the center.*

2. *Cut back the remaining stems. Make slanting cuts to outward-facing buds, which will help to keep the center of the bush open.*

Old Garden and Shrub Roses *(right)*

1. *Thin the bush by cutting out a few old, woody stems at the base of the plant. Remove any dead, damaged, or weak canes, and any that rub against or cross one another.*

2. *Cut back the remaining canes lightly, pruning just the tips. If the center of the bush is crowded, shorten the side shoots to outward-facing buds.*

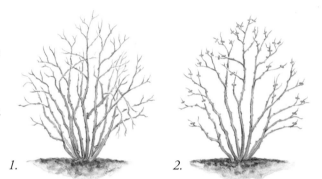

1.   2.

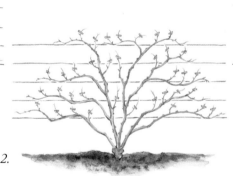

1.

2.

Climbing Roses *(left)*

1. *Remove only the old and obviously unproductive canes, leaving the basic framework of strong, healthy canes.*

2. *Cut back remaining canes to two or three buds on all the side branches (called laterals) that flowered during the last year; this encourages new blooms all along the canes.*

Winter Chill

In cold-winter regions of the West—at high elevations and east of the Sierra Nevada–Cascade mountains—winter low temperatures may damage exposed rose canes. Generally speaking, modern hybrid teas, grandifloras, miniatures, and climbers run little risk of damage as long as winter lows seldom go below 10°F/−12°C. Some floribundas and many shrub and old garden roses are tough enough to withstand exposure to 0°F/−18°C. Occasional dips below stated minimums may or may not hurt exposed canes; prolonged low-temperature episodes, though, are sure to be harmful. To succeed with these roses in areas colder than their threshold temperatures, you'll need to protect plants. Protection keeps plants dormant by keeping them evenly cold; it also shields them from desiccation by cold, dry winds (see page 305).

To protect roses by mounding, first clear away all old leaves and spent flowers on and around the plant. Cut back any dead or diseased canes, then cut healthy canes back to 3 feet and tie them together. Build a mound of soil at least 1 foot high over the base of the bush. After the soil freezes, surround it with an insulating layer of straw, hay, cut conifer boughs, or other noncompacting organic material. Hold the material in place with a wire-mesh cylinder.

Vines

As frosting is to a cake, vines are to a garden: that finishing touch. Whether you use them to frame an entry, soften a fence or trellis, envelop a pillar, cover arbor, or simply let them spread out to cover the soil, vines *adorn* their host. The plants we call vines share only the trait of relatively lax stems; it is this flexible growth that gives them such versatility. Within the vine category are vigorous growers that can cover the side of a two-story house or smother a pergola, demure sorts that offer traceries of foliage on head-high plants, and the entire in-between range of sizes and densities. Many vines are famous for their floral displays—think bougainvillea and wisteria, for example—others, like Virginia creeper, are famous for foliage alone.

Without support, all vines sprawl, but they have developed their abilities to climb and meander by a variety of climbing methods. *Twining* vines (such as wisteria) have stems that spiral or twist as they grow, encircling their own stems and those of other plants as well as strings or wires strategically placed to guide their growth. *Clinging* vines (ivy and Boston ivy are examples) have specialized structures that automatically attach to all but absolutely smooth, slick surfaces. Other types of specialized structures are *coiling tendrils* (as in grape vines) that reach out and wrap around

ABOVE *Some vines reserve their big display for the season's finale. Virginia creeper* (Parthenocissus quinquefolia) *forms a curtain of green foliage that becomes a tapestry of orange, red, and burgundy with the arrival of autumnal chill.*

RIGHT *Wherever frost is rare or light, you can count on bougainvillea to tirelessly give you masses of color. Numerous named sorts are available, ranging from blinding reds and oranges to vivid purples and softer tones of lavender, pink, and yellow.*

whatever is close by, and *coiling leaf-stalks* (clematis, for example) that function in the same way. *Clambering* vines have no means of attachment, instead poking their stems through other plants in order to gain a foothold; some have thorns or prickles (as climbing roses do) which help secure the stems in place.

How a vine climbs tells you what kind of support you must provide. Clinging types just need a flat surface—wall, fence, or structure. Vines with twining stems, tendrils, and coiling leafstalks must have something to coil around: string (for annual vines), wire, or small-diameter doweling. With clambering vines, you need to tie stems into place against their backdrop; on openwork supports (treillage, wire fencing) all you need is soft twine or plant ties, but against solid surfaces (wooden fencing, for example) you'll need to affix screw eyes or staples for securing the ties that position the stems.

ABOVE *For combined beauty and elegance, nothing beats the large-flowered clematis hybrids. Use them wherever you need a splash of purple, lavender, blue, wine red, pink, or white—either by themselves or in tandem with their classic partner, climbing roses—to adorn fences, trellises, and pillars.*

RIGHT *Despite their willful, undisciplined tendencies, vines can be coaxed into rigidly formal positions. Here, star jasmine* (Trachelospermum jasminoides), *carefully trained and trimmed, forms a foliage bas-relief in a diamond pattern against this patio wall.*

Lawns & Alternatives

In much of the West, lawns are a luxury. But even where drought conditions are common, there are times when lawns make sense. Turfgrass is an attractive way to cover bare earth, and offers a safe and inviting surface for recreation. A lawn need not be large to enhance a property. Studies done for the Arizona Department of Water Resources show that 600 square feet of lawn is sufficient for most activities. Unless you plan to play football, a patch 20 by 30 feet is enough lawn. (In drought-prone areas, your city or county may have restrictions on lawn size.)

When planning a new lawn or renovating an existing one, think outside a box shape; lawn, like fabric, can be cut to any shape. A small circle of grass, for example, ringed by trees and flowers can be the centerpiece of a formal garden. A curving or kidney-shaped lawn can direct the eye to a focal point, while a grassy pathway can lead to a secret garden.

Seed or Sod?

There are two ways to plant a new lawn. A lawn grown from seed is more work to establish, but far less expensive than installing sod. Seeded lawns establish deep roots and are generally more durable than sod. In addition, the wide variety of seed available allows you to choose the grass or mixture.

The primary advantages of sod are easy installation and immediate gratification. Sod lawns can be planted during any season, except when the ground is frozen.

Whether you choose seed or sod, the end result will be more successful if the area is first tilled, weeded, amended, fertilized, and leveled.

BELOW *Looking like green cookies on a pebbly baking sheet, precise circles of turfgrass serve as steppingstones in a gravel pathway. Flush mowing strips keep the grass from spreading beyond the prescribed confines.*

Be sure you select a grass suited to your region (see pages 206–207) and the site. A shady spot beneath a tree may call for a shade-tolerant (and tree-root tolerant) ground cover. Also consider maintenance. All lawns need water, so will a simple hose and hose-end sprinkler serve your purposes, or should you install an automatic sprinkler or drip irrigation system? If you have an existing system, does it need upgrading? To eliminate tedious hand-trimming, install a ribbon of concrete, brick, or flat pavers, just wide enough to accommodate the wheels of a mower, around the perimeter. In the absence of a mowing strip, you still may want to contain your lawn with an edging of plastic, metal, or wood benderboard. Particularly if you intend to plant a grass that spreads by stolons or runners, you'll need an edging about 8 inches wide.

Choosing the Right Grass

Climate determines the sort of grass that will perform best in your garden. Although the velvety green look of cool-season bluegrass, bent grass, and fine fescue was long held as the standard of lawn perfection, those grasses are at their best only with abundant summer rainfall. A recent movement toward more climate-sensible lawn grasses has given Western gardeners an array of turfgrass choices.

Turfgrasses divide into two categories. The *cool-season* grasses withstand cold winters, but most of them languish where summer is hot. The *warm-season* grasses grow vigorously during hot weather but go dormant (often turning brownish) when winter temperatures drop to freezing. Here is a rundown of the grasses available to Western gardeners.

Fine fescues and *Kentucky bluegrass* are recommended for cool mountain regions, although drought-tolerant natives such as buffalo grass are also ideal for informal settings. Once established, buffalo grass forms a dense, often clumpy turf; blades are colored gray-green from spring to frost, golden tan during winter. *Crested wheatgrass, blue grama grass*, and similar native grasses are found in seed mixes with *ryegrass* or *fescue*; these mixes are good for creating grassy meadows.

In dry-summer climates, the less-thirsty *tall fescues* are the most popular of the cool-season grasses, thriving even in shade; in warm-winter regions, they'll remain green year-round.

New hybrids, including the dwarf tall fescues such as 'Bonsai' and 'Twilight', have finer, softer blades and are the premier choices for home lawns.

In mild-winter, warm- to hot-summer Southern California, warm-season *Bermuda, St. Augustine,* and *zoysia* are the top performers. Despite its reputation for being weedy and invasive, Bermuda grass has the virtue of thriving in heat—even in the desert. Hybrid strains of it have better color and finer texture. Because Bermuda grass turns brown during winter, overseed it each fall with cool-season perennial ryegrass which provides green color until warm weather returns.

RIGHT *Even surrounded by tall conifers in Bruce Wakefield's Portland, Oregon, garden, this sweep of lawn is the perfect foil for the billowing borders that surround it.*

St. Augustine grass is the most shade-tolerant of the warm-season types, growing well in both dry and humid summer regions where winters are largely frost-free. Rapid spread and very coarse texture are its drawbacks, though selected forms offer finer textured blades. Turf will turn brown when temperatures drop below 55°F/13°F and during summer drought (but greens up with water). For sunny exposures in humid-summer, mild-winter regions, *Bahia grass* and *centipede grass* make similar, coarse-textured lawns.

Zoysia grass is fine-textured but tough, well-suited to regions with hot, humid summers. It has a long winter dormancy and spreads slowly, though some improved forms (such as 'El Toro') are faster growing. Established lawns are durable and quite drought-tolerant.

Turf Alternatives

Not every property is suited to a bright green lawn of turf-grass. In many areas, lawns consume too much water and require too much care to be practical. Elsewhere, a native grass or sedge lawn simply looks better in a particular garden design. In this mountain garden, Hershberger Design planted a variety of grasses in place of traditional lawns. Here, a row of blue fescue *(Festuca glauca)* lines the path and continues up a stone wall. Under the aspens is a new planting of tufted hair grass *(Deschampsia cespitosa)*. Once the grasses have filled in, they'll require only occasional grooming and no supplemental irrigation.

Less-thirsty Lawns

Switch grasses. If your lawn is a water-guzzler in your climate, look for a less-thirsty grass. In hard-to-water spots—like slopes and narrow parking strips—replace lawn with unthirsty ground covers.

Monitor water use. Place at least five straight-sided cans or cups randomly on your lawn. Run the sprinklers for 15 minutes, then measure the water in each cup. For example, if ¼ inch of water collects in 15 minutes, your sprinklers deliver 1 inch an hour. If necessary, make adjustments in sprinkler placement to assure even coverage. Also fix any leaks, clogs, obstructions, and broken heads.

Check evapotranspiration (ET) guidelines. ET is the amount of water that evaporates from soil and transpires from leaves. Your local water department should have ET figures which will help you determine how long to water.

Prevent runoff. To avoid wetting the soil more quickly than it can be absorbed, water for several short intervals rather than one longer period. Another solution is to change to low-volume sprinklers, then let them run long enough to deliver the required amount.

Increase penetration. Rent a power aerator and run it over the lawn to reduce water-repellant thatch and enhance penetration of water into soil.

Adjust watering to exposure. Shaded areas of lawn can go for longer intervals between waterings than can sunny areas.

Cut back on fertilizer. Too much nitrogen encourages water-thirsty new growth.

Mow higher. Set your mower at 2 to 2 ½ inches for bluegrass, 2 to 3 inches for tall fescue, and 1 inch for warm-season grasses such as Bermuda and zoysia.

Let the lawn go dry. Many lawn grasses—including Bermuda, tall fescue, and zoysia—will green up when they can be watered again. If not, replant with a less thirsty grass.

Lawn Alternatives

Where the ground slopes more than gently, in shaded areas, or where there's root competition for water and nutrients, ground cover is a better option than turfgrass. Ground-cover plants share one common trait: they grow low to the soil, spreading widely and densely to cover the ground with a solid blanket of foliage. Among the grab bag of ground-cover plants are perennials, shrubs, or even vines. Water needs vary; some thrive in shade, others prefer sun. Some ground covers even control erosion by making extensive root networks that bind soil. Some easily endure light foot traffic; others become traffic barriers due to plant height or thorny stems. Some ground covers easily grow with tree-root competition.

You also have a wide variety of appearance choices. Those with showy flowers may go on to give a conspicuous crop of berries. Foliage textures run from

LEFT *Mexican feather grass quickly forms a drought-tolerant, shaggy meadow on sunny ground. Beige to tan during summer, the plants green up with the onset of cool weather and rainfall.*

grasslike fineness to plants with leaves that look nearly tropical. Color also varies; in addition to shades of green, you'll find plants with leaves of yellow, blue, bronze, and burgundy, as well as green variegated in white or yellow. By combining ground covers you can create stunning tapestry effects, either by using different flower colors of the same plant or by mixing entirely different types of plants.

FACING PAGE, ABOVE *A riotous mix of wildflowers smothers a hard-to-water slope, where they thrive on rainfall alone. After a dazzling seasonal bloom the flowers set seeds, which become the plants for the following year's display.*

FACING PAGE, BELOW *Rocky terrain perfectly suits a variety of low-growing ground covers and accent shrubs. Lithodora diffusa 'Grace Ward' accounts for the showy patches of brilliant blue.*

RIGHT *Although creeping thyme (*Thymus serpyllum *'Reiter's') needs an occasional mowing to remain uniform, this minimal maintenance is just a fraction of what lawn requires.*

Choosing Ground Covers

When choosing ground covers, don't be seduced by appearance alone. Just as with lawn grasses, you need to match the ground cover to your climate and to the conditions it will encounter in your garden. The lists here highlight ground cover favorites in the disparate Western climate regions. Plants marked with an asterisk (*) are mat-like spreaders forming a fairly even surface no greater than 1 foot high.

LEFT *Why settle for just one ground cover? Here, a potpourri of low-spreading perennials has been artfully combined with gravel pathways to produce an ever-changing tapestry of colors and textures.*

NORTHWEST

Arctostaphylos × media Manzanita
Calluna vulgaris Scotch heather
Cotoneaster salicifolius 'Emerald Carpet' Willowleaf cotoneaster
Epimedium and *Vancouveria*
Erica carnea 'Springwood' Heath*
Erica 'Dawn' Heath
Juniperus conferta Shore juniper*
Pachysandra terminalis Japanese spurge*
Potentilla neumanniana
Rubus pentalobus Bramble*

MOUNTAIN & GREAT BASIN

Aegopodium podagraria Bishop's weed*
Arctostaphylos uva-ursi Bearberry*
Cotoneaster adpressus praecox
Cotoneaster dammeri Bearberry cotoneaster*
Duchesnea indica Indian mock strawberry*

Euonymus fortunei 'Colorata' Purple-leaf winter creeper
Juniperus horizontalis cultivars Juniper*
Juniperus procumbens cultivars Japanese garden juniper
Paxistima canbyi
Verbena 'Homestead Purple'

NORTHERN & CENTRAL CALIFORNIA

Arctostaphylos 'Emerald Carpet' Manzanita
Baccharis pilularis 'Pigeon Point', 'Twin Peaks' Dwarf coyote brush
Ceanothus 'Centennial' Wild lilac
Ceanothus griseus horizontalis 'Yankee Point' Carmel creeper
Ceratostigma plumbaginoides Dwarf plumbago*
Cistus salviifolius Sageleaf rockrose
Convolvulus sabatius Ground morning glory

Fragaria chiloensis Beach strawberry*
Hypericum calycinum Aaron's beard*
Rosmarinus officinalis 'Irene', 'Prostratus' Rosemary

SOUTHERN CALIFORNIA & SOUTHWEST

Arctotheca calendula Cape weed*
Cerastium tomentosum Snow-in-summer*
*Gazania**
Hedera canariensis Algerian ivy
Ice plants*
Lantana montevidensis
Osteospermum fruticosum Trailing African daisy*
Pelargonium peltatum Ivy geranium
Trachelospermum jasminoides Star jasmine
Verbena lilacina Cedros Island verbena*

ABOVE *Flagstone pavers are held together not by mortar but by ribbons of woolly thyme* (Thymus pseudolanuginosus). *Here and there, fountains of common blue fescue* (Festuca glauca) *punctuate the overall flatness.*

LEFT *Irregularly shaped concrete steppingstones are relieved of starkness by the connecting "glue" provided by* Pratia angulata, *which oozes between and around the pavers.*

BELOW, LEFT *A mowing strip would have made a stark demarcation between lawn and flowers. In its place, a band of stones set into blue star creeper* (Pratia pedunculata) *creates a gradual transition.*

Plants for Paths

A smooth, swift course is a virtue on a speedway but not in a garden. One of the best ways to slow down traffic on a path is to intersperse pavers with plants. As a bonus, plantings between pavers make a garden appear more lush—which is especially valuable in a small garden where the proportion of hardscape to planting areas is always greater.

To get ground covers between pavers off to a good start, you'll need at least 6 inches of high quality planting mix under the path. Before you position the pavers, consider the pedestrian impact. Where there's heavy foot traffic, create narrow gaps between pavers; where it is more occasional, leave up to 4 inches between stones.

Choose the lowest-growing ground covers for well-used areas and the taller, more sprawling plants for side paths. Buy the ground covers as plugs, and place them as close together as possible, planting densely to get the plants off to a good start. Most ground-cover plants don't require fertilizer, but regular watering is essential; overhead sprinklers are best.

211

Perennials

Flowering perennials stage a comeback year after year. Only after several seasons do you need to rejuvenate them—either by dividing and replanting or by replacing them. Some favorites can remain in place for so many years as to qualify as permanent. Routine maintenance includes yearly cleanup of old leaves and flower stems, a spring fertilizer application, and usually some watering during the growing period. Some perennials will flower longer if you remove spent blossoms.

Many perennials give you immediate gratification the year you plant them; others need a year or two to get established before reaching their full potential. All Western climates are hospitable to perennials, but adaptability varies, so be sure the plants you want are adapted to the conditions in your garden.

Because perennials make up such a diverse group, it pays to know something about the plants before you choose. *Herbaceous* perennials die down to the ground in fall, then put up new growth the following year. Others are *evergreen* and remain leafy and virtually unchanged throughout the year. Some fall between the two extremes—not disappearing from view but dying back to low tufts of foliage during the winter months. And finally, you have *shrubby* perennials with woody-based stems.

Perennials are sold by mail-order firms as well as in retail nurseries. For mail-order purchase, deal with reputable nurseries and place orders in time for shipment at proper planting time in your area. At retail nurseries, try to buy plants before they're in bloom so they get established before they have to devote energies to flowering. (However, this doesn't mean you *never* should buy blooming perennials; often you'll find favorite kinds available only when they're in full flower.) Small sizes really are the better value. Healthy young plants (not root-bound or leggy) in small containers (cell-packs and 2- to 4-inch pots) experience less transplant shock and establish roots faster than do plants in 1- and 2-gallon containers.

Beds & Borders

The perennial border, an idea originally borrowed from English gardens, traditionally mixes perennials in a wide bed against a fence or wall; put one on either side of a walk and you have a double border. Mixing plants with varied bloom times, plant shapes, foliage textures—and flower colors, sizes, and shapes—is what gives borders their distinctive looks. Perennials also can serve in mixed borders that include shrubs, roses, bulbs, annuals, ornamental grasses, or even small trees. Eye-catching perennial plantings don't "just happen." Here are six points to address in the planning phase.

Shape. A bed in the shape of a circle, square, or octagon looks formal, while one with a free-form shape has a casual look. To experiment with shapes, lay a hose on the ground and adjust it to form potential outlines.

A Variety of Borders

View. Angle the bed for best viewing from different parts of the garden and house—from paths, a patio or other outdoor-living space, or indoors through prominent view windows.

Height. One simple way to guarantee variation is to use plants that mature at different heights—placing taller ones at the rear of one-sided borders or toward the center of island beds. You also can add the illusion of height by mounding soil to create a gentle berm with its high point toward the center or nearer one end, then using it as a stage for an accent plant or a piece of sculpture.

Color and texture. Flowering perennials have their individual moments of glory, then retreat from center stage, so intersperse them with permanent foliage plants for visual constants during the growing season. Shrubs with colored or variegated foliage are especially good candidates for mixing with colorful perennials.

Accents. A shapely boulder, a well-placed piece of garden art, or a low-growing Japanese maple can make just the needed finishing touch when it rises above the surrounding lower plants.

Edging. If you want a bed to look crisp, outline it with pavers like brick or stone. For a decidedly informal, fuzzy margin, plant billowy, spreading perennials such as catmint or dwarf morning glory.

A gently winding entry walk that links the driveway and the front door can be flanked by irregular beds planted for multiple seasons of color.

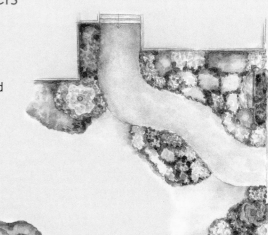

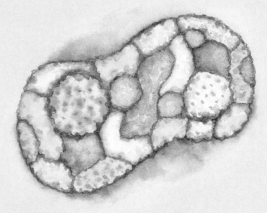

To surround a mature tree (such as a live oak) without strangling or overwatering its roots, create a long, curving bed beyond the tree's drip line.

A more recent variation on the border plan is the "island bed," usually of irregular shape, set into a lawn or paving. Compose the bed with plants of varying heights, anchoring the bed with the tallest plants in the center.

Place an arbor over an entryway walk, then plant small beds on either side. Add a few climbing vines in complementary colors to clamber up the structure.

ABOVE *Great swathes of contrasting colors and textures create a dynamic landscape picture. Bristly grass clumps appear at left, merging into a pink sea of* Sedum 'Autumn Joy'. *Santa Barbara daisy* (Erigeron karvinskianus) *forms a billowy ribbon along the pathway edge.*

ABOVE, INSET *For total contrast, all you need are two perfect perennials. Purple-flowered globe thistle* (Echinops)—*angular and spiky—wends its way through a meadow of gracefully wispy Mexican feather grass* (Nassella tenuissima).

RIGHT *Bold and bright—that's the key in this hot-colored planting. In the background, a dramatic clump of cannas sets the tone, the color theme picked up by red-flowered bedding dahlias toward the foreground. Gray-blue* Melianthus major *cools down the foreground.*

FACING PAGE *This picture-perfect planting consists entirely of perennials. Clumps of feather reed grass* (Calamagrostis × acutiflora) *provide vertical accent behind daylilies* (Hemerocallis), *mounds of catmint* (Nepeta), *and a gray foreground carpet of lamb's ears* (Stachys byzantina).

ABOVE *A cottage-garden planting need not be complex. Here just a few plants provide contrast and informality: grassy clumps of purple-flowered Siberian iris, pink-blossomed coral bells (Heuchera), orange geum, and a dramatic clump of purple-leafed Japanese barberry (Berberis thunbergii atropurpurea).*

LEFT *In the spirit of old cottage gardens, this planting presents a pleasing hodge-podge of perennials and annuals. Prominent in the foreground are dense spikes of lupine and pincushion flower (Scabiosa).*

Plant It: Perennial Plenty

This colorful group of easygoing late-spring and summer bloomers offers treats for all comers, including birds, butterflies, and human visitors. It is a widely adapted planting suitable for much of the West. Most of the plants can remain in place for many years, requiring only a yearly late-winter cleanup. The annuals can be replaced each spring.

A *Agastache rugosa* Korean hummingbird mint *(1)*

B *Alcea rosea* Hollyhock *(6)*

C *Centranthus ruber* 'Albus' Jupiter's beard *(1)*

D *Asclepias tuberosa* Butterfly weed *(3)*

E *Achillea filipendulina* 'Coronation Gold' Fernleaf yarrow *(2)*

F *A. millefolium* Common yarrow *(4)*

G *Echinacea purpurea* Purple coneflower *(3)*

H *Chrysanthemum maximum* 'Alaska' Shasta daisy *(7)*

I *Coreopsis grandiflora* 'Early Sunrise' or 'Sunburst' *(12)*

J *Liatris spicata* Gayfeather *(1)*

K *Sedum* 'Autumn Joy' *(3)*

L *Salvia nemorosa* 'Ostfriesland' *(3)*

M *Heuchera sanguinea* Coral bells *(9)*

N *Cleome hasslerana* Spider flower *(1)*

O *Dianthus gratianopolitanus* Cheddar pink *(4)*

P *Iberis sempervirens* 'Snowflake' Evergreen candytuft *(4)*

Q *Antirrhinum majus,* Rocket strain Snapdragon *(6)*

R *Tagetes erecta* African marigold *(4)*

S *T. patula* French marigold *(6)*

T *Nicotiana alata,* Nicki strain Flowering tobacco *(10)*

U *Salvia splendens* Scarlet sage *(4)*

V *Cosmos bipinnatus,* Sonata series *(4)*

W *Petunia* × *hybrida (5)*

X *Lobularia maritima* Sweet alyssum *(8)*

Annuals

Flowering annuals are garden racehorses: they grow easily and quickly from seed, bloom soon after, then die. In spring and summer (plus fall and winter in mild-winter low elevations) nurseries are filled with a vast array of colorful annuals in cell-packs, pots, and flats. (Note: some of the most popular annuals—impatiens and petunia, for example—really are fast-growing tender perennials but they are treated as annuals nearly everywhere.)

Because annuals come in a wide range of plant sizes, shapes, and flower colors, *versatility* is their hallmark. You can use them as showy components in mixed borders, for the cutting garden, as temporary color between slower-growing plants, as mass-effect

Cool-season annuals

Calendula	Larkspur
Clarkia	Nemesia
Cornflower	Pansy, viola
Fairy primrose	Snapdragon
Forget-me-not	Sweet pea

Warm-season annuals

Cosmos	Marigold
Garden verbena	Petunia
Impatiens	Pincushion flower
Lobelia	Scarlet sage
Madagascar periwinkle	Zinnia

Annuals for naturalizing

California poppy	Love-in-a-mist
Clarkia	Moss rose
Corn cockle	Shirley poppy
Cornflower	Sweet alyssum
Desert marigold	
Larkspur	

plantings, and as stellar container subjects. Even the kitchen garden offers a
home for annuals.

In low-elevation, mild-winter
gardens, annual color is possible for
much of the year. *Cool-season* types
flower in late winter and early spring
from fall planting. *Warm-season* types,
planted in spring after the last frost,
carry on the bloom show from late
spring through summer to fall. A
number of spring-blooming annuals
will, if you let them, reseed year after
year, adding impromptu sparkle
among more permanent plants.

Breeders continue to improve plant
vigor, disease resistance, flower quality,
and color ranges. In recent years,
explorers have enriched gardens with
new annuals, often natives suited to
the Southwest, where heat and water
scarcity are gardening issues. Here are
the West's proven performers.

ABOVE *For connoisseurs of fragrance, sweet peas are indis-
pensable in any planting of cool-weather annuals. Their
distinctive blossoms come in white plus a variety of shades
of pink, red, purple, lavender, and bicolor combinations.*

LEFT *Vibrant California poppy* (Eschscholzia californica)
*comes not only in traditional yellow and orange tones but also
in white, cream, apricot, pink, red, and purple. Technically
perennial (though short-lived), it seeds itself freely to produce
a new crop of plants each year.*

FACING PAGE, ABOVE *After winter rains give way to warmer
weather, many annuals burst into bloom. Clockwise from bottom are pink* Scabiosa anthemifolia, *salmon farewell-to-spring
(*Clarkia amoena *'Aurora'), red* Clarkia rubicunda *'Shamini',
spiky* Verbascum chaixii *and dark blue* Nigella. *The orange
note is provided by perennial* Alstroemeria *'Third Harmonic'.*

FACING PAGE, BELOW *Easy-growing, prolific cosmos (*Cosmos
bipinnatus) *is an old-fashioned favorite annual still beloved
in modern gardens. Fernlike foliage forms a backdrop to
satin-finished daisy flowers in white as well as shades of pink,
lavender, and purple.*

Bulbs

Bulbs are a wonderfully varied group. Think of daffodils, tulips, lilies, cannas, callas, and irises and you'll clearly see the diversity in appearance and season. Like perennials, bulbs reappear year after year. What sets them apart lies beneath the soil: all bulbs grow from an underground structure that stores nutrients for growth and bloom. In addition to true bulbs, we use the term to refer to corms, tubers, rhizomes, and tuberous roots.

The majority of bulbs have a distinct dormant period during which they are totally leafless. That makes them easy to purchase and handle: in most cases you have no roots or soil to deal with, and there's no rush to plant. Spring-flowering bulbs usually appear in nurseries in early fall; summer bloomers are sold in late winter and early spring. Whatever bulb

you buy, it's important to plant at the proper depth for the particular plant and to locate the bulbs where the climate and garden conditions will meet their needs. (One exception to that caution: most tulips need distinct winter chill; in warm-winter regions, plant them as annuals.) If you live where winters are mild and you want to plant bulbs that will naturalize (spread), choose species tulips, such as *Tulipa chrysantha* or *T. clusiana*, or bulbs from South Africa such as *Babiana,* crocosmia, freesia, and *Sparaxis.*

Bulbs are sociable plants, best planted in multiples. Mass them in isolated clumps to form dramatic punctuation marks, or set them out in larger drifts. Some bulbs will naturalize; scatter these randomly to appear as seasonal accents under trees, in meadows, or in mixed plantings. Many bulbs also serve in more structured settings: as border color along walkways or massed in geometric beds. And, of course, many bulbs make spectacular container subjects.

After flowering, most bulbs prepare for dormancy: foliage grows a bit to manufacture nutrients for storage in the bulb, then it yellows and dies down. With spring-flowering types, you have to deal with yellowing bulb leaves just when the rest of the garden starts looking lush. Where bulbs are grown in naturalized plantings, this may pose no problem. In mixed plantings, interplant spring-blooming bulbs with annuals or perennials that cover or hide the bulb foliage as it dies.

ABOVE *Dramatic leaves and brightly colored flowers make cannas ideal as prominent accents. Here,* Canna 'Tropicanna' *is complemented by bright orange flowers of annual garden nasturtium* (Tropaeolum majus).

FACING PAGE *Randomly scattered as though native, clumps of tall bearded irises spring from a gravel bed beneath silvery olive trees.*

FACING PAGE, INSET *Multicolored blossoms of harlequin flower* (Sparaxis tricolor), *another South African native.*

RIGHT *A South African favorite,* Watsonia, *lifts its vivid blossoms on tall spires above clumps of upright, sword-shaped leaves.* Watsonia pillansii *has evergreen foliage;* W. borbonica *goes dormant in summer.*

Can't-miss Combos

Whenever they flower, bulbs are the undisputed stars of the show. What shouldn't be overlooked, however, is their value as ensemble players. By pairing bulbs with other plants that flower with them, you can allow bulbs to remain the stars, using the other plants as supporting cast members. You can go for total color contrast—yellow daffodils and red pansies, for example—or something more harmonious like apricot tulips and cream violas. You can vary the color impact in several ways: combine plants with equally brilliant or equally soft colors, or let the bulb flowers shine in brilliance and choose a softer-hued companion.

However you mix colors, the key to successful combinations lies in choosing companion plants that need the same conditions as the bulbs they will accompany. Look for plants that will thrive in your climate and that have the same water and sunlight needs as their bulb associates.

Winter, early spring. Daffodils and tulips are this period's mainstay bulbs; hyacinths, grape hyacinths, bluebells, Dutch irises, and freesias are other seasonal favorites. Their best companion plants are found among the cool-season annuals. Pansies and violas embrace the full color spectrum, some in bright hues, some in softer tones, many with bicolor blossoms. Nemesias come in all colors except green, including both solid-color and bicolor flowers. Polyanthus primroses also feature a broad color range with emphasis on the warm side of the spectrum; fairy primroses, on the other hand, offer only white, lavender, and pink. English wallflowers encompass an unusual range of warm shades, from cream through yellow, orange, red, and brown. For pure blue, nothing touches forget-me-nots and baby blue eyes.

Late spring, summer. The warmer part of the growing season brings on bulb favorites such as lilies, cannas, crocosmias, and alstroemerias. To complement them is an array of warm-season annuals as well as summer-blooming perennials. For largely warm-toned flowers, look to these annuals: annual coreopsis, marigolds, and zinnias; among perennials are blanket flower, coreopsis, and yarrow. Annuals in cool colors and white include cosmos, garden verbena, lobelia, Madagascar periwinkle, nicotiana, petunia, and sweet alyssum; in cool-colored perennials you have *Anchusa,* baby's breath, geranium, Jupiter's beard, perennial candytuft, perennial verbenas, Santa Barbara daisy, and snow-in-summer.

FACING PAGE *Double-flowered pale pink tulips emerge from a sea of mixed-color pansies in an early spring tour-de-force display. By midspring, both tulips and pansies can be replaced by other bulbs or annual flowers for summer color.*

BELOW *White and maroon Darwin tulips create a springtime complement to pink blossoms and wine-colored leaves of shrubby* Loropetalum chinense.

'Sweet 100'
cherry tomato.

ABOVE *In the style of a French* potager, *this garden features symmetrical beds filled with herbs and vegetables. Brick pathways offer easy access to the beds for tending and harvesting.*

Edibles

Gardening tradition used to relegate vegetables and herbs to separate gardens, to hide their workaday appearance from the ornamental landscape. But where space is limited, edibles can be beautiful when combined with flowers. A model for this is the French *potager* (culinary) garden where small beds are separated by walkways for easy crop tending and harvesting.

In creating a Western version of a *potager,* remember that for at-home consumption you'll need very few plants of each chosen edible. One zucchini plant, one teepee of pole beans, and one tomato cylinder, for example, can satisfy a household of four, freeing up garden space for other plants.

To integrate edibles into the overall garden plan, use each type where it will look good within the general planting scheme, making attractive combinations with purely ornamental plants. Chives, for example, are a classic edging plant, perfect for a foreground show with lobelias or sweet alyssum; clumps of bronze-tinted lettuce can add foliage contrast. Bell peppers and sweet basil make neat, shrubby accents that can complement colorful, fine-textured marigolds or cosmos. And for pure foliage drama, you can't go wrong with rhubarb, Swiss chard (especially the colored-leaf types), or even the humble zucchini.

The majority of vegetables are annual plants, so think of them as you do flowering annuals and provide them with similar exposure, soil, watering, and fertilizing. Some of the favorite herbs also are annuals (sweet basil, for example) but others are perennials and shrubs. Use these as permanent landscape components, pruning and feeding on a yearly basis.

The simple plan shown below integrates vegetables and strawberries with flowering plants. A graceful border that would look good anywhere, the main requirement of this planting is a spot that receives at least six hours of direct sun per day.

RIGHT *Even if you have no ground to garden, you can grow edibles in containers. Here 'Sunburst' squash, 'Early Girl' tomato, and 'Lemon' cucumber thrive in big glazed pots.*

Plant It: *Pretty Edible Medley*

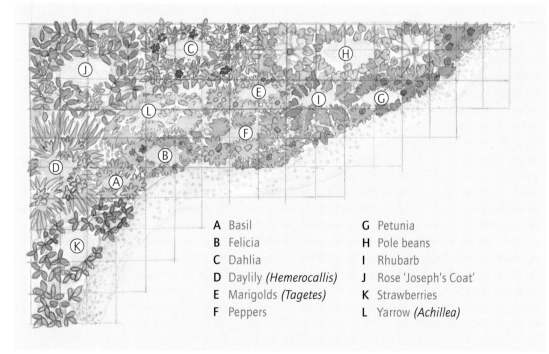

A Basil	**G** Petunia
B Felicia	**H** Pole beans
C Dahlia	**I** Rhubarb
D Daylily *(Hemerocallis)*	**J** Rose 'Joseph's Coat'
E Marigolds *(Tagetes)*	**K** Strawberries
F Peppers	**L** Yarrow *(Achillea)*

LEFT *'Fairy Wings' Spanish lavender* (Lavandula stoechas) *thrives equally well in containers or in the ground. Pretty winged flower heads are its prime feature, but you can also use the leaves for potpourri, soap, or cooking.*

BELOW *Culinary sage* (Salvia officinalis) *comes in several foliage variants. Here, S. o. 'Purpurascens' spreads its purple-flushed leaves between clumps of a violet-flowered ornamental sage,* S. nemorosa.

BOTTOM *A mixed planting of herbs neatly tucks into the corner of a lawn. Taking its cue from classic knot gardens, carefully clipped boxwood provides geometric separation between the different herb plants.*

Plant It: Savory Corner

With this modest cornucopia of culinary herbs *just a few steps away from the kitchen, you can stop and snip a few sprigs to add to the dishes simmering on the stove. This frequent clipping also helps to keep the shrubby herbs compact and bushy. Two favorites get special treatment: spearmint is confined to a container to keep its invasive nature in check. And the bay tree is displayed in its own terracotta pot, so that it can be taken indoors during winter in colder zones.*

A Parsley
B Basil
C Chives
D Sage, common
E Oregano
F French tarragon
G Sweet marjoram
H Winter savory
I Rosemary
J Thyme, common
K Thyme, lemon
L Spearmint
M Sweet bay

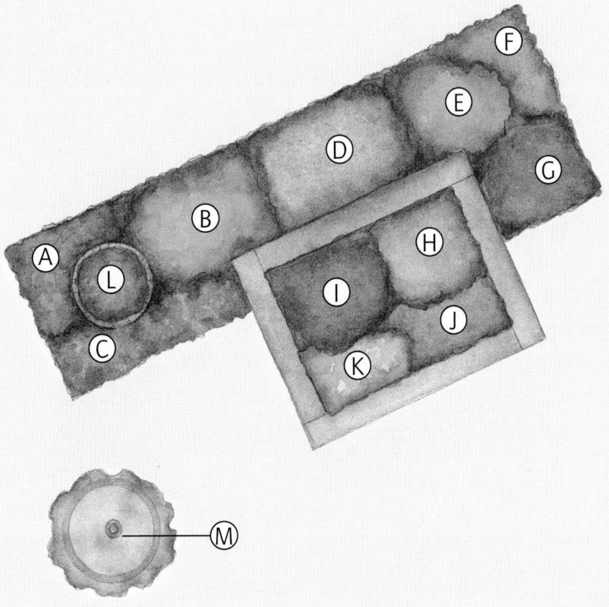

ABOVE *Bold, lush foliage, big flowers, and bright color combine to suggest the tropics. In this patio planting, giant bird of paradise* (Strelitzia nicolai) *provides the major foliage accent; angel's trumpet* (Brugmansia, *in background*) *offers dramatic, trumpet-shaped blossoms; flaming red dahlias set the equatorial color scheme.*

Tropicals

The word *tropical* suggests a riotous array of lush greenery, showy and fragrant flowers, brilliant birds, and exotic perfumed fruits. It's no wonder that travelers try to recreate the steamy luxuriance of the Caribbean, Hawaii, and the South Pacific in their own backyards. Fortunately, this is possible in regions of the West where frosts are light or non-existent. Even where winter is nippier—inland, and in higher elevations—gardeners can create a convincing illusion of the tropics (see facing page).

The first step toward a junglelike garden is choosing plants that will thrive in your climate. Look for large-leafed ones that suggest warm, moist climes. Wildly colorful flowers—and large ones of any color—are another tropical feature. You can amplify the color impact by using plants with leaves striped red, green, and bronze. And don't overlook striking plants with unusual shapes: palms, tree ferns, dracaenas, even phormium, for example. Vines, too, enhance a jungle look; particularly if they thread through other plants, they underscore the sense of luxuriance—of almost overgrown rampancy—that typifies tropical vegetation. Passion vine and giant Burmese honeysuckle fit the profile.

Finally, arrange the plants as they might appear in the tropics. Layer them, with the tallest ones—palms and bananas, perhaps—rising above mid-level flowering shrubs that are underplanted with low-growing plants. In tropical gardens, the mass effect of foliage carries the show. Be sure to mix the planting to contrast foliage shapes, sizes, and textures.

BELOW *Frangipani* (Plumeria) *has a fragrance truly redolent of the tropics.* Plumeria rubra *makes a sparse shrub to small tree and is hardy enough to grow in coastal Southern California as well as desert regions. Colors range from white through cream, yellow, orange, red, and pink.*

Tropicals in Colder Zones

A surprising number of tropical-appearing plants will tolerate frosts and even actual freezes. So gardeners in places as far from the tropics as Seattle, Vancouver, Salt Lake City, Denver, and Albuquerque still create the mood of balmy, equatorial climes. These hardier "tropicals" are highlighted by an asterisk (*) in the lists on page 232.

Start by selecting plants that will survive the winter lows in your area. Then, increase your chances of success with marginally hardy and tender plants in these colder-winter climes by placing them in the garden hot spots—under roof overhangs and beneath arbors where it can be warmer than exposed garden areas. Plantings against walls benefit from reflected heat, as do those placed at the top of slopes. (Because cold air sinks, plants at the bottom of a sloping garden are at greater freezing risk than are plants higher up the slope.)

Some gardeners grow tropicals in large nursery containers that can be placed in the ground in garden beds during the warm summer months, then pulled out and stored in a protected spot over winter. Bulbous plants such as calla, canna, ginger, and taro can be planted directly in the ground after danger of frost is past; you can dig them in fall, then store their rhizomes or tubers over winter for planting out after the last frost of the following year.

THE WEST'S BEST TROPICALS

Fashion your own South Pacific oasis from the broad array of subtropical natives and a selection of hardier but tropically lush individuals. Those marked with an asterisk (*) will thrive outdoors all year, at least in the Pacific Northwest west of the Cascade Mountains; some (such as *Aralia* and *Catalpa*) endure even harsher winters.

Trees and treelike plants

Aralia *
Bauhinia Orchid tree
Catalpa *
Chorisia Floss silk tree
Ensete ventricosum Abyssinian banana
Erythrina Coral tree
Ficus
F. carica Fig (edible)*
Firmiana simplex Chinese parasol tree
Musa Banana
M. basjoo Japanese banana*
Palms (many; some*)
Paulownia tomentosa Empress tree*
Tabebuia Trumpet tree

Shrubs and shrublike plants

Abutilon Flowering maple
Brugmansia Angel's trumpet
Cycas revoluta Sago palm
Euphorbia cotinifolia Caribbean copper plant
Fatsia japonica Japanese aralia*
Hibiscus rosa-sinensis Chinese hibiscus
Melianthus major Honey bush
Plumeria Frangipani
Schefflera
Sparmannia africana African linden
Tecoma stans Yellow bells
Tibouchina urvilleana Princess flower

Vines

Beaumontia grandiflora Herald's trumpet
Bougainvillea
Campsis Trumpet creeper*
× *Fatshedera lizei*
Lonicera hildebrandiana Giant Burmese honeysuckle
Mandevilla
M. laxa Chilean jasmine*
Monstera deliciosa Split-leaf philodendron
Pandorea
Passiflora Passion vine
P. incarnata Wild passion vine*
Solandra maxima Cup-of-gold vine

Perennials

Acanthus mollis Bear's breech
Alocasia Elephant's ear
Alpinia
Aspidistra elatior Cast-iron plant*
Bamboo
Caladium bicolor Fancy-leafed caladium
Canna
Clivia miniata
Colocasia esculenta Taro
Crinum
Epiphyllum Orchid cactus
Gunnera *
Hedychium Ginger lily
Hosta Plantain lily*
Ligularia *
Philodendron
Strelitzia Bird of paradise
Zantedeschia aethiopica Common calla

Annuals

Coleus × *hybridus* Coleus
Impatiens New Guinea hybrids
Ricinus communis Castor bean

ABOVE *Brazen colors and compelling foliage convey a sense of junglelike exuberance. Hot yellow and red dahlias are joined by an orange-flowered canna; foliage drama comes from bronzy canna leaves as well as Abyssinian banana (rear) and ginger (foreground).*

RIGHT *Canna blossoms are a colorful bonus carried in spikes over broad, paddle-shaped leaves. Colors include the range of warm and hot hues plus pink shades, as well as striking bicolor combinations like 'Cleopatra'.*

FAR RIGHT *Rampant passion vines embody that peculiar tropical mingling of exotic beauty and the vaguely sinister. This banana passion vine* (Passiflora mollissima) *also bears flavorful, oblong yellow fruits.*

Grasses

Versatile ornamental grasses offer beauty and grace, yet demand minimal care in return. Not all plants we commonly place in this category are true grasses; sedges *(Carex)* and rushes are usually considered to be ornamental grasses in the garden.

We often classify grasses according to growth habit. Most grasses are *perennial*, but a few are *annual* growers, lasting just a single season. Among perennial types, some grasses are *evergreen* (especially in warmer climates), while *deciduous* types die back in winter. Further, most perennial grasses are classified as either *warm-* or *cool-season* growers. Warm-season types grow

rapidly in the heat of summer and produce long-lasting, showy seedheads; cool-season types start to grow early in the spring and then flower in spring and summer, only to fade away in fall.

Like bamboo, the aggressive nature of some grasses has made gardeners wary, but most grasses are *clumping* types that stay where you put them. Those types that grow by runners, such as ribbon grass *(Phalaris arundinacea picta),* can be contained with barrier edgings.

Massed groups of clumping grasses can create the same impact of heft and color as landscape shrubs. Taller plants, such as zebra grass or giant feather grass, can make effective hedges and privacy screens. In smaller gardens, use grasses as specimens or accents in borders—warm-season types are especially valuable in later-summer and fall displays. If you have a pond, surround it with moisture-loving sedges, where they lend a naturalistic look to the setting.

ABOVE *This showy border includes arching pampas grass* (Cortaderia selloana 'Monvin') *behind 'Maori Maiden' phormium. To the left is a variegated cordyline.*

FACING PAGE, TOP *Needle grass* (Nassella) *and fountain grass* (Pennisetum) *are prominent in the foreground of this natural-looking California hillside.*

FACING PAGE, BELOW *Thriving clumps of deer grass* (Muhlenbergia rigens) *soften a desert landscape of native cacti and palo verde trees.*

Off-season Care

All grasses benefit from—and look better for—an annual grooming. What you do depends on whether the grass is deciduous or evergreen. One of the beauties of many ornamental grasses is their winter appearance. Unless beaten down by snow, their foliage and flower stems remain upright and subtly showy throughout the coldest months. This means you can delay cleanup until late winter or early spring.

Foliage of deciduous grasses dies down in fall and is replaced by new growth in early spring. To keep clumps neat, you'll need to cut down old foliage to make way for the new. Beginning in mid- to late winter (depending on how mild or cold your climate is), look for the start of new growth showing at the base of the clump. At that time, cut dead leaves down to 1 to 3 inches (for smaller grasses) or 3 to 6 inches (for the taller growers). Use hand pruners, hedge shears (either manual or electric), or even a bow saw; be sure to wear sturdy gloves, as blades of some grasses can inflict nasty cuts.

Evergreen grasses remain uniformly leafy throughout the year but individual leaves die and brown. With these grasses, you have to clean out the dead leaves and spent flower stems by hand. In some cases you can pull out the dead material (wearing gloves, of course); for stubborn leaves and stems, use hand shears to cut them out. If an entire clump appears ratty after several years, cut it down as described above for deciduous types.

ABOVE *Tawny clumps of Mexican feather grass and arching plumes of purple fountain grass* (Pennisetum setaceum *'Rubrum') provide textural contrast in harmonizing colors to the dominant clump of bronze-leafed New Zealand flax* (Phormium tenax *'Bronze Baby') and burgundy foliage of smoke tree* (Cotinus coggygria *'Velvet Cloak').*

Plant It: Grassy Blend

The decorative grasses in this plan come in all forms: foliage in fountains, shafts, and tussocks; blossoms and seed heads in spikes and plumes. And not all are green. You'll see steely blue-gray, rusty red, and even variegation. Many change still more in autumn. Mixing the grasses with bright flowers and a dramatic shrubby annual serves to further highlight the grasses.

A *Miscanthus sinensis* 'Strictus' Porcupine grass *(2)*

B *Calamagrostis* × *acutiflora* 'Karl Foerster'
Feather reed grass *(1)*

C *Panicum virgatum* 'Haense Herms'
Switch grass *(2)*

D *Pennisetum orientale* Oriental fountain grass *(2)*

E *M. s.* 'Yaku Jima' Eulalia grass

F *Helictotrichon sempervirens* Blue oat grass *(1)*

G *Pennisetum alopecuroides* 'Hameln'
Fountain grass *(1)*

H *Imperata cylindrica* 'Red Baron' Japanese blood grass *(3)*

I *Deschampsia cespitosa* Tufted hair grass *(2)*

J *Festuca glauca* 'Elijah Blue' Common blue fescue *(5)*

K *Rhynchelytrum nerviglume* 'Pink Crystals'
Natal ruby grass *(2)*

L *Rudbeckia fulgiva* Coneflower *(3)*

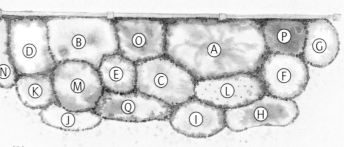

M *Phlomis russeliana* *(2)*

N *Hemerocallis* 'Stella de Oro' Daylily *(4)*

O *Tithonia rotundifolia* Mexican sunflower *(1)*

P *Ricinus communis* 'Dwarf Red Spire' Castor bean *(1)*

Q *Celosia*, Castle series Plume cockscomb *(7)*

Leopard skin bamboo, Phyllostachys nigra *'Bory', reinforces the exotic mood in an Asian-themed garden. Plantings spread freely to form irregular, forestlike groves of mottled culms to 50 feet tall.*

Bamboo

Bamboos are at once distinctive, varied, and amazing. Botanically, they are true grasses of enormous diversity; you'll find rain-forest natives that revel in shady situations as well as dry-chaparral denizens that thrive in full sun. Some form knee-high ground-covering mats, but the giant timber types can shoot up 4 feet a day. They're the plants *par excellence* for creating an Asian garden ambience, yet you'll find bamboos suited to almost every Western climate—including where temperatures drop to –20°F/–28°C.

All bamboo stems (called 'culms') grow from underground rhizomes that spread laterally beneath the soil surface, but there are two distinct growth types.

ABOVE *Although green is the prevailing color in bamboo, you can find distinct variations on the norm.* Himalaya-calamus falconeri *'Damarapa',* the candy cane bamboo, is a striking Himalayan clumping bamboo with culms striped with lavender-pink, green, and yellow.

LEFT *No bamboo is more graceful than Mexican weeping bamboo,* Otatea acuminata aztecorum, *whose foliage mimics the languid droop of weeping willow leaves. One plant makes an accent clump, but this bamboo is equally effective planted as a billowy tall screen.*

Clumping bamboos. Rhizomes grow just a short distance, then send up stems; clumps slowly increase in diameter over the years. These types make excellent focal points and container subjects; planted close together, they form attractive screens or hedges. Many are frost-tender tropical species.

Running bamboos. Rhizomes spread rapidly, then send up stems. By nature these form groves, but can be contained by subsoil root barriers. This group contains most of the cold-tolerant bamboos.

Clumping

Bambusa multiplex cultivars ('Alphonse Karr', 'Fernleaf', 'Golden Goddess', *B. m. riviereorum*): Mostly upright, some with colored culms, 8 to 20 ft.; hardy to 15°F/−9°C.

B. oldhamii: Upright, timber type 25 to 40 ft.; hardy to 15°F/−9°C.

Chusquea culeou: Upright to 20 ft.; hardy to 20°F/−7°C.

Fargesia murielae: Upright, arching at top, 6 to 15 ft.; hardy to −20°F/−28°C.

Otatea acuminata aztecorum: Upright 10 to 20 ft. but gracefully drooping; hardy to 15°F/−9°C.

Running

Phyllostachys aurea: Upright and dense, 10 to 20 ft, aggressive; hardy to 0°F/−18°C.

P. nigra: Upright 8 to 15 ft., culms turn black in second year; hardy to 0°F/−18°C.

P. vivax: Giant timber type to 50 ft.; hardy to −5°F/−20°C.

Pleioblastus variegata: Rapid-spreading ground cover type to 2 ft. with white-edged leaves; hardy to 5°F/−15°C.

Semiarundinaria fastuosa: Upright 10 to 25 ft., slow spreader; hardy to −5°F/−20°C.

Native Plants

"Go native!" is a rallying cry that not only expresses regional pride, it makes good sense. Just as the West encompasses a broad spectrum of climates, Western gardeners have a smorgasbord of native choices at their disposal, from towering forest trees to lowly desert annuals. So whether you live in Washington's rain-soaked Olympic Peninsula or Arizona's sun-baked Salt River Valley, you can find native plants that not only accept the existing conditions but *love* them!

In choosing native plants, there's one caveat: just because a plant is native to your *state* doesn't ensure its success in your particular area. All Western states include mountains and lowlands, and four of the mainland states also have extensive oceanic coastlines. Even the islands of Hawaii vary enormously from each other, as well as between their windward and leeward sides.

ABOVE, TOP *Bright California fuchsia (Zauschneria) adorns hillsides beyond its namesake state into all other arid regions of the West and Southwest. Typical colors are red and orange, but pink and white forms also are available.*

ABOVE *Common flannel bush (Fremontodendron californicum).*

LEFT *Redwoods may be better known, but coast live oak (Quercus agrifolia) is California's signature tree. From north to south, coast to inland, it forms distinctive mounds of dark green foliage as it spreads its rough-barked limbs over summer-dry hillsides.*

PACIFIC NORTHWEST

Trees

Acer circinatum Vine maple
Arbutus menziesii Madrone
Cornus nuttallii Pacific dogwood
Pseudotsuga menziesii Douglas fir
Thuja plicata Western red cedar

Shrubs

Arctostaphylos columbiana Hairy
    manzanita
Gaultheria shallon Salal
Mahonia aquifolium Oregon grape
Rhododendron occidentale Western azalea
Vaccinium ovatum Evergreen huckleberry

Perennials, Ferns, Bulbs

Adiantum aleuticum Five-finger fern
Aquilegia formosa Western columbine
Camassia quamash Camass
Dryas octopetala
Vancouveria

CALIFORNIA

Trees

Calocedrus decurrens Incense cedar
Pinus contorta contorta Beach pine
Platanus racemosa California sycamore
Quercus (many) Oak
Umbellularia californica California laurel

Shrubs

Arctostaphylos (many) Manzanita
Baccharis pilularis Dwarf coyote brush
Carpenteria californica Bush anemone
Ceanothus (many) Wild lilac
Cercis occidentalis Western redbud
Fremontodendron Flannel bush
Garrya elliptica Coast silktassel
Heteromeles arbutifolia Toyon
Prunus ilicifolia ilicifolia Hollyleaf cherry
Rhamnus californica Coffeeberry
Ribes sanguineum Pink winter currant

Perennials

Eriogonum (several) Wild buckwheat
Iris douglasiana Douglas iris
Mimulus aurantiacus Sticky monkey
    flower
Romneya coulteri Matilija poppy
Zauschneria California fuchsia

Regional Bests

Despite the variety of Western climates and topography, the region can be broadly segregated into four distinct climatic regions—each with its own palette of specially adapted native plants. Plants listed for the Pacific Northwest are particularly at home in the territory west of the Cascade Mountains, where rainfall and mild temperatures are the norm. The California plant picks are for a dryer climate regime with a significant low-temperature variation from coast to mountains and north to south. Southwestern natives exemplify adaptation to extremes of both dryness and heat. And the Mountain/Great Basin choices feature the rugged individuals that find snowy, frozen-solid winters just to their liking.

BELOW *Northwestern native vine maple (Acer circinatum) is an edge-of-forest denizen where it unfailingly inflames the autumn scene with a foliage display in sharp contrast to the somber green of its conifer and fern associates.*

ABOVE *Southwest-adapted landscape features a classic native pair. Massive spikes of white blossoms spring from the foliage tuft of a small Joshua tree (*Yucca brevifolia, *left), while spiny stems of ocotillo (*Fouquieria splendens, *right) make a skeletal tracery against the background wall.*

RIGHT *Fragrant evening primrose (*Oenothera caespitosa) *thrives on next to no water yet flowers heavily from spring into summer, offering its beauty and scent to the evening air.*

FACING PAGE, ABOVE *Showy blossoms of Rocky Mountain columbine (*Aquilegia caerulea) *encapsulate colors of the sky, snow, and water of its native region.*

FACING PAGE, BELOW *In autumn, brilliant foliage complements the stems of redtwig dogwood (*Cornus stolonifera) *while clusters of white berries stand in stark contrast.*

SOUTHWEST

Trees

Acacia smallii
Cercidium (several) Palo verde
Chilopsis linearis Desert willow
Cupressus arizonica Arizona cypress
Prosopis (several) Mesquite

Shrubs and shrublike plants

Anisacanthus thurberi Chuparosa
Dalea (several)
Dodonaea viscosa Hop bush
Encelia farinosa Brittlebush
Fallugia paradoxa Apache plume
Fouquieria splendens Ocotillo
Larrea tridentata Creosote bush
Leucophyllum (several) Texas ranger
Salvia greggii Autumn sage
Yucca (several)

Perennials

Calylophus hartwegii Sundrops
Melampodium leucanthum Blackfoot
   daisy
Oenothera (several) Evening primrose
Penstemon (several) Beard tongue
Verbena (several)

ROCKY MOUNTAIN, GREAT BASIN

Trees

Acer saccharum grandidentatum
   Wasatch maple
Picea pungens Colorado spruce

Populus angustifolia Narrowleaf poplar
P. tremuloides Quaking aspen
Pseudotsuga menziesii glauca Rocky
   Mountain Douglas fir

Shrubs

Amelanchier alnifolia Saskatoon
Cercocarpus ledifolius Curl-leaf
   mountain mahogany
Cornus stolonifera Redtwig dogwood
Elaeagnus commutata Silverberry
Philadelphus lewisii Wild mock orange
Quercus gambellii Gambell oak
Ribes aureum Golden currant
Rubus deliciosus Rocky Mountain
   thimbleberry
Shepherdia argentea Silver
   buffaloberry

Perennials

Aquilegia caerulea Rocky Mountain
   columbine
Callirhoe involucrata Poppy mallow
Eriogonum umbellatum Sulfur flower
Oenothera caespitosa Tufted evening
   primrose
Penstemon (several) Beard tongue

HAWAII

Trees

Acacia koa Koa
Erythrina sandwicensis Wiliwili
Metrosideros polymorphus 'Ohi'a lehua
Pritchardia hillebrandii Loulu lelo

Shrubs

Artemisia australis Ahinahina
Hibiscus waimeae White Kauai hibiscus
Scaevola taccada Beach naupaka
Sida fallax 'Ilima

Perennials

*Gnaphalium sandwicensium
   sandwicensium* 'Ena 'ena
Plectranthus parviflorus 'Ala 'ala wai nui

Ground covers

Alyxia oliviformis Maile
Heliotropium anomalum argentum
   Hinahina

ALASKA

Trees

Abies lasiocarpa Alpine fir
Betula papyrifera Paper birch
Picea glauca White spruce
Pinus contorta murrayana Lodgepole
   pine
Populus tremuloides Quaking aspen
Tsuga mertensiana Mountain hemlock

Shrubs, Ground covers

Amelanchier alnifolia Saskatoon
Arctostaphylos uva-ursi Bearberry
Cornus stolonifera Redtwig dogwood
Elaeagnus commutata Silverberry
Juniperus communis 'Effusa'
Juniperus horizontalis
Rosa rugosa Ramanas rose
Rubus arcticus 'Kenai Carpet'
   Nagoonberry
Vaccinium vitis-idaea Cowberry
Viburnum edule Highbush cranberry

Perennials, Ferns

Adiantum aleuticum Five-finger fern
Allium schoenoprasum Chives
Aquilegia formosa Western columbine
Chrysanthemum arcticum Arctic
   chrysanthemum
Cornus canadensis Bunchberry
Iris setosa
Maianthemum dilatatum False lily-of-
   the-valley
Matteuccia struthiopteris Ostrich fern
Polemonium pulcherrimum
Polystichum × setigerum Alaska holly
   fern
Pulsatilla patens Eastern pasque flower
Tiarella trifoliata unifoliata Western
   foamflower

Plants for Pots

Containers are a part of gardening life in the West. You can celebrate the seasons by displaying "portable color" on entry porches and decks: petunias and impatiens from summer into fall, pansies and Iceland poppies in winter (climate permitting) and spring. But it's also possible to have container plantings that look good all year. This is no magic trick, just common sense. First choose a small shrub, grass, or perhaps a dwarf tree as an anchor, then build a composition—whether composed of ephemeral annuals or more permanent choices—around it.

Start by choosing an appropriate container. In addition to good looks, the container must accommodate the permanent plant with room left over to plug in seasonal changes. The lists (opposite) suggest a variety of suitable candidates for that permanent resident in a range of Western climates. Then you can select surrounding plants that need the same care and exposure as the principal resident.

ABOVE *Flaming 'Tropicanna' canna is paired with* Phormium *'Guardsman' for a blaze of foliage color. Below them are rosy pink impatiens and sweet potato vine.*

RIGHT *The sweetly fragrant yellow flowers of angel's trumpet* (Brugmansia × candida) *are surrounded by a colorful tapestry of shorter flowers and foliage plants, including 'Dragon Wing' semperflorens begonias, coleus, variegated vinca* (Vinca *'Wojo's Jem'), and chartreuse sweet potato* (Ipomoea batata).

FACING PAGE, LEFT *Smoldering shades of orange, yellow, and burgundy reflect the first heralds of autumn. Phormium 'Platt's Black' forms a stunning centerpiece in the midst of yellow gloriosa daisies and 'Profusion Orange' zinnias. Loropetalum chinense 'Plum Delight' spills from two of the pots.*

ABOVE *A rusted, long-necked urn makes a stately home for fountainlike* Puya coerulea, Helichrysum argyrophyllum *'Moe's Gold', and lavender-flowered* campanula. *Designers Freeland and Sabrina Tanner raised the urn up on a pedestal so the plants could "grab more sunlight."*

Trees

Acer palmatum Japanese maple
Apple (dwarf)
Citrus (orange, lemon, kumquat)
Ficus carica Fig (edible)
Laurus nobilis Sweet bay
Podocarpus macrophyllus Yew pine
Podocarpus nagi

Shrubs

Abutilon Flowering maple
Aucuba japonica Japanese aucuba
Bougainvillea (shrubby types)
Brugmansia Angel's trumpet
Buxus Boxwood
Camellia
Euonymus fortunei

Euonymus japonicus Evergreen euonymus
Euryops pectinatus
Fatsia japonica Japanese aralia
Fuchsia
Gardenia
Hibiscus rosa-sinensis Chinese hibiscus
Hydrangea macrophylla Bigleaf hydrangea
Justicia brandegeeana Shrimp plant
Lagerstroemia indica (dwarf kinds) Crape myrtle
Lantana
Melianthus major Honey bush
Nandina domestica Heavenly bamboo
Nerium oleander (dwarf kinds) Oleander

Picea glauca albertiana 'Conica' Dwarf Alberta spruce
Punica granatum (dwarf kinds) Pomegranate
Rhododendron, Azalea
Rosa Rose
Solanum rantonnetii

Perennials, Grasses

Agave
Aspidistra elatior Cast-iron plant
Clivia miniata
Cordyline
Pelargonium Geranium
Pennisetum Fountain grass
Phormium tenax New Zealand flax
Puya

Easy Plants

If you're new to gardening in the West, choosing the best plants from the vast array available at nurseries can seem overwhelming. Fortunately, you don't have to be an expert to plant your first garden; within each broad Western climate region, there are key plants that perform reliably with no special attention. These "starter plants" are tried and true; given basic care, they'll thrive in your garden year after year. These are a garden's permanent plants, the ones that establish its framework and provide long-term stability.

FACING PAGE *Decked out in seasonal color, a Japanese maple,* Acer palmatum *'Osakuzki', sets the garden ablaze in fall. Below it is the yellow-orange foliage of diminutive* A. p. dissectum *'Filigree'. In the background, right, are purple leaves of* Prunus × cistena *and the red foliage of* A. p. *'Garnet'.*

FACING PAGE, BELOW, LEFT TO RIGHT Bougainvillea *'Hawaii',* Salvia × superba, *large-flowered hybrid clematis, and* Euphorbia characias wulfenii.

CALIFORNIA

Trees

Acacia baileyana Bailey acacia
Albizia julibrissin Silk tree
Erythrina Coral tree
Lagerstroemia indica Crape myrtle
Liquidambar styraciflua American sweet gum
Magnolia grandiflora Southern magnolia
Olea europaea Olive
Pistacia chinensis Chinese pistache
Prunus Flowering plum
Pyrus calleryana Ornamental pear

Shrubs

Callistemon Bottlebrush
Camellia
Ceanothus Wild lilac
Cistus Rockrose
Lavandula Lavender
Leptospermum scoparium New Zealand tea tree
Nerium oleander Oleander
Rhaphiolepis indica Indian hawthorn
Rosa Rose
Rosmarinus officinalis Rosemary

Vines, Ground covers

Bougainvillea
Clytostoma callistegioides Violet trumpet vine
Gazania
Hardenbergia Lilac vine
Hypericum calycinum Aaron's beard
Lantana montevidensis

Osteospermum fruticosa Trailing African daisy
Pelargonium peltatum Ivy geranium
Trachelospermum jasminoides Star jasmine
Wisteria

Perennials, Bulbs

Agapanthus Lily-of-the-Nile
Canna
Dietes Fortnight lily
Erigeron karvinskianus Mexican daisy
Euphorbia characias wulfenii
Gaura lindheimeri
Hemerocallis Daylily
Iris (tall bearded)
Narcissus Daffodil
Penstemon × gloxinioides Border penstemon

NORTHWEST

Trees

Acer palmatum Japanese maple
Betula jacquemontii Birch
Cercidiphyllum japonicum Katsura tree
Cercis canadensis Eastern redbud
Cornus Dogwood
Magnolia kobus Kobus magnolia
Oxydendrum arboreum Sourwood
Pinus thunbergii Japanese black pine
Prunus Flowering cherry
Sorbus Mountain ash

Shrubs

Calluna vulgaris and *Erica* Scotch heather; heath
Camellia

Hamamelis Witch hazel
Hydrangea macrophylla Bigleaf hydrangea
Mahonia aquifolium Oregon grape
Nandina domestica Heavenly bamboo
Pieris
Rhododendron
Rosa Rose
Viburnum plicatum tomentosum Doublefile viburnum

Vines, Ground covers

Actinidia kolomikta
Arctostaphylos uva-ursi Bearberry
Clematis
Cornus canadensis Bunchberry
Cotoneaster salicifolius 'Emerald Carpet' Willowleaf cotoneaster
Genista pilosa 'Vancouver Gold' Broom
Lonicera Honeysuckle
Parthenocissus
Vancouveria
Wisteria

Perennials, Bulbs

Dahlia
Epimedium
Geranium Cranesbill
Helleborus Hellebore
Hosta Plantain lily
Iris
Lilium Lily
Narcissus Daffodil
Paeonia (herbaceous hybrids) Peony
Tulipa Tulip

SOUTHWEST

Trees

Callistemon citrinus Lemon bottlebrush
Cercidium Palo verde
Chilopsis linearis Desert willow
× *Chitalpa tashkentensis*
Citrus (grapefruit, lemon, mandarin, orange)
Olneya tesota Desert ironwood
Palms (several)
Parkinsonia aculeata Jerusalem thorn
Pithecellobium flexicaule Texas ebony
Prosopis Mesquite

Shrubs

Anisacanthus thurberi Chuparosa
Caesalpinia pulcherrima
   Red bird of paradise
Calliandra californica Baja fairy duster
Cotinus coggygria Smoke tree
Dodonaea viscosa Hop bush
Euryops pectinatus
Justicia brandegeeana Shrimp plant
Lantana
Nerium oleander Oleander
Plumbago auriculata Cape plumbago

Vines, Ground covers

Arctotheca calendula Cape weed
Bougainvillea
Dalea greggii Trailing indigo bush

Macfadyena unguis-cati Cat's claw
Mascagnia Orchid vine
Podranea ricasoliana
   Pink trumpet vine
Rosmarinus officinalis 'Irene',
   'Prostratus'
Santolina chamaecyparissus
   Lavender cotton
Tecoma capensis Cape honeysuckle

Perennials

Agastache
Agave
Coreopsis grandiflora
Erigeron karvinskianus
   Mexican daisy
Gaillardia × *grandiflora*
Gaura lindheimeri
Hesperaloe parviflora Red yucca
Lobelia laxiflora
Melampodium leucanthum
   Blackfoot daisy
Oenothera (several) Evening primrose

MOUNTAIN

Trees

Acer griseum Paperbark maple
Amelanchier × *grandiflora* Juneberry
Betula nigra River birch
Carpinus caroliniana American
   hornbeam
Crataegus phaenopyrum Washington
   thorn
Elaeagnus angustifolia Russian olive
Picea engelmanii Engelmann spruce
Picea pungens Colorado spruce
Pseudotsuga menziesii glauca Rocky
   Mountain Douglas fir
Robinia × *ambigua* Locust

Shrubs

Berberis thunbergii Japanese barberry
Buddleia davidii Butterfly bush
Cornus alba 'Sibirica' Siberian
   dogwood
Forsythia (hardy hybrids)
Hydrangea paniculata 'Grandiflora'
   Peegee hydrangea
Juniperus Juniper
Philadelphus × *virginalis* Mock orange

Rubus deliciosus Rocky Mountain
   thimbleberry
Spiraea × *vanhouttei*
Syringa vulgaris Common lilac

Vines, Ground covers

Aegopodium podagraria Bishop's weed
Ampelopsis brevipedunculata
   Porcelain berry
Celastrus scandens American
   bittersweet
Gazania linearis 'Colorado Gold'
Juniperus (many) Juniper
Lonicera × *brownii* Scarlet trumpet
   honeysuckle
Pachysandra terminalis Japanese
   spurge
Parthenocissus tricuspidata Boston ivy
Verbena 'Homestead Purple'
Wisteria floribunda Japanese wisteria

Perennials, bulbs

Alchemilla mollis Lady's-mantle
Aquilegia Columbine
Asclepias tuberosa Butterfly weed
Centranthus ruber Jupiter's beard
Echinacea purpurea Purple coneflower
Iris
Paeonia (herbaceous hybrids) Peony
Penstemon (many) Beard tongue
Rudbeckia fulgida
Sedum 'Autumn Joy'

FACING PAGE, ABOVE *Rosy pink desert beard tongue* (Penstemon pseudo-spectabilis), *a shrubby plant to 4 feet tall, is one of many showy penstemons native to water-scarce parts of the West.*

FACING PAGE, BELOW *Century plant* (Agave americana) *thrives beyond the Southwest into much of California and Hawaii, where its spiny foliage rosettes are popular as pieces of living sculpture.*

ABOVE *For lush landscapes in the arid Southwest, all you need is water-thrifty plants. This lavish display features purple coneflower (*Echinacea purpurea, *rear) and* Sedum *'Autumn Joy', foreground.*

décor

ART | BIRDHOUSES |
BIRDBATHS | CONTAINERS |
FURNITURE | HAMMOCKS |
UMBRELLAS | PAINT | TILE |
PORTABLE LIGHTING |
WATER FEATURES | RETREATS

Art

Like icing on a cake, the right garden art—in the right place—can transform a seemingly ordinary garden into a magical hideaway. An outdoor sculpture can serve as a soothing oasis among a riot of blooms or as an accent that visually breaks up long stretches of foliage. It may be a playful rainman statue dancing across a pond, or small leaf-shaped rocks nestled on the ground among baby's tears. Even a topiary can turn a humble herb garden into a charming outdoor room.

Shopping for garden art is half the fun. Where you begin is mostly determined by your resources. Size, shape, and cost vary as much as the art itself. The key is to select pieces that fit your garden's style. For larger, more expensive pieces, look in outdoor sculpture galleries. Major metropolitan areas and small towns known as artists' havens usually have at least one such gallery.

For the budget-minded, mail-order catalogs offer a selection of sundials, birdhouses, painted or sculpted wall plaques, and sculptures of wood, metal, or stone. And wonderful surprises are always awaiting discovery in salvage yards, antique shops, and thrift stores.

FACING PAGE *Looking like a relic from ancient times, this faux wall "ruin" was actually built from cinder block, cement, and stucco to frame a pair of centuries-old Tunisian doors.* Colonel Mustard, *a metal sculpture, perches on a rock in the pond.*

ABOVE *Vashon Island artist Claire Dohna crafted a tile mosaic shell for this turtle in shades of seawater-blue, turquoise, and kiwi-green. She fires and glazes the tiles herself, then uses them to create her colorful and weatherproof mosaic designs.*

ABOVE RIGHT *In Terry Welch's Asian-style garden, a grouping of craggy, monolithic boulders mimics a natural rock formation.*

RIGHT *Faux bamboo culms, topped with decorative caps, rise out of a bed of greenery. These ceramic "bambones" were devised by Berkeley, California, artist Marcia Donahue.*

Display Basics

The size and shape of the piece help determine how best to set it off. Large sculptures can sit on the ground, stand on a pedestal or platform, or bask in the center of a fountain or pool.

If you collect a variety of objects, vary their positions and heights in the garden. A carved rock placed on the ground or a birdhouse hanging from a branch can add cheerful touches in otherwise overlooked parts of the garden.

Keep the backdrop simple. No matter where you put garden art, make sure the surroundings are simple enough to display it properly (hedges and solid-colored walls work well).

Check it out. After you buy a piece of art and take it home, place it in different locations to see where it looks best. If the piece is too heavy to move around, walk around the garden and imagine it in various positions.

Keep scale in mind. A massive piece requires plenty of space to stop it from dwarfing its neighbors. A small piece can get lost in a jungle of foliage.

ABOVE *In a celebration of adventure, Cevan Forristt designed Bob and Linda Shelby's backyard with Roman columns, Asian lanterns, and Indonesian décor. Bob Shelby describes the exuberant clash of cultures as "Noisy but wonderful."*

LEFT *A wall of cinnabar red makes a rich backdrop for a sculptural painted metal light fixture designed by Jeff Zischke, Scottsdale, Arizona.*

BELOW *Fabric fashion has taken over this garden, where a sweep of bold tangerine-colored cloth is suspended from long poles to shelter a sitting area. Equally vibrant orange spheres dot the lawn.*

RIGHT *Rising from a drift of scarlet roses, this bird feeder makes both a beautiful garden accent and a spot for birds to find some tasty treats.*

BELOW *A log-cabin birdhouse hanging from the branches of an apple tree brings a rustic touch to the garden.*

Birdhouses

Like weathervanes and sundials, birdhouses can be as much garden art as living quarters for feathered friends. They come in many styles, although flashy or whimsical houses are often more decorative than functional.

Only cavity-nesting birds (those that nest in tree hollows) use birdhouses. This group includes bluebirds, chickadees, nuthatches, swallows, and wrens. The kind of house you install determines the kinds of birds you'll attract, but this is a most inexact science: while a birdhouse may be intended for a wren or a bluebird, it will be fair game for any birds of similar size.

Small birds like chickadees, nuthatches, and most wrens prefer a hole that's 1⅛ inches across. Medium-size birds like bluebirds and swallows need a nest box with a hole of 1½ inches. White-breasted nuthatches need 1¼ inches; mountain bluebirds need 1⁹⁄₁₆ inches.

Tree swallows and violet-green swallows accept a wider variety of habitats, often stealing houses from bluebirds. Larger birds such as purple martins and flickers take boxes with 2¼- and 2½-inch entry holes, respectively. Flickers usually like to dig out their own nests, but sometimes you can attract them with a large nest box. Fill it with wood chips; they'll dig it out.

RIGHT *Brilliantly colored nesting houses such as these are attractive to smaller species like sparrows, chickadees, and finches. Golden hop vine provides a bright color contrast.*

BELOW *Bird-friendly perennials billow at the base of this bird feeder in a garden in Hailey, Idaho. A surround of chicken wire protects the contents from hungry squirrels and raccoons.*

Birdhouse Basics

To keep birdhouses safe from raccoons and cats, mount them atop metal poles. If you want to put a birdhouse in a tree, hang it from a branch.

Keep houses away from feeders (the mealtime bustle makes nesting birds nervous).

Face the entrance away from any prevailing winds, and remove any perch your birdhouse came with (it's unnecessary, and house sparrows use it to heckle birds inside).

Birdhouses should be made from materials that insulate well, such as 1-inch-thick wood (plastic and cartons are too thin and have poor ventilation; heat can bake chicks inside or make them fledge too early).

Nest boxes need an openable side or top for easy cleaning, drain holes on the bottom, and, in hot-summer areas, ventilation holes high in the sides.

If you put up more than one, keep birdhouses well separated and out of sight of one another. Houses must go up early, since migrant birds start returning in late February.

RIGHT *Lightweight concrete bowls fashioned by Quinterra Cement Works have a rustic simplicity. Textural spheres of the same material are light enough to float in the water alongside feathered visitors.*

FACING PAGE, LEFT *Birds are drawn to the burbling water in this 19-inch-high glazed urn. A recirculating pump is hidden in an underground reservoir beneath a layer of river rocks.*

INSET *A thirsty goldfinch takes a sip of water in Bob Wigand's garden.*

Birdbaths

If you set out a birdbath, it's a sure bet feathered visitors will come flocking—especially on warm summer days. While birds will gladly frolic in a streambed or puddle, a birdbath is their preferred watering hole.

Birdbaths run the range from utilitarian to eccentric. Some are basic bowls that either sit atop pedestals or hang from chains. Others are designed as much for people to look at as for birds to splash in; you can display them much like sculpture among garden plants.

Once birds discover your bath as a reliable water source—in the right spot, kept filled and clean—your garden will come alive with the creatures' color, music, and activity. And you'll discover the quiet pleasure of watching finches, wrens, and other songbirds swoop into the bath for a splashing good time.

ABOVE *Annual flowers such as larkspur and cosmos are easy-to-grow bird favorites. The feasting begins when the blooms are allowed to form seedheads. A birdbath provides a sheltered spot in which to splash.*

BELOW *Carved granite birdbaths stand 2 feet high; the stone's rough surface is nonslip, and the shallow dish is suitable for even small birds.*

Birdbath Basics

While a bath cools birds in summer, it can also help them keep warm in winter: frequent bathing insulates birds by keeping their feathers clean and fluffed up.

Keep it shallow but roomy. Ideally, baths should be 2 to 3 inches deep and 24 to 36 inches across. The sides should slope gradually.

Consider materials. Plastic and metal are often too slippery for birds. Some plastics can crack with age; metal dishes should be stainless steel or other rust-resistant material.

Keep it clean. Use a strong jet of water from the hose to clean the bowl. If the bottom is dirty, scrub it.

Keep it safe. Put the birdbath next to shrubs or trees that provide cover and escape routes. Place ground-level baths where they have 10 to 20 feet of open space around them—but no more, or you'll leave damp birds exposed to hawks, owls, and cats.

Keep it moving. Running water attracts birds. Some baths come with built-in fountains. Or you can create a small fountain by adding a submersible pump with a spray head.

Keep it from freezing. In colder climates in winter, add a heating element to keep the bath water thawed.

Containers

Almost any container that will hold soil can be used to grow plants. But those that make the biggest statements in the landscape are large, artfully crafted, and full of character. Smaller vessels can make their mark, too, if they're clustered to form a single focal point.

Nurseries offer plenty of good pots in wood, terracotta, and concrete. Styles range from elegant urns to whimsical terracotta frogs. Specialty pottery stores—with containers from places such as China, Greece, Italy, Mexico, and Thailand—have sprung up in many urban areas. And mail-order catalogs are offering a wide selection, from cheerful handpainted vessels to sophisticated, lightweight fiberglass pots. Some of the best containers can be found in antique shops and even at garage sales.

Choose containers that complement your home or that accent your landscape. Then plant them with flowers and shrubs that offset the pots' style.

ABOVE *Groupings of glazed pots in bold hues can be garden standouts, even when they are empty of flowers or foliage.*

LEFT *A gate of wrought iron, a carriage lamp, climbing roses, and a voluptuous Mediterranean urn combine to form a vignette of romantic beauty.*

RIGHT *This collection of Mexican containers includes (at left) Talavera ginger jars—a majolica-type of pottery; rope-necked urns and half-pots from Tonala (foreground); and an impressive 5-foot-tall urn from Chalapa (behind).*

INSET *Rosemary spills from a cone-shaped pot atop a sculptural pedestal.*

BELOW *Galvanized steel tanks originally used as watering troughs have been transformed into raised beds for Greg Corman's carefree but abundant edible garden in Tucson.*

CLOCKWISE FROM LEFT *Concrete makes a sturdy and durable material for holding plants, and it can be cast and stained in a variety of shapes and colors. A collection of assorted containers in buff, cream, and soft gray awaits planting. Plum, purple, and black coleus fill a little pot in the seat of a heart-shaped chair. Massive stoneware urns flank a doorway on either side of a gate in a Phoenix courtyard. A pair of vintage jars holds fragrant antique roses. A dwarf conifer forms the center of this trough planting in Roberta and Scott Bolling's garden in Eugene, Oregon.*

Succulents in Pots

When it comes to containers, succulents have the stage presence of stars but the undemanding dispositions of chorus members. Their architectural shapes look good with any material. Leaf drop and other plant litter are slight. And they have amazing details when viewed up close. Here are some tips:

- **Try wide, shallow containers.** Because many succulents are wider than they are tall, planters of the same proportions are often the most aesthetically pleasing.

- **Set plants close together;** if one succulent overtakes its companions in a container, simply take cuttings and plant them in a new pot.

- **Provide good drainage.** Succulents will forgive most failures—too much or not enough water or lack of fertilizer—but they do like their roots in quick-draining soil.

- **Water more in hot weather.** Regular irrigation during summer months will keep succulents looking their best—especially in the desert.

ABOVE LEFT *Tapered aluminum containers hold neat rows of succulents. A mulch of gravel keeps the arrangement looking tidy and prevents weeds from sprouting.*

ABOVE *An angular trough the color of lava holds succulents and beach pebbles.*

LEFT *A playful pot with a painted checkerboard base sits in front of a striped wall.*

LEFT *These three-tiered planters rise from a sea of ground covers. Pink-flowered kalanchoe is tucked into the top of recycled clay pipes, which in turn hold terracotta pots. Perched on top of the pots are squat figurines, each of which sports a single succulent topknot.*

BELOW *A pair of tabletop containers holds easy-to-care-for* Sempervivum *and* Sedum.

Furniture

There's an enduring graciousness to outdoor furniture. It evokes images of rolling lawns, intimate gardens, and lemonade in the afternoon. But deciding which furniture to buy can be a challenge.

Many styles are available in materials that include teak, woven willow, and cast iron. Rustic furniture blends well with natural surroundings. Other styles are more finely crafted to complement patios and decks. Still other outdoor "furniture" comes not from a showroom but from a gardener's imagination: well-placed boulders, stones, or wooden planks can also provide outdoor seating.

ABOVE *Traditional and contemporary blend together in this outdoor room in Santa Fe. Beneath a pair of star-shaped* estrella *light fixtures, a custom chaise lounge and antique table add textural richness.*

RIGHT *This modernist oversized chair and footrest complement the garden's sleek design and its contemporary hardscape.*

Manufactured lounges, chairs, and tables are often designed in sets. The price range can be wide; in general, wooden furniture is more expensive than its cast-resin or metal counterparts.

Whichever type you choose, keep in mind that outdoor furniture must be suited to year-round use outdoors; sun, rain, insects, mold, smog, and people dole out heavy wear and tear.

ABOVE *Furniture should work with garden structures and style. The clean lines of these poolside lounge chairs, for instance, suit the large square pavers and the nearby simple, natural-looking plantings.*

LEFT *This all-in-white back porch is an oasis of calm. Antiqued bistro chairs surround a small table; an elegant chandelier hangs overhead. White and silver plantings just beside the porch echo the color scheme.*

Furniture Materials

With so many styles available, the choice of garden furniture can bewilder even decisive shoppers. One good way to narrow the field is to narrow your range of materials.

Metal. If you like heavy metal but your budget doesn't, you can buy cast aluminum or steel that looks like wrought iron. Consider also enameled or powder-coated, aluminum-frame furniture. It won't rust, and it's durable and lightweight.

Wood. Teak and redwood are favored for their beauty, strength, and resistance to insects and rot. (To avoid depleting natural supplies, purchase only plantation-grown teak or recycled redwood.) Other woods include jarrah, a member of the eucalyptus family that performs and weathers like teak; Honduran cedar, the

FACING PAGE, ABOVE *A grouping of graceful metal chairs adds a decorative touch to a grove of trees.*

FACING PAGE BELOW *Encircled by a jungly planting of bamboo and grasses, this firepit and surrounding comfortable chairs make an inviting spot for conversation on summer evenings.*

RIGHT *Painted furniture is one way to bring color to any spot in the garden. These dark mauve chairs enliven a shady corner.*

BELOW *Natural materials such as wicker, rattan, and bamboo call to mind tropical verandas and cool drinks on hot days.*

pink-brown wood with the distinctive "cigar-box" smell; and jatroba (also known as courbaril), a tight-grained wood from the West Indies and Central and South America. Willow, bamboo, and cypress also appear in outdoor furniture. Willow is less durable; a yearly application of water sealer will extend its life.

As woods weather, they turn to shades of gray unless you seal them with marine varnish or semitransparent stain.

Synthetics. Synthetic wicker looks and feels like natural wicker, but it's made of cellulose, resin, or latex-coated fibers and is undaunted by the weather. Wicker and rattan made of natural fibers are less durable and are better suited to sheltered patios or enclosed porches.

Joinery 101

When shopping for outdoor furniture, pay close attention to the joinery. A good joint—where a chair leg or arm meets the seat, for example—looks nearly seamless. And it is strong: it gives a chair, bench, or table the staying power needed to withstand weight and lateral movement.

RIGHT *Found materials can be put to new use in the garden. A hefty block of granite topped with glass makes a fine table for a patio paved with equally substantial granite slabs.*

FACING PAGE, ABOVE *Incorporating a few seaside treasures helped Carole McElwee to create this charming seating area. A set of rustic chairs and a table are fashioned out of bent branches; the table holds an urn covered with shells.*

FACING PAGE, BELOW *Shelly Coglizer created this cozy hilltop sitting area for her Lafayette, California, garden. A casual rattan swing dangles from a steel arbor, and oversize cushions complement the rusty patina of the metal.*

BELOW *In the garden of Martha Sturdy in Pemberton, B.C., a large outdoor terrace is furnished for lounging no matter the weather. Comfortable chairs, chaises, and benches are all amply supplied with cushions.*

This tasseled hammock invites relaxation in a secluded patio niche. The fabric's stripes in shades of blue contrast against a warm terracotta-colored wall.

Hammocks

The world slows down when you stretch out in a hammock. Suspended and supine, you notice more keenly the pleasures of summer: the soft air wafting across your cheeks, a swaying view into the branches of a tree, chirping birds, the scent of sun-warmed flowers.

Today's hammocks have evolved well beyond the trusty versions made of cotton rope. New synthetic materials are softer, more comfortable, and more durable than traditional materials. The variety of colors and patterns can be easily coordinated with contemporary outdoor furniture. Sizes now range from subcompact to behemoth.

If your garden lacks trees or posts at just the right distance apart (12 to 15 feet) to hang a hammock, you can choose from sturdy frames made of such materials as wood or aluminum.

Sources include outdoor furniture dealers, home supply stores, and mail-order companies.

ABOVE *Traditional castaway rope hammocks can be suspended almost anywhere, including a shaded porch. Wooden spacer bars keep the hammock spread open at all times, ready for a drowsy inhabitant.*

LEFT *Set just inside a pair of wooden doors, this patterned fabric hammock is shaded from the sun, yet it is positioned to allow views of the garden beyond.*

Hammock Basics

Hammocks take many forms:

- Synthetic rope hammocks are usually made of durable, soft-spun materials, such as polyester, that resist moisture and are available in a range of colors. As with any woven rope, this type will emboss its pattern on your arms and legs if you lie on it for a while.

- Cloth hammocks are often made of the same fabric that covers contemporary umbrellas and outdoor chairs. It's strong and mildew resistant, and it stands up to harsh sun.

- Screen or mesh hammocks are made of a soft shadecloth-type material that allows good air circulation, can be cleaned easily, and is water and stain resistant.

- Quilted hammocks are typically made of two layers of weather-resistant polyester with batting between.

- Most hammocks come with sturdy metal chains, S-hooks, and oversize threaded hooks you can attach to posts. Some suppliers sell these separately. Frames enable you to place a hammock almost anywhere—on a deck or patio or in the middle of a lawn. Other hammock extras include storage bags, canopy tops, and add-on wheels for the frames, which make moving the hammock easy.

Umbrellas

If the backyard is as much a part of the house as the family room or kitchen, it makes sense that a shade structure should look as if it belongs there, not at a campsite. Many good-looking shade structures are now available, including sleek, high-quality fabric gazebos and crisp, pyramid-shaped canvas parasols like those that dot the Mediterranean coastal resorts. Some umbrellas come with fabric walls designed to filter low sunlight; others are equipped with tiny lights that add sparkle over a table long after the sun has set. Some are designed to drape and hang, with no center pole to obscure the view. A freestanding structure that supports a fabric roof with perimeter posts can create an outdoor room. Corner supports don't require the large weighted bases that center-supported umbrellas must have, and, of course, the center of the shaded area isn't taken up with a post. Although such structures set up and knock down easily, they can be fixed in place on a lawn, deck, or patio for as long as you like.

ABOVE, TOP *Classic white market umbrellas are so versatile they suit almost any garden design. In this contemporary coastal garden, the fabric tops of the umbrellas appear to soar like kites above a viewing patio.*

ABOVE *A mirror image of the garden—complete with towering palms—graces this umbrella with a view. Artist Ken Parker of Palm Springs used fade-proof billboard paint for this vibrant design.*

FACING PAGE, ABOVE *Dressed up for a party, this once-plain umbrella is bedecked with ribbons and hung with tassled, glowing lanterns.*

Umbrella Basics

If you plan to set the umbrella over a table, make sure the pole fits in the opening in the table, or buy a swivel umbrella to set beside the table.

Fabrics should provide UV protection and resist fading, rot, and mildew. Some also repel rain, although even the most water-resistant types aren't entirely waterproof. For a large canopy, look for a canopy fabric that not only shades but also breathes, allowing air to pass through its weave.

Check the workmanship of the frame and struts (canopy ribs). Whether hardwood or metal, the frame should firmly snap the struts into place, and the structure should hold the canopy taut. Metal fittings should have an anticorrosion finish.

Look for a guarantee that covers mechanical parts for the duration of the umbrella's life.

Build It: Umbrella Pot

1. Measure pot depth and cut ABS pipe to extend 8 inches above top (left). Cover the drainage holes in the pot with screening and add a 1-inch layer of gravel or lava rocks. Position the pipe and add the remaining stone to anchor the pipe.

2. Mix concrete; shovel in 2 to 3 inches of concrete over the stone, sloping it slightly away from the pipe. While the concrete is still wet, use levels to check that the pot is horizontal and the pipe is vertical (right).

3. Insert 6-inch wooden dowels into the wet concrete (left) to create drainage holes. Let the concrete dry overnight; remove the dowels. Use a dolly to move the pot to its final location before filling with potting mix. Add plants, then slide in an umbrella.

Paint

When you're looking to enhance your garden, consider the power of color. Imagine a sky blue wall behind a row of bright yellow and orange nasturtiums and blue cornflowers. Or a mint green wall behind a cluster of metal cafe chairs painted the color of strawberry sherbet. Such arresting color schemes are at home in Mexico and southern Arizona—especially in gardens that surround Mediterranean, contemporary, or adobe-style houses.

Color can highlight many garden features. A low white wall, for example, might more readily invite sitting if you paint its top azure blue or another color that blends

with your garden's décor and the color of your house. Paint can brighten pots, outdoor furniture, or other garden accessories. It can add texture to a plain wall by mimicking brick or wood. It can even embellish a wall with a delicate tracery of faux vines.

Paint Basics

Make sure surfaces are free of dirt, grease, rust, and paint flakes (scrape and sand the surface, if necessary, to achieve this).

For plaster and stucco, use exterior latex or acrylic paint. Rolling will force paint into crevices for a more uniform surface (or mix a tint into wet stucco).

For new wood, seal all exposed surfaces with one or two coats of latex or exterior wood primer. Then paint it with flat latex acrylic or vinyl exterior enamel or house paint in the desired sheen.

Paint in fair (above 50°F/10°C), dry weather, out of direct sun.

To avoid wrinkling, fading, or loss of gloss in solvent-thinned paints and streaking of latex paints, apply after morning dew and at least two hours before evening damp.

To paint faux bricks on a white stucco wall, glue a horizontal row of three brick-size sponges onto a piece of scrap wood, leaving 1/2-inch spaces between them. Then dip them into a tray of paint and stamp them onto the wall.

ABOVE *A plain wooden structure might disappear from view under the weight of climbing vines, but this pretty blue gate and arbor stand out at the end of a curved pathway.*

ABOVE, LEFT *A sunflower-yellow wall is a vibrant backdrop for a river of blue fescue. Pebbles, painted purple, outline the grass.*

FACING PAGE, ABOVE *A freestanding wall painted cerulean blue sets off the butter-yellow flowers of a red-hot poker (Kniphofia).*

FACING PAGE, BELOW *In this San Diego children's garden designed by Topher Delaney, bold painted walls alternate with steel panels peppered with cheerful animal cutouts.*

ABOVE *Indian saris inspired these dazzling walls in Fremont, California. Designer Topher Delaney first selected the paint colors, then chose plants with compatible hues, including the purple Mexican sage in the background. A copper firepit warms the scene.*

ABOVE RIGHT *Startling Southwest motifs in bright colors decorate this wooden bench. Furthering the bold design is a Navajo rug made from natural-dye yarns.*

RIGHT *Adirondack chairs painted a vivid magenta pink complement a glazed blue urn and rose-colored flowers in Linda Cochran's garden.*

FACING PAGE *Landscape architect Chad Robert uses strong colors to add accents to a spare design. In this Phoenix court-yard, bright coral walls make a vivid backdrop for the pool's blue tiles and echo the hues of the potted geraniums.*

Tile

Ceramic tile works well in many gardens especially those with a Spanish or Moorish flair. Tiles can be used for much more than covering floors and walls; you can use them to face fountains or raised beds, as finishing touches on steps, pool decks, and spas, or as colorful accents for containers.

Choose tiles that are proven to survive winters in your area. If you are covering steps, bear in mind that tiles with a glazed surface are slick when wet, while quarry tiles and other types have a slip-resistant surface. Installing smaller tiles results in more grout lines, which improve slip resistance. Some tiles can be cut easily with a hand-held snap tile cutter; others require a wet saw. On a stairway or other highly visible area, choose bullnose tiles, which have one edge that is rounded off and finished.

Set tiles in latex- or polymer-reinforced thinset mortar, and use grout specified for outdoor use.

LEFT *A wall fountain features hand-made embossed tiles of cool blue with unembellished tiles in buff tones.*

BELOW *Pieces of broken pottery enliven the edges of a 16-foot-long concrete table. For best effects with such mosaics, use pottery bits sparingly and in a limited palette of colors.*

FACING PAGE, ABOVE *A decorative tile frieze edges a swimming pool and is reflected in the still surface of the water.*

FACING PAGE, BELOW *An entryway reveals Spanish-Moorish influences through the use of glazed terracotta floor tiles, stuccoed walls, and decorative tile-work on the step risers and fountain.*

Mosaics

Handmade mosaics created from pieces of tile or pottery can add special charm and a very personal touch to your garden, especially if the pieces have fond associations for you. Perhaps you've broken a favorite dish or pottery piece, or maybe you have colorful tiles left over from a remodeling project.

There are two basic methods for making mosaics. In the grouting method, you stick pieces of tile to a surface with tile adhesive, either in a free-form pattern or by following a sketch you have done beforehand. When the adhesive has dried, press tile grout evenly into the spaces between the pieces. After about 10 minutes, wipe off any excess grout with a damp sponge. When dry, seal the mosaic with an outdoor sealer.

If your tile pieces vary in shape and size, you may find it easier to create a mosaic without grouting. First you spread a 1- to 2-inch bed of preset mortar mix of "high early" concrete on a clean, dry surface. While the mix is still wet, set the tile pieces directly into the mix. After the mix has cured, seal the mosaic.

Portable Lighting

When night falls, the garden becomes a perfect stage for outdoor lighting. Each spot, beam, and burst of light brings daylight to darkness, yet it does so in a selective fashion: by controlling the source of light, you can accentuate the positive in your garden while leaving the negative in darkness or deep shadow.

Outdoor lighting can also visually enlarge indoor rooms. If at night you peer out at an unlighted garden, your windows seem little more than black holes or dark mirrors. Landscape lighting makes the windows transparent again, and your home feels more spacious because the eye is drawn outdoors.

Good outdoor lighting has a practical use, too. Lights can outline paths for safe and easy walking, and they can brighten dark areas to discourage intruders. Lighting can be subtle, dramatic, and anything in between. Lighting a pond underwater or silhouetting a single shrub or tree can add ethereal magic to nighttime gardens. Carefully placed lights can even mimic the play of moonlight and shadow across pavings.

FACING PAGE *Protected from wind by tall glass cylinders, these candles light the way from garden to beach. Scatterings of sea glass add color and enhance the coastal effect.*

RIGHT *To make these solar lights look like candlelit torches, Greg Rubin screwed off the lids (which contain the illuminating device) and set them on clear votive glasses atop metal stakes.*

BELOW *Hold candles in place—and add a custom touch—by filling the base of clear glass cylinders with nuts, pebbles, shells, marbles, or colored sand.*

Lighting Basics

Outdoor lighting fixtures are either decorative or functional. Decorative lights—lanterns, hanging and post- or wall-mounted units, path lights, and strip lights—can add some fill light, but they're primarily meant to be seen and to set an architectural tone.

A functional fixture's job is to light the garden unnoticed. Although some manufacturers make attractive versions, the less visible these fixtures are, the more successful your lighting will be.

- Backlighting a lacy shrub makes it glow delicately.
- Path lights can flank walks or go high under eaves.
- Sidelighting dense trees defines their details.
- Shadowing magnifies plant silhouettes on walls.
- "Moonlighting" casts soft pools of light below trees.
- "Grazing" lights aim upward to highlight architecture.
- Uplighting trees reveals form; canopy reflects glow.

Candles and Lanterns

Special occasions such as holidays or outdoor parties often call for temporary lighting that can be put into place nearly instantly. A broad range of lanterns is available, from hurricane lamps that burn oil to glass-sided lanterns that house candles. Classic New Mexican *luminarias*—open paper bags that contain votive candles set in sand—have now been electrified, adding to the growing field of specialty outdoor lighting. Tiny hat lights on strings can bring a carnival atmosphere to a patio or deck. And lanterns on stakes can add drama along the path to a gate or door.

No matter which lantern you choose, you'll need to place it with care; this is especially true for lanterns with open flames. Unless snow covers the ground around them, avoid placing lanterns along a path or among foliage where they can pose a fire hazard. Also, make sure that they're sturdy and will not topple in a breeze. And avoid putting metal lanterns that could become hot near dry plant material.

ABOVE *Lidless mason jars and antique carriage lamps are suspended by wires from Jeff Zischke's backyard ramada in Scottsdale, Arizona. Candles glow seductively within these improvised "light pendants."*

LEFT *This unusual effect in Laura Morton's garden is created by a gas-and-sand firepit. The gas percolates up through the sand to create flames that dance over the surface of the sand.*

FAR RIGHT *Flickering torches atop tall copper stakes echo the shape of native organ-pipe cactus.*

RIGHT *A serene-looking Buddha statue sits in the flickering light between two hurricane lamps fitted with candles.*

Water Features

Sparkling, splashing, dripping, or still, water brings tranquility to a garden. Even the smallest water feature can calm the surroundings. And the sounds of falling water can mask traffic and other neighborhood noises.

A pleasing water feature can be as modest as a wall-mounted terracotta basin from a nursery or as big and pricey as a 6-foot granite sculpture that dribbles water into a pool. You can convert a wooden planter box, metal basin, or large pot into a small fountain. Coat the inside of a wooden container with asphalt emulsion or epoxy paint, or use a liner of heavy-gauge plastic sheeting. If you're using an unglazed pan or clay pot, coat the interior with asphalt emulsion, epoxy, or polyester resin. Then drop in a submersible pump and add water.

ABOVE *Water trickles through a rusty pipe onto a stone basin in the Capistrano Beach garden of artist Maria del Carmen Calvo. Grasses growing in front and back add to the rustic setting.*

INSET *Peach-colored water lily.*

RIGHT *Water gently sprays out the top of a concrete pedestal fountain and spills over the edge into a pool. Mosses create the look of a miniature garden atop the pedestal.*

BELOW *A slender, continuous stream emerges from a simple bamboo spout and spills into a copper basin.*

Classic terracotta jars tucked in the foliage lend a timeless quality. A recirculating pump pulls water up a length of flexible tubing into the jar.

ABOVE *Water burbles up a threaded pipe in stacked concrete disks.*

LEFT *A shallow stream cascades over a stacked-stone wall in this San Luis Obispo, California, back garden.*

RIGHT *Japanese fishing-net floats spin in circles around a turquoise Bauer oil jar in a shallow fountain.*

BELOW *This two-tiered Italianate fountain is the centerpiece of a 13-foot-wide sideyard in a San Diego housing development. Landscape designer Linda Chisari and architect Stephen Arnold Brown surrounded the base of the fountain with 'Gourmet Popcorn' miniature roses; Indian hawthorn standards line the path and emphasize the garden's linear geometry.*

Retreats

In a world that often whirls too rapidly around us, our gardens are among the few places where we can find peace and tranquility.

No matter how small your lot, chances are you can still find space in your backyard, sideyard, and front yard for a personal retreat that can expand your living space outward from the house to the edges of your property. A corner of a large garden—tucked away from hubs of activity such as dining terraces, firepits, swimming pools, or play areas—can be a retreat when enclosed with billowy curtains, a rose-covered trellis, or a screen of woven bamboo. An entire garden, if small enough, becomes a sanctuary when surrounded with tall trees and climbing vines that give it privacy from street traffic and neighboring houses.

Whether your retreat is an elaborate structure or a simple grouping of furniture, orient it to face a favorite view of water or mountains or to capture a sunrise or sunset. Then make the space your own. Furnish it for comfort with cushions, a tabletop fountain, or lanterns or candles for soft evening light. Bring in pots of fragrant flowers—cottage pinks or stock or whispery grasses that shimmer in sunlight. Fill your retreat with things you love, whether pillows covered in colorful Indian saris or paper parasols from China. Then relax and allow your retreat to spin its magic.

RIGHT *Towering palms call for sculptural drama, and it is provided by this structure. Tall poles hold aloft a length of draped fabric, creating a cool and restful place to lounge while the palms sway overhead.*

LEFT *Big pots filled with cannas and flowering maple dress up a fir-plank deck in Vi and Don Kono's Redmond, Washington, garden. The deck looks out over a fish pond; a pair of Adirondack chairs complete the serene retreat.*

ABOVE *Leafy green curtains of trumpet vine hang over this outdoor daybed, which makes a perfect spot to curl up when afternoons turn warm and drowsy. Garden designer Brenda Gousha situated her "napping arbor" facing west, so she could watch the sun set behind distant hills.*

LEFT *Resembling a Balinese hideaway, this retreat—designed by Bud Stuckey—was built in a weekend. The 10-by-10-foot platform is topped by a palapa of bamboo poles hung with mosquito netting. Cannas, oriental lilies, and bright cushions add to the exotic effect.*

FACING PAGE, ABOVE *Camping out never felt so good. An open-air bed nestled beneath giant cedars has been fitted out with comfortable linens and overhead lamps for settling in with a good book.*

FACING PAGE, BELOW *Once an aging shed, this structure is now a relaxing hideaway. Designer Francesca Harris installed a raised platform and a cushy foam mattress; a mirror behind this daybed reflects the light, and Indian saris cover the pillows. Shutters pivot closed for warmth.*

ABOVE *A 6-by-13-foot pavilion occupies a wooden platform near a small pond. Designer Marni Leis hung gauzy curtains from the front and furnished the space with comfortable pieces found at a flea market.*

RIGHT *Sliding doors open onto a poolside deck in this Japanese-style British Columbia garden. The water, rocks, and distant mountains provide all the elements for restful meditation.*

ABOVE *A fountain is the focal point of Cindy Jo Rose's backyard haven in Capitola, California. The surrounding stone circle is paved with gravel, marbles, and beach pebbles. Paper umbrellas and stone statuary add to the magic.*

ABOVE RIGHT *Bathing in an indoor-outdoor tub is probably the ultimate luxury. In the Henry Virgil garden—designed by Paul Repetowski—a tub sits in an Asian-style guest house over-looking a private garden.*

RIGHT *All the elements for a cozy retreat—comfortable seating, shade, privacy, and layers of lush plantings—are found in this serene patio.*

solutions

FIRE | FROST & SNOW |

PETS | POLLEN | PRIVACY |

SLOPES | SMOG DAMAGE |

SMALL SPACES | SOIL |

SUN | WILDLIFE |

WATER | WIND

Fire

Bone-dry air. Drought-stressed vegetation. Hot, parching winds. Add a spark and you have the potential for raging wildfires like those that ravaged Southern California during October 2003. Fifteen separate blazes raged then throughout Southern California—the Cedar Fire in San Diego causing the largest loss of lives and homes.

But over the years, wildfires have devastated many parts of the West, from New Mexico to Montana. California, with its hot, dry winds and low humidity, is especially vulnerable. Below are some of the factors that create a disastrous fire season.

Rainfall. Heavy winter rains encourage abundant grass growth, which increases the hazard of grass fires later in the summer. Low rainfall increases the amount of dead foliage (known as dead fuel).

Drought. Consecutive years of scant rainfall leave parts of the West drier than usual.

Freeze. In open spaces, killing freezes turn live-fuel plants into crackling-dry fuel.

Population growth. Some fast-growing communities have ignored fire threats in the rush for development. More thoughtfully designed, fire-safe subdivisions reduce fire hazards by providing buffers between wild land and houses.

Wind. Foehns, sundowners, monos, Santa Anas—these hot, dry winds start in the interior and blow out to the coast. Heavy onshore winds, though cooler and moister, can fan small fires in coastal sage and chaparral, creating infernos.

Fuel loading. Coastal sage becomes tinder 7 to 10 years after a burn (chaparral 15 to 20 years after a burn). Unless this crackling-dry growth is trimmed or burned, it builds up, creating conditions that favor more damaging fires.

Native plant communities. Dry chaparral produces fast-moving firestorms, particularly during Santa Ana wind conditions. Ponderosa pine and mixed-conifer forests are vulnerable to catastrophic crown fires due to fuel loading.

Lightning. Warm air that cools as it rises into the western mountain ranges creates thunderstorms. As lightning strikes at higher elevations, it sparks fires.

Ironically, the most wildfire-prone areas in the West have some of the very same characteristics that define

RIGHT *A defensible landscape helped firefighters save a rural home from wildfire in San Diego County in 2000.*

the "good life" in this part of the country. They tend to be on hillsides, surrounded by thick stands of trees and brushy open spaces, or packed close together in canyons. Making matters worse, firefighters have difficulty reaching properties up narrow, curvy, tree-lined roads or dead-end streets with bridges that can't support fire engines.

How do we protect our homes and gardens from future threats? As has been seen in recent fires, a good start is to install the right landscaping in the first place. Fire officials advise that you halve the odds of your home being destroyed when you clear the brush within 30 to 400 feet of the house; the exact distance is determined by slope, wind, neighborhood density, and house architecture and materials.

Follow the guidelines described on the pages that follow and be sure to avoid highly flammable plants (below). These contain high levels of oil or resin, have foliage with low moisture content, or tend to accumulate large amounts of dead foliage.

HIGHLY FLAMMABLE PLANTS

Trees, Shrubs

Abies Fir
Acacia
Adenostoma fasciculatum
  Chamise
Arctostaphylos Manzanita
Artemisia californica
  California sagebrush
Cedrus Cedar
Cupressus Cypress
Cytisus scoparius Scotch
  broom
Eriogonum fasciculatum
  California buckwheat
Eucalyptus (many
  species, especially
  E. camaldulensis,
  E. globulus, E. rudis,
  E. viminalis)

Heteromeles arbutifolia
  Toyon
Juniperus Juniper
Palms
Pinus Pine
Pseudotsuga menziesii
  Douglas fir
Rhus laurina Laurel sumac
Rosmarinus officinalis
  Rosemary
Taxus Yew
Thuja Arborvitae
Umbellularia californica
  California laurel

Western Fires 1988–2003

1. Firestorm 1991
2. Awbrey Hall 1990
3. Biscuit 2002
4. Winema National Forest 2001
5. Big Bar 1999
6. Tunnel 1991
7. Kirk Complex 1999
8. Paint 1990
9. McNally 2002
10. Simi-Piru 2003
11. Topanga 1993
12. Laguna Canyon 1993
13. Viejas 2001

14. Cedar 2003
15. Rodeo-Chediski 2002
16. Hochderffer 1996
17. Cero Grande 2000
18. Hayman 2002
19. South Canyon 1994
20. Yellowstone Park 1988
21. Cox Wells 1996
22. Clear Creek 2000
23. Valley Complex 2000
24. Dunn Glenn Complex 1999

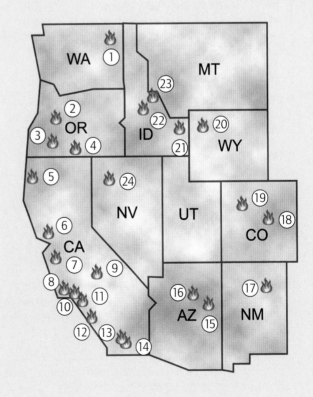

A Fire-retardant House & Garden

A. Hydrant. Near the street, you can install a standpipe for firefighters' use; check size with fire department. Make sure it's accessible. If possible, use a gravity feed from pool.

B. Siding. Nonflammable material such as stucco is preferred. Avoid wooden siding.

C. Eaves and vents. Eliminate eaves or enclose them with stucco or other nonflammable material. Place vents at outer edge of soffit and cover them with 1/4-inch wire mesh. If feasible, when fire approaches, block the vents with precut plywood panels.

D. Roof. Use noncombustible materials.

E. Glass. Thermal-pane and safety glass are the most resistant to heat damage. If fire threatens, cover the glass outside with shutters, fire curtains, or plywood panels.

F. Pump. Have a well-maintained pump (gas, diesel, or propane) of at least 100-gpm capacity, with standard 1 1/2-inch threaded standpipe. Keep a plastic or cotton-jacket fire hose (long enough to reach the far side of house) and nozzle at hand.

G. Walls, fences, and railings. Use nonflammable masonry or wrought iron—particularly adjoining the house. Make wooden arbors or trellises of 4-by-4 or larger lumber.

H. Deck. Nonflammable brick, tile, or concrete decking is safest. If you use wood, recommended 1-hour fire ratings require overscaled decking—at least 1 1/2-inch-thick tongue-and-groove boards over a solid substructure.

I. Substructure. Decks in wildland areas should be either enclosed with a nonflammable solid skirt—concrete block, gypsum board, stucco, or other exterior sheathing—or built with oversize timbers (6-by-6-inch posts and beams).

J. Pool, hot tub. Can serve as a reservoir (a typical hot tub holds about 500 gallons—as much as a tank truck). If possible, make the water source drainable to an accessible hydrant or pumphouse.

K. Four-hundred-foot reduced fuel zone. Plant low-growing, deep-rooted, drought-tolerant ground covers. Prune them regularly to remove woody undergrowth.

L. Access. Keep fire lanes (preferably on both sides of the house) clear enough for firefighters to bring in trucks and other equipment.

West of Boulder, Colorado, this fire-safe landscape features materials and plant configurations that serve as a firebreak around the house. A series of landscaped concentric rings correspond to the plants' irrigation needs. A stacked-stone wall separates the outermost ring of unirrigated plants such as California poppy and purple thyme from the irrigated plants within.

The Fire-safe Demonstration Garden, in the north San Diego community of Elfin Forest, features drifts of water-retaining low-growing plants such as ice plants and ivy geraniums. These segue into drifts of larger succulents and shrubs, as well as trees like coast live oaks.

Landscaping for Fire

Eliminate fire "ladders"—plants of different heights that form a continual fuel supply from the ground up into the tree canopy.

Create a defensible space around your home. Starting from the perimeter of your property and working inward: Selectively thin native vegetation. Plant low-growing, drought-tolerant ground covers on the perimeter of your property. Arrange plants into islands, 50 to 400 feet from the house, and widely space any trees or large shrubs (the distance between shrubs should be three to five times their height). Close to the house, maintain a well-watered greenbelt. Install a buffer of hardscape (paving, decomposed granite) right next to the house. Or plant this area sparingly, using only low-growing, fire-resistant plants.

Clean up the yard. Regularly clean up leaves and other plant litter and remove brush that grows with winter rains. Keep gutters clear of dead leaves and other debris. Situate firewood and propane tanks at least 30 feet from the house.

Keep plants well irrigated and well maintained, especially those within 30 feet of the house (if water supplies permit). Keep grasses watered and green year-round, or let them dry out and cut them back to 4 inches.

Prune vegetation next to the house to under $1\frac{1}{2}$ feet high. In early spring, prune or mow down low ground covers, such as ceanothus and *Coprosma* × *kirkii*. Fertilize and water afterward. Periodically cut back chaparral plants hard.

Thin crowns of clustered trees, trim limbs up off the ground to 20 feet or more, and cut back any branches to 15 or 20 feet from the house. Prune out all dead branches; remove all dead plants.

Clear out overhanging tree branches along the driveway, and prune back bushy shrubs (so that fire trucks have easy access).

ABOVE *Frost damage to a magnolia blossom.*

Frost & Snow

Mild winters are one of the main reasons that people live at low elevations in the West. But despite the comfortable winter temperatures, occasional frosts can strike even the mildest coastal strip of Southern California. So whether you live where freezing temperatures are the norm or where short sleeves are standard winter attire, it pays to protect your plants from cold damage.

Of course, the best way to avoid cold damage in your garden is to choose permanent landscape plants—trees, shrubs, vines, ground covers—that can survive normal low temperatures in your area. However, unusual invasions of frigid air flowing south from the Arctic can call for special protection for the more vulnerable plants.

Freezes that come when plants are unprepared for the cold—in early fall or in spring—can be the most dangerous. It's worth paying attention to weather forecasts at these times; if unseasonal frost is predicted, you can apply protection (see facing page)—especially to plants at borderline hardiness.

Get Ready for Winter

During the main growth period—from spring to midsummer—water and fertilize plants as needed. But starting in late summer, withhold nitrogen feeding, which promotes frost-susceptible new growth.

Likewise, as the days grow shorter, reduce watering and avoid pruning, which leaves plants vulnerable to freeze damage. Let plants form seeds, bringing to a close the plant's yearly growth cycle.

During winter, keep soil moist. Dry winter winds and cold temperatures hasten evaporation from leaf surfaces and from the soil. Plants weakened by wilting are more susceptible to damage from freezing temperatures. Keep planting beds weeded. Bare soil absorbs heat more easily than weedy soil, and the weeds needlessly draw moisture from the soil.

Post-freeze Measures

When unusual freezes strike, you can minimize frost damage. Early in the morning after the freeze, use shade cloth, sheets, or burlap to keep plants shaded and protect them from sunburn. Irrigate frost-damaged woody plants immediately and continue watering to keep soil moist. (However, don't irrigate damaged soft-tissue plants like banana until spring; wet soil can lead to rot.)

Winter Protection

Roses. Protect the bud union from the cold. After pruning for winter, mount up soil around the base, covering up the bud union, then surround with straw (left). Wrap with netting or hardware cloth (right).

Snow. To prevent heavy, wet snow from breaking upright branches, wrap conifers with a spiral of twine (left). A frame of bamboo stakes covered with burlap (right) shelters plants from snow and wind.

Resist the impulse to prune out frozen parts of the plant and, instead, wait until new growth starts and the actual damage becomes obvious. When you can determine what is really dead, cut all of it out. For evergreens—both conifers and broad-leaf plants—delay any pruning until plants are actively growing.

To determine if a deciduous tree or shrub has survived, check the growth buds on the bare stems. Live buds are greenish, not withered and brown. If you can't see the buds readily, carefully scratch through bark with your thumbnail. Dead tissue will be brownish and dry; live tissue will be greenish to whitish and moist.

Don't immediately give up hope on any plants killed to the ground by freezing temperatures; some may still have live root systems. Give the plant a year to see if it will regrow. If the apparently dead plant was budded or grafted onto an understock, make sure the new growth comes from the grafted portion and not the rootstock. For older, established trees, it may take several years to determine the full extent of damage.

Microclimates Matter

When it comes to marginally hardy plants, location is everything. Stretches of open ground, exposed to air from all sides (especially from the north) and to open sky, are risky spots. Warmth stored in the ground during the day rises quickly and is replaced by cold air, resulting in "radiation freezes." Cold air also sinks, so the lowest parts of a sloping garden or valley will be colder. If a fence or wall runs at right angles to a slope, cold air flowing downward will collect on the uphill side of the wall; plants growing there will be colder than plants farther uphill or even just below the wall. The warmest part of any garden is usually beside a south-facing wall and beneath a roof overhang. Second-safest locations are beneath overhead lath structures or where branches of evergreen trees shelter plantings beneath; in both cases, heat rising from the ground is intercepted, resulting in slower cooling.

Cold air collects

Cold air drains

South-facing wall

Pets

Get a dog and—doggone it—there goes the garden. That's what many homeowners conclude, but it doesn't have to be that way. A garden can provide both a safe, comfortable environment for dogs and an attractive space for plants and people. Fido can romp and race without injuring himself or trampling your flowers— most of the time, anyway. Owning a dog also means giving up perfectionism and learning forgiveness.

The first step in creating a "dogscape" is to think like a canine. If you were a dog, what would you want? Spaniels, terriers, retrievers—each breed has a different personality. The better you can accommodate its particular traits, the happier your dog.

Paths to Run and Patrol

Dogs need exercise; paths give them a designated space to do it as well as a venue to perform their perceived job—to patrol your property line and keep out intruders. If your dogs have already created their own paths through your garden, don't try to redirect them. Instead, turn their well-worn routes into proper pathways.

A 3-foot-wide clearance is sufficient for most canines. Plant a screen to hide this dog run if you like; pets seem to like having their own "secret garden." If you have a Houdini and need to keep your escape artist from tunneling under the fence, you may need to install an underground barrier made of rebar, chicken wire, or poured concrete.

Shade and Shelter

Like humans, dogs enjoy basking in the sun. So give them a deck or patch of lawn for sunbathing. But remember that dogs can overheat easily, so it's more important to provide them with cooling retreats. They'll happily share arbors, pergolas, and other shade structures with their owners. But most dogs seem to appreciate having a shelter of their own, such as a doghouse.

Answering Nature's Call

Your dog needs to relieve himself, but it doesn't have to be on your flower beds. Set aside a corner of your yard as a comfort station, and train your pet to eliminate there and nowhere else. This learning process may take a puppy about three weeks and an adult dog even longer.

Cover the designated area with material the dog will accept and you can clean easily. If you have a male dog, consider adding a marking post so he can define his territory.

LEFT *Good long runs along a well-built fence keep dogs in shape—and out of the neighbor's property. Sturdy boards along the base of the fence and a mulch of rounded pebbles deter digging.*

Plant Wisely

If you plant landscaped areas densely, dogs will stay out. Still, most dog owners recommend additional precautions: plant in raised beds or on mounds, and start with 1-gallon or larger plants. Put temporary fencing around newly landscaped areas; when you remove it, add a rock border or low fencing as a reminder to stay out.

Plant romp-proof shrubs and perennials like ornamental grasses around the edge of the garden. Put plants with brittle stems like salvias in the center, where they'll be protected.

Choose Plants Carefully

Avoid thorny and spiny plants, which can cause serious eye injuries. Many wild mushrooms produce aflatoxins, which can be fatal if ingested by dogs; if mushrooms appear, dig and dispose of them immediately. Your compost pile should be off limits for the same reason. Weeds can be dangerous, especially foxtail grasses with barbed seed heads, which dogs can accidentally inhale with serious consequences. (Foxtails can also work their way into dogs' ears, causing pain, infection, and possibly deafness if not treated in time.)

ABOVE LEFT *Small cedar chips are easy on paws yet large enough so they won't stick to silky cocker spaniel coats; smooth flagstones set in pebbles form a path where dogs can comfortably tread. Pieces of driftwood persuade the canines to stay out of planted areas.*

INSET *Dogs enjoy a change of viewpoint just as much as do humans. Hester, a pug, likes to survey the world from her rocky perch in a West Seattle garden.*

ABOVE RIGHT *Welsh springer spaniels wade into a cool, safe pond in Battle Ground, Washington.*

Safety Matters

If you have a dog or cat, be very cautious about growing poisonous plants like *Amaryllis belladonna,* castor bean, foxglove, or hellebore in readily accessible areas. Other potentially hazardous plants—including avocado (fruits), grape (fruits and raisins), onions and garlic, rhubarb (foliage), and tomato (especially immature fruits and foliage)—can cause gastric distress if ingested by pets, or have a sap that's an irritant beneath the skin (aloe). Some common plants to think twice about growing if you have pets are listed opposite. Grow favorites like onions, garlic, and tomatoes in raised beds or in fenced-off areas. Visit *www.aspca.org/toxicplants* for a complete list.

BELOW *Zorro the cat loves to lounge on this circular "pool" mirror in Lynne Blackman's Del Mar, California, garden.*

PLANTS TO AVOID

Aloe

*Asparagus
    setaceus* Fern
    asparagus

Avocado

Caladium bicolor
    Caladium

Clematis

*Colocasia
    esculenta*
    Elephant's ear

*Convallaria
    majalis* Lily-of-
    the-valley

Cycas

Cyclamen

Digitalis Foxglove

Dracaena fragrans
    Corn plant

Hedera helix
    English ivy

Hemerocallis
    Daylily

Hippeastrum
    Amaryllis

Hyacinthus
    Hyacinth

Hydrangea

Ilex Holly

Ipomoea
    Morning
    glory

Kalanchoe

Lilium Lily
    (Asiatic
    hybrids,
    oriental hybrid
    'Stargazer')

Narcissus
    Daffodil

Nerium oleander
    Oleander

Rhododendron
    Azalea,
    rhododendron

Solanum (most)

Strelitzia reginae
    Bird of
    paradise

Taxus Yew
    Tomato

Yucca

Zantedeschia
    Calla

Problems with Cats?

As cute and cuddly as kitties are to their owners, neighbors may look upon the roaming furballs as midnight marauders who dig up seedlings in freshly tilled raised beds, use sandboxes as litterboxes, and chew the tips from lush, lance-shaped leaves. Or a neighbor might view your cat as a predator who stalks and kills songbirds. What to do?

First, follow the advice of veterinarians everywhere: Cats live longer and healthier lives indoors than they do outdoors. Restrict your cat's daytime sunbathing to a windowsill, or limit its treks into the garden to times when you're nearby. Also:

- Cover sandboxes that are not being used. Or fit the sandbox with a small portable deck that can be easily removed for children's play.

- Put row covers over newly planted seedlings, or cover the soil around them with a mulch such as fir bark or straw. Or plant thickly to cover loamy soil.

- Hang bird feeders from house eaves or mount them atop poles to keep them well out of the cat's reach. Put birdbaths near dense foliage plants so birds have a quick escape to safety, and raise the baths out of cats' reach. Put a bell on your cat's collar—even though a stealthy cat can move toward birds with barely a tinkle, it's an added precaution.

- Add deterrents. Plant things that many cats love to nibble or roll in: catnip *(Nepeta cataria)* or catmint *(N. × faassenii)*. If necessary, protect the crowns of these plants with an inverted wire basket or short sticks.

Pollen

Itchy eyes, runny nose, near-constant sneezing—to many, this is a yearly affliction; up to 60 percent of it is caused by airborne pollen from trees, grasses, and flowers. Depending on where you live in the West, allergy season can start as early as mid- to late winter and run into summer. The problem of airborne pollen is on the rise in the West, largely the result of population increase and landscaping with exotic pollen-bearing plants. Because some of these pollens are wind-distributed, they're difficult to escape.

Reducing Pollen

Although some communities now prohibit the planting of the worst pollen producers, there's no way to completely eliminate offending plants in your neighborhood or to remove grasses from nearby fields. But to enjoy your own garden without aggravating your allergies, you can choose plants known not to produce airborne pollen. The two lists on these pages will help you make your landscape choices. The first list contains the classic allergenic plants—those to avoid at all costs. The second list is a sampling of popular trees, shrubs, and perennials you can plant with confidence.

How you maintain your garden also can reduce its allergenic potential. When you tidy up, use a rake; nothing makes pollen (as well as allergy-causing dust and fungal spores) spread faster than leaf blowers. Lawn grasses—particularly Bermuda grass—are among the most common causes of allergies. Mow frequently at the proper height for the grass to remove all flowering stems. Keeping the lawn growing vigorously with regular water and fertilizer will almost guarantee no blooming stems will form between mowings. As a final resort, replace the lawn with a ground cover (see pages 210–211) or relandscape.

Other Allergy Causes

Airborne pollens are only one source of allergic reactions. Fungal spores, dust mites, and animal dander also cause allergies, particularly in fall. If you're especially afflicted, consult an allergist to identify your allergens. If plant pollens are not the cause of your misery, the professional diagnosis could save you from the effort and expense of relandscaping.

Acacia

ALLERGENIC PLANTS

Trees, Shrubs

Acacia
Acer Maple
Adenostoma fasciculatum Chamise
Almond
Alnus Alder
Betula Birch
Carya illinoensis Pecan
Castanea Chestnut
Chrysolepis chrysophylla Chinquapin
Ceanothus Wild lilac
Cupressus Cypress
Fraxinus Ash
Juglans Walnut
Juniperus Juniper
Ligustrum Privet
Liquidambar Sweet gum
Morus Mulberry
Olea europaea Olive
Platanus Plane tree, sycamore
Populus Poplar
Quercus Oak
Rhamnus
Salix Willow
Schinus molle California pepper tree

Syringa vulgaris Common lilac
Ulmus Elm

Perennials, Annuals

Amaranthus Amaranth
Carex Sedge
Chrysanthemum
Dahlia
Helianthus Sunflower
Lamium Dead nettle
Rudbeckia hirta Gloriosa daisy
Trifolium Clover
Zinnia

Sedge (Carex)

Amaranth (Amaranthus)

NONALLERGENIC PLANTS

Trees

Arbutus unedo Strawberry tree
Catalpa speciosa
Celtis Hackberry
Cercis occidentalis Western redbud
Chilopsis linearis Desert willow
Cornus Dogwood
Eriobotrya Loquat
Eucalyptus sideroxylon 'Rosea'
  Red ironbark
Fouquieria splendens Ocotillo
Ginkgo biloba Maidenhair tree
Jacaranda mimosifolia Jacaranda
Lagerstroemia indica Crape myrtle
Leptospermum laevigatum Australian
  tea tree
Liriodendron tulipifera Tulip tree
Magnolia × soulangeana Saucer
  magnolia
Maytenus boaria Mayten
Pittosporum phillyreoides Willow
  pittosporum
Podocarpus gracilior Fern pine
Prunus caroliniana Carolina laurel cherry
P. × subhirtella 'Pendula' Single weeping
  cherry
Pyrus Ornamental pear
Sapium sebiferum Chinese tallow tree
Sequoia sempervirens Redwood
Umbellularia californica California laurel
Vitex agnus-castus Chaste tree

Shrubs

Arctostaphylos Manzanita
Aucuba japonica Japanese aucuba
Berberis Barberry
Caesalpinia
Calluna vulgaris Scotch heather
Camellia
Carpenteria californica Bush anemone
Chaenomeles Flowering quince
Choisya ternata Mexican orange
Cistus Rockrose
Escallonia
Heteromeles arbutifolia Toyon
Hibiscus
Hydrangea
Ilex Holly
Leucophyllum frutescens Texas ranger
Mahonia
Myrtus communis Myrtle
Nandina domestica Heavenly bamboo
Plumbago auriculata Cape plumbago
Potentilla Cinquefoil
Rhaphiolepis indica Indian hawthorn
Rhododendron Azalea, Rhodondendron
Senna artemisioides Feathery cassia
Spiraea

Perennials, Bulbs

Alcea rosea Hollyhock
Aquilegia Columbine
Campanula Bellflower
Canna
Dianthus Pink
Dicentra Bleeding heart
Ferns
Gladiolus
Hemerocallis Daylily
Iris
Oenothera Evening primrose
Penstemon Beard tongue
Phormium tenax New Zealand flax
Platycodon grandiflorus Balloon flower
Potentilla Cinquefoil
Romneya coulteri Matilija poppy
Strelitzia reginae Bird of paradise
Tradescantia virginiana Spiderwort
Verbena
Zantedeschia Calla

Bellflower (Campanula)

Mahonia

Canna

Bird of paradise (Strelitzia reginae)

ABOVE *Partially hidden from the street, this dining alcove provides a measure of privacy from a busy neighborhood. A curved wall planter that wraps around the pocket-size space is only waist-high, but strategically placed plants—including a strawberry tree and several sweet gums (Liquidambar)—lend a feeling of seclusion.*

Privacy

Growing populations that crowd today's cities and housing developments make many of us feel like overexposed goldfish every time we walk into our yards. For better or worse, many of us have homes that take up most of our lots. What's left, typically, are narrow strips of ground in front, sideyards barely wide enough to walk through, and backyards that neighbors can peer into from second-story windows.

Fortunately, most privacy problems can be solved with some creative landscaping. Well-positioned hedges, fences, or leafy screens can shield your house from the street or from neighbors. A tree or an arbor can block the view of your property from a hillside above. Walls and berms, carefully placed, can create privacy as well, especially in front yards.

Identify Intrusions

Before you can create privacy, determine exactly what you want to block out or be shielded from. Walk around your property, identifying areas that require covers or screens. Also try to evaluate how plantings and additional structures will affect your neighbors, the patterns of sun and shade in your garden, and any views you want to preserve.

A really annoying privacy problem might seem to call for fast-growing, closely spaced trees or shrubs. But don't overdo it. You may end up replacing or removing such plants because fast-growers are often not long-lived. You can, however, plan for selective removal, such as every other shrub in a closely spaced hedge. Or combine fast- and slow-growing plants, knowing that you'll remove the less desirable ones as the better species mature.

RIGHT *The trees along this allée double the height of the stone wall, providing leafy screening.*

Privacy Solutions

Vine-covered arbor blocks views from second-story windows next door.

Clipped hedge screens neighbor's view.

Berm, or mound of soil, planted with ground covers, low-growing shrubs, and perhaps a small tree, provides privacy from the street.

Single tree placed at the front corner of a driveway blocks views of an entry.

Layers of plants—pillowy perennials, shrubs, and small trees—create privacy and soften a fence or wall.

Low-level shrubs conceal the trunks of mature trees.

Fence shields you from view when it is slightly higher than eye level, or approximately 6 feet tall. To add privacy without extending a fence, mount a trellis on top.

Keep It Down

What can you do to foster quiet in the garden? Plants alone won't deflect noise generated by street traffic or neighbors, although layers of them can help. It takes a solid barrier—a fence, earth, or even a thick wall. But keep security concerns in mind. If barriers create shadows near entrances, for example, install outdoor lights for night visibility.

The soothing burble of falling water is effective in masking nearby noise. The water doesn't so much drown out other sounds as focus attention on a gentler one.

LEFT *This east-facing front courtyard has become a favorite place to escape the hot afternoon heat for Art and Rachel McCausland of Sacramento. The 16-by-36-foot space has a 6-foot-high wall with a built-in fountain to block both the sight and sound of the street beyond. Terra-cotta pavers extend from the breakfast room, blending the spaces together.*

Good-neighbor Gardening

Before you begin any building, planting, or pruning along shared property lines, consider your neighbors.

First, find out exactly where the boundaries of your property are, so you don't build or plant on your neighbors' land. Also check local ordinances, restrictions, and easements that could affect your plans. Many communities have guidelines that protect solar access or beautiful views.

Any fences, hedges, or plantings on the property line belong to you and your neighbor as tenants-in-common. So before you begin, talk to your neighbor about what you'd like to do and how it will look or be maintained. If you can't come to an agreement, you may need to install your fence or screen just inside the boundary of your property.

Under certain circumstances, you can prune branches and roots that extend over your property from a neighbor's tree, but only up to the boundary line. You may not trespass on your neighbor's property to prune a tree.

If the construction or pruning you do on your property affects the health of plants that are growing on your neighbor's property, or alters the integrity of their shapes, you may be liable for damages.

Use common sense when planting near property lines. Don't plant trees or shrubs that will eventually outgrow their space or extend too far into neighbors' yards or rob them of sunlight. Avoid planting species that drop a lot of debris (such as fruit trees, Monterey pine, privet, silk tree, and sycamore) and those that have weak branches (poplar and Monterey cypress) or aggressive roots (camphor tree and coral tree).

Build It: A Berm

A mound of soil planted with shrubs and trees buffers sound from a neighbor's garden or a busy street. It also provides a leafy privacy screen. Even though it's only a low hill of earth, a berm can elevate plants so that even young trees and shrubs can screen out unwanted views and enhance privacy. Dense evergreen plants are best for this use; this one is planted with fast-growing incense cedars. When locating a berm, consider how it will affect drainage patterns. On a slope, water can accumulate on the uphill side of the berm, so don't put one where it will interfere with runoff. On any lot—flat or sloping—a dry creek bed built into the berm can channel water in the right direction.

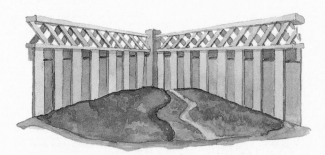

1. Pile soil for the berm, then spread it into a mound about 2 feet tall. (You'll need 8 cubic yards of sandy loam to cover about 200 square feet.) Firm the soil with a manual tamper. Dig out a 6-inch-deep depression in the berm for a dry creek bed (shown).

2. Set boulders on the berm, anchoring their bases about 8 inches deep into the soil. (Have them moved into place by professionals, or use a small tractor to place them.) You can lay river rocks for a creek bed at this point.

3. Plant the berm, mixing an all-purpose fertilizer (such as a 15–15–15 formula) into the backfill. Cover the soil with a layer of bark chips or other mulch.

Slopes

Rolling hills and rugged mountains give the West beauty and character, but they can also be the source of landscaping challenges. A slope that begins a few feet from the back of the house makes it difficult to find outdoor living space. It can also be hard to plant and maintain and, unless retained by a sturdy wall, can allow mud to slide downward toward the house during rains.

Vast areas of the West are underlain with clay soils that often expand and heave when wet and shrink and crack when dry. Other areas have silty and sandy soils that are easily eroded. The Pacific Coast strip and western Colorado are two of the most landslide-prone areas of the country, but housing developments there continue to sprawl up hillsides that may be unstable.

When the terrain is cut and graded (flattened or reshaped for construction), weighted down by houses and swimming pools, and soaked by rain or landscape irrigation, it needs special care.

Evaluating Your Slopes

Is the slope above or below the house or site? If the street is below the property, do runoff and debris have a clear channel to the street? Are there gullies on the base of a slope? These indicate poor drainage, which may be caused by erosion from insufficient ground cover, improperly compacted fill, or bedrock fractures below the face of the slope. Is there surface "ponding" on flat ground? If so, it can mean poor grading or uneven soil settlement. Do poorly placed downdrains empty into gardens unintentionally (washes

and water channels are exceptions)? Are slopes flecked with softball-size holes? The burrows of gophers and ground squirrels can increase a slope's susceptibility to saturation and slumping.

Surface drains, berms, retaining walls, and terraces are all effective erosion controls. Many plants—including California buckwheat, ceanothus, Japanese honeysuckle, kinnikinnick, and periwinkle—are all fast growing and have dense, strong roots. Careful maintenance can help stop erosion, too. Make sure all the soil beside the house slopes away from the foundation and regularly clear debris from drains, gutters, and weep holes in retaining walls.

Above all, if you suspect a serious erosion problem on your property (or a neighboring one), seek professional advice from a private or public structural or soils engineer, an erosion control specialist, or an engineering geologist.

RIGHT *Foliage plants were chosen for toughness, texture, and year-round good looks on this steep slope in Oakland.* Rubus pentalobus *'Emerald Carpet' covers the slope and creeps between sturdy stone steps. At the top of the hill,* Loropetalum chinense *provides a bright contrast.*

Dealing with Slopes

Shallow slope. Several terraces with steps between create separate level areas for a lawn, play yard, and planting beds.

Medium slope. Low retaining walls create four different levels in the backyard. Lawn is a gentle slope, so that the mower need not be lifted or pulled up and down steps.

Steep slope. The simplest and least expensive way to create level space is to build a deck. Trees planted at deck height lessen the feeling of being perched above ground level.

Hill Taming

There are several ways to landscape a slope. You can build retaining walls to create terraces, and then connect the terraces with zigzag pathways. (Before construction on steep slopes, it's a good idea to review your plans with a structural engineer.)

Install jute erosion-control netting before planting steep slopes. Unfurl the rolls on the slope across the grade; secure them to the ground with U-shaped galvanized or plastic-coated pins (usually sold with the jute). Cut small, X-shaped holes in the jute and plant the seedlings or plants through them.

Choose plants with dense, strong roots that help hold the soil. Examples include *Artemisia,* ceanothus, cotoneaster, creeping mahonia *(Mahonia repens),* ice plants, juniper, rockrose, and rugosa roses. Arrange the plants in staggered rows.

Install drip irrigation so plants get the amount of water they need without a lot of runoff. Place emitters uphill of the plants. To catch rainwater, build berms on the downhill side of the plants using soil from the planting hole.

LEFT *Agaves punctuate a gently sloping hillside. A stepped stone wall at the base doubles as seating.*

RIGHT *Rustic materials such as Napa basalt, bricks, and concrete recycled from an old driveway make up a retaining wall to hold back the slope in Suzette and Bob Ferguson's Oakland garden. Brightly colored perennials and roses stand out against a background of ferns, Japanese maple, and flowering maple.*

FACING PAGE, ABOVE *Steps curve up a hill above a flagstone-covered retaining wall and concrete-and-flagstone patio in Lafayette, California. The hillside is planted with California-friendly plants, including lavenders, penstemon, Mexican feather grass, and Santa Barbara daisy.*

FACING PAGE, BELOW *Horizontal pathways and rock walls help hold the hillside of this hot, dry garden. Cloaking the ground are tough, unthirsty perennials, including lavender, society garlic* (Tulbaghia violacea), *pride of Madeira* (Echium candicans), *and salvias.*

Smog Damage

Plants breathe air just as we do—except they take it in through their leaf pores. When the air looks dingy, smells oily, stings your eyes, and hurts your lungs, plants suffer too. Air quality in the West has improved markedly over the last 30 years, but even so, you still see smog-damaged plants, particularly in California's more densely populated areas and in its Central Valley (blown eastward by the prevailing winds). Susceptible plants are affected in any of several ways. Smog can weaken or stunt growth and is most damaging to young, rapidly growing annuals, vegetables, and perennials. It can cause leaves to take on a tannish to yellowish cast, with small stippled or bleached-looking areas on the surfaces; the leaves' undersides may appear silvery. Flowers and fruits may drop, or overall fruit production may be reduced. The decline of a plant's health makes it more susceptible to attack by insects and diseases.

Smog damage means financial losses to growers of nursery plants and edible crops—which is the reason most research on damage has been focused on these plants.

Anecdotal evidence from growers has been confirmed and expanded upon by research conducted in Los Angeles. This research has generated the list of smog-susceptible plants shown here. Because the focus has been on smog susceptibility, resistant plants are identified indirectly by their apparent ability to thrive in smoggy areas without showing signs of damage. To learn which smog-tolerant plants flourish in your particular area, ask at an established, reputable nursery or consult your local Cooperative Extension Service.

RIGHT *Los Angeles freeways are notoriously crowded, but there are also other causes of smog damage, ranging from leaf blowers to airplanes.*

Roadside Pollution

Airborne particulates—small particles of dust and debris from cars, trucks, and buses—can harm plants. When particulates settle on plants, they reduce the amount of light that reaches the leaves, providing breeding grounds for insect pests. To help keep roadside plants healthy, wash them off frequently with strong jets of water from the hose, thoroughly rinsing both the top and bottom surfaces of leaves.

In cold-winter climates, salts used to melt snow and ice on roads and walkways can accumulate in the soil nearby and damage plants growing there. If the soil is well drained, heavy irrigation in spring may help leach out salts and reduce damage to plants.

Ask a local nursery about plants that resist salt damage and use them beside roadways and driveways. Apply sand or sawdust to control ice, rather than salt. If you must use salt, try to avoid it in late spring, when plants are emerging from dormancy. Don't pile salted or dirty snow around plants.

Apple

Dahlia

Chrysanthemum (Shasta daisy)

SMOG-SUSCEPTIBLE PLANTS

Vegetables

Beans
Broccoli
Cantaloupe
Carrot
Corn
Cucumber
Lettuce
   (head and
   romaine)
Onion
Parsley
Pepper
Radish
Spinach
Tomato

Fruits, Nuts

Almond
Apple
Apricot

Avocado
Cherry
Citrus
Fig
Grapes
Peach and nectarine
Plum and prune

Annuals, Perennials

Adiantum Maidenhair fern
Ageratum houstonianum
   Floss flower
Antirrhinum majus
   Snapdragon
Begonia
Browallia Amethyst flower
Calceolaria
Calendula officinalis
Chrysanthemum
Coleus × hybridus
Cyclamen

Dahlia
Dianthus caryophyllus
   Carnation
Impatiens
Lobularia maritima Sweet
   alyssum
Matthiola Stock
Mentha Mint
Orchids
Petunia × hybrida
Primula Primrose
Salvia splendens Scarlet sage
Senecio × hybridus Florists'
   cineraria
Tagetes Marigold
Viola Pansy, viola, violet
Zinnia

Shrubs, Trees

Acer saccharum Sugar maple

Betula pendula European
   white birch
Catalpa speciosa
Hibiscus rosa-sinensis
   Chinese hibiscus
Lantana
Liquidambar Sweet gum
Morus Mulberry
Philadelphus Mock orange
Philodendron
Pinus Pine
Platanus Plane tree,
   sycamore
Rhododendron Azalea,
   rhododendron
Rosa Rose
Schinus molle California
   pepper tree

Impatiens

Rhododendron

Small Spaces

A typical backyard in a new housing development is about the same size and shape as a two-car garage. And it generally receives about as much attention. Most of us look out our patio doors, see the slabs of concrete and a few yards of dirt, and shut the blinds again, quickly. These uninspiring little rectangles don't exactly resonate with possibility for us.

Older houses often share the small-yard dilemma with tract houses. As their owners remodel them by raising the roof a story or two and pushing out walls as far as municipal codes allow, little space is left over for outdoor living, playing, or planting.

How do you make the best use of the space that remains around your house while accommodating multiple functions—a personal retreat, play area, and entertaining patio, for example? It can be done, in as little as 600 square feet.

First, tiny gardens need focal points, especially if they have no sweeping views to borrow over the back fence. A great water feature, a simple urn, or a garden sculpture can serve that purpose. Pay attention to details; they show more in small spaces. Indulge in premium materials—pavers, art pieces, tiles, furnishings—for highly visible areas. Use vertical plants such as climbing roses and other vines to soften peripheral walls.

Finally, keep the color scheme restrained. Choose a strong color—red-orange, for example—and use it judiciously. Then add one or two colors to harmonize with it. Repeat that color—in pillows and tiles that accent the patio. Or, choose all one color that's easy on the eyes—white, for instance—and play it off foliage in silvery gray and deep shades.

RIGHT *Complementary paving materials define each space in this long, narrow garden in Walnut Creek, California. The slate patio, edged with raised planters, offers a cozy setting for outdoor dining. The planters are filled with blooming plants to soften the tall fence; white wisteria covers the sturdy overhead arbor. A wooden walkway (above) set flush with the patio acts as a bridge to link the patio and the sideyard.*

FACING PAGE *Several visual tricks make Christine Moore's Los Angeles garden seem larger than its 590 square feet. A winding path suggests movement through a larger space (top), while a dining patio fits snugly in a corner (bottom).*

ABOVE *This zigzag patio of square pavers and gravel makes a small garden appear larger. The playful water columns in the foreground are bold accents.*

ABOVE RIGHT *Liven a wall by hanging up some interesting objects. The peaked roofs, solid colors, and simple shapes of these birdhouses add rich detail to a tight space.*

RIGHT *A mirror reflects a rose allée and makes it appear to be a neighboring garden. A frame painted on the wall around the mirror and urn enhances the illusion.*

Big Ideas

There are a number of techniques that garden designers use to make small spaces feel a bit larger. Here are a few:

Blur the boundaries. Use trees, vines, and shrubs to obscure the fences and walls that define your property. You can also imply that there is more beyond by constructing a pathway that disappears around a bend.

Change levels. A new level, even if it's just a few inches, offers a different perspective, which creates the illusion of greater space. Consider raising or lowering patios, or creating gentle berms (mounds) and swales (depressions).

Plant in layers. Espalier a first row of plants against the wall. That way you can squeeze in two or three layers, making the space appear multidimensional.

Embellish walls and paved pockets. A pocket garden off the side of the house entered through French doors calls for artistic detailing, even if it encloses only 5 square feet. Consider a small café table and a pair of chairs, a wall fountain, or miniature art gallery—such as an array of colorful, hand-crafted birdhouses—hung on the wall.

Pattern the paving. Paving set on the diagonal or a path stamped or colored with bold diamond shapes can make a garden seem deeper than it really is. Boldly curving paths keep the eye from racing to the periphery of the property.

Use water as a reflector. Finding space in a small garden for a water feature isn't always easy. But even the tiniest ponds and pools can make a garden appear larger by adding the illusion of depth, and by reflecting the sky and surrounding surfaces.

Design Tricks

Family party space. The 20-by-22-foot deck (A) in this teenager-friendly garden is set on a diagonal to the house to make the space seem larger. Set at a 30° angle from the home's rear wall, it has space-saving perimeter seating (B) and is perfect for sunbathing. Raised beds fit into the yard's back corner (C); they hold a changing cast of herbs and flowers. Small lawn areas (D) soften the hardscape.

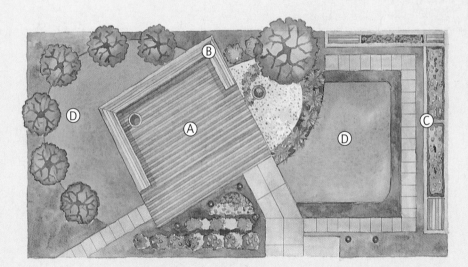

Place for play. A wide flagstone path (A) curves through the garden, visually expanding the space and making a great surface for tricycle riding. It circles a sand pit (B) and passes a play structure (C). Just off the main patio is a firepit (D) flanked by chairs. The garden's focal point is a simple fountain (E) that fills the air with the sound of water.

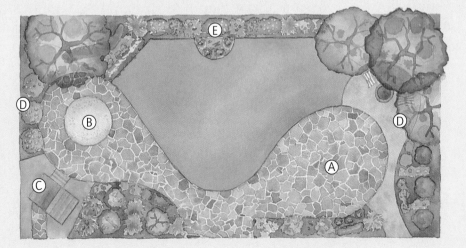

Small-garden Anatomy

When outdoor living space is limited, think big. That's the message of this little patio, which occupies a mere 450 square feet, yet doesn't feel cramped. Private and comfortable, the well-planted patio invites guests to linger over a leisurely meal. What makes it so appealing? Quality materials and rich details, for starters. The trees and vines enhance a sense of enclosure, and antiques and artistic touches are carefully positioned. To make the space appear larger, the designers, Ellerie Designs and Jeanne McNeil and Associates, Bainbridge Island, employed a number of visual tricks.

Minimal color palette

The spectrum of silvery grays, greens, and white is uncomplicated and soothing. "In a small garden, sweeps of the same plants make bold statements," says the designer.

Containers in varied sizes

Unmatched urns shift the sense of proportion, making the patio seem bigger. Dominated by a 30-inch-tall pot of lavender, smaller pots contain gardenia, jasmine, and miniature rhododendrons.

Intriguing touches of art

A leafy curtain of variegated ivy flanks a pair of French antique wood doors against the far wall. A rusted metal bird cage adds interest in the background at left.

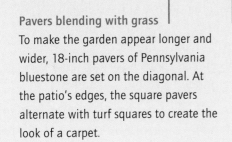

Pavers blending with grass
To make the garden appear longer and wider, 18-inch pavers of Pennsylvania bluestone are set on the diagonal. At the patio's edges, the square pavers alternate with turf squares to create the look of a carpet.

Bold yet graceful furnishings
The charcoal-gray concrete table is large in scale—7 feet long and 3 feet wide—but fits in with the color scheme, so it doesn't overwhelm the space. The creamy white umbrella measures 11 feet across.

Plants arranged in layers
Arranging plants from short to tall against a wall creates a feeling of depth. A row of callery pears cloaked with snowy spring bloom grows in raised beds. Pots of jasmine dangle between trees, while white-flowered azaleas bloom at their bases.

ABOVE *Homemade compost is one of the best sources of inexpensive organic matter for the garden. A simple wooden bin works just fine—though you should occasionally aerate the compost with a fork. Finished compost is dark and crumbly (inset), with a pleasant, earthy aroma.*

Soil

The West's soils can present gardeners with some of their most frustrating dilemmas. Not always easy to recognize, these problems may be caused by microscopic disease organisms such as oak root fungus or *Phytophthora*. The problem may lie well below the surface—an impenetrable hardpan that prevents water drainage, for example. Or the topsoil may have been removed during construction of your home, and what's left is devoid of nutrients.

The key to dealing with bad soil is to evaluate it before planting. Then you can choose whether to correct the problem or select plants that will grow despite it.

Soil texture. The soil in your garden may be too sandy or too clayey. Sandy soils absorb water quickly, dry fast, and don't hold onto nutrients. If you pick up a handful of moist, sandy soil and squeeze it into a ball, it will break apart easily when you let it go. Clay soils are the opposite of sandy soils. Water is slow to be absorbed, but once it is, the soil stays wet for a long time—often too long for healthy root growth. If you form a handful of wet clay soil into a ball, it will hold its shape.

The best way to improve sandy soils and clay soils is to add organic matter and work it as deeply into the ground as possible, but at least 6 to 8 inches.

Drainage. Soils that drain poorly reduce the availability of air to roots. Without air, roots suffocate and the plant can't absorb water and dies; molds and rots can take over. Overwatering can suffocate plant roots growing in clay soils, but often a further problem lies below the soil's surface.

Hardpan is an impervious layer of hard soil or clay that does not allow water to drain through. *Caliche,* a common type of hardpan in the Southwest, is a layer of white calcium carbonate, or lime.

To evaluate drainage, dig a hole 12 to 24 inches deep and fill it with water. If the hole does not drain in 24 hours, drainage is poor.

If you discover hardpan in your soil, a landscape professional can sometimes bring in special equipment that will break up a thin layer. Another option is to dig a drainage "chimney" through the hardpan at the base of each planting hole.

Thick hardpans may require the installation of subsurface drainage, usually by a landscape contractor. Or you can plant in raised beds or berms (see page 315). Berms are less expensive and can be made of topsoil, firmly tamped down, and amended with organic matter.

Salinity. Where annual rainfall is low, soils are alkaline and irrigation water is on the saline side—all common conditions in the Southwest. Excess salts often accumulate in the soil and damage plants. Yellowing foliage and burnt leaf edges, especially on acid-loving plants like azaleas and camellias, are signs of salinity. Leaching the salts out of the soil with heavy irrigation is effective only if you have good drainage. You can help to lower the soil's pH by adding organic matter and acidifying fertilizers, such as ammonium sulfate, sulfur, or gypsum.

Topsoil. The top layer of native soil, which is usually best for plant growth, is often redistributed or removed during grading and construction of a new home. What's left is a problem soil: rocky, hard, sandy, or slippery, and low in organic matter and nutrients. The addition of organic matter will help if the problem is not severe, but often the best solution is to replace the topsoil that was removed. Choose a replacement soil that is as close as possible to your native soil and that is free of weeds, salts, and herbicides. Put the topsoil down in layers, tilling each layer into the ground.

RIGHT *This healthy vegetable garden is generously mulched with straw to keep down weeds and retain moisture in the soil.*

Amending Soil

Adding organic amendments is the most effective way to improve your soil's texture, giving water- and nutrient-holding capacity to sandy soil and aerating and loosening clay soils. There are many different amendments to choose from, including compost, composted manure or "zoo doo," wood shavings, ground bark, and peat moss. Locally available agricultural by-products such as grape and apple pomace are also useful and usually inexpensive.

To get the best results, use generous amounts—about 25 to 50 percent of the total soil volume to be amended. For example, to amend soil to a depth of 6 to 8 inches, you should add 2 to 4 inches of organic matter. The chart at right can help you estimate how much soil amendment you'll need for large areas.

Most soil amendments can be purchased in bags or in bulk at nurseries and garden centers. If you need a lot, buying in bulk is usually less expensive. For additional sources, look in the Yellow Pages under Topsoil, Soil Amendments, or Building and Garden Supply.

Adding organic matter to soil does more than improve soil's texture. In general, most organic matter acidifies the soil (lowers the pH), which in much of the West has a positive effect. But as it breaks down, some raw organic matter, like wood shavings and ground bark, can rob the soil of nitrogen—an element important for plant nutrition. To counter this, some amendments are nitrogen fortified. If you use one that isn't, dig in 1 pound of ammonium sulfate for each 1-inch layer of raw organic matter spread over 100 square feet. A year later, apply about half as much ammonium sulfate. After that, watch for nitrogen deficiency (yellowing, stunted growth) and amend as necessary. Alternatively, you can simply plant species that are native to alkaline soil.

How Much to Amend?

To cover this area	2 inches deep	3 inches deep	4 inches deep
100 sq. ft.	$\frac{2}{3}$ cu. yd.	1 cu. yd.	$1\frac{1}{3}$ cu. yd.
250 sq. ft.	$1\frac{2}{3}$ cu. yd.	$2\frac{1}{2}$ cu. yd.	$3\frac{1}{3}$ cu. yd.
500 sq. ft.	$3\frac{1}{3}$ cu. yd.	5 cu. yd.	$6\frac{2}{3}$ cu. yd.
1,000 sq. ft.	$6\frac{2}{3}$ cu. yd.	10 cu. yd.	$13\frac{1}{3}$ cu. yd.

Fabric Mulches

Various sorts of plastic sheeting can warm the soil, control weed growth, conserve moisture, and keep developing fruits clean. After preparing the soil for planting, cover it with sheeting; use soil, pieces of lumber, or staples to hold down its edges. Cut small Xs in the fabric and plant through them.

The most familiar sheeting, black plastic (above right) absorbs heat to warm the soil in spring, allowing you to plant heat-loving crops. Infrared-transmitting (IRT) mulch sheeting is green plastic that allows infrared light to penetrate. It is very effective at warming the soil, leading to greater crop yields. Developed especially for tomatoes, red plastic selective reflecting mulch (SRM-Red) bounces light waves in the red spectrum up into the foliage (below right), leading to larger plants and increased production.

FACING PAGE *Before planting vegetable or flower beds, add a helping of compost to enrich the soil. Pour it onto the soil, evenly distribute it with a rake, then dig it in.*

RIGHT *You can get a general idea of your soil's pH—its degree of acidity or alkalinity—with an inexpensive pH testing kit. For a more precise reading, have the test done at a laboratory.*

Testing Soil

A soil test may be in order if you're planning to put in a new lawn, a vegetable plot, or ornamentals. The time to correct fertility, pH, or other soil problems is before you put plants in the ground.

But if a cluster of established, unrelated ornamental plants suddenly and mysteriously starts to die, you might also want to test the soil. Before getting a test, ask neighbors about any problems they've had with their soil. Your county's Cooperative Extension Service or local nursery can let you know about soil problems common to your area. If your lawn or ornamental plants are dying, check first to make sure the cause is not overwatering, poor drainage, insects, or disease.

In some Western states, you can have your soil tested through the Cooperative Extension Service. In other areas, the service can recommend a private soil laboratory. Before sending your sample, find out what tests are available, their cost, and whether the lab will recommend specific soil improvements. Laboratory soil testing can be expensive—more than $50 for a basic fertility test—so be sure to get a reliable sample.

- Dig samples from different areas of the garden separately, using a soil probe or shovel and scraping away surface residue such as rocks.

- Cut a ½-inch-thick vertical slice; dig down about 12 inches for unplanted areas, 3 to 6 inches for turf. Cut out a 1-inch-wide core from each shovel slice. Place the samples in clean paper or plastic bags.

- Collect 5 to 10 samples per 1,000 square feet in each area, all similar in texture and type.

- Thoroughly mix samples from one area, breaking up any clods. If soil is too wet to mix, spread it out to air-dry.

- Label the sample with your name, contact information, the general sample location, the types of plants that grow in the sample location, the date and depth of sample, and any special problems you know about. Generally, the more detailed information you provide, the more specific remedies the tester is able to give you.

Soilborne Diseases

Plant diseases that live in the soil are especially insidious: by the time the plant shows clear evidence of infection, the root system has been extensively damaged. Four such diseases—oak root fungus, *Pythium* and *Phytophthora*, Texas root rot, and verticillium wilt—can be serious problems in various parts of the West. Each disease is encouraged by overwatering in poorly-drained soil, especially during warm weather. Soil management can help to some extent, but your best approach is prevention: Grow plants that have known resistance to each disease.

Oak Root Fungus

This fungus *(Armillaria mellea)* is a problem in low-elevation, nondesert California, particularly in housing developments created in former oak woodlands. The fungus sustains itself on buried wood—mostly dead roots—from which it can infect nearby live roots of susceptible plants. Each new infection leads to a new reservoir of dead root tissue that perpetuates the fungus.

The fungus kills its host by gradually decaying the roots and moving into the main stem where it girdles the plant; the first symptoms above ground may be dull or yellowed leaves and/or sparse foliage. Leaves may wilt and entire branches die; eventually, the plant dies. To identify oak root fungus, check the bark of the stem or trunk (or large roots) at or below ground level; a mat of whitish fungus tissue just beneath the bark is the indicator. In late fall or early winter, clumps of tan mushrooms may appear around infected plants.

You can try to remove all woody tissue from the soil, but in *Armillaria*-infested neighborhoods, it is far safer to choose plants that are resistant to the disease.

PLANTS RESISTANT TO OAK ROOT FUNGUS

Trees

Abies concolor White fir
Acer macrophyllum Bigleaf maple
A. palmatum Japanese maple
A. tataricum ginnala Amur maple
Ailanthus altissima Tree-of-heaven
Apple
Arbutus menziesii Madrone
Avocado
Brachychiton populneus Bottle tree
Calocedrus decurrens Incense cedar
Carya illinoensis Pecan
Catalpa
Celtis australis European hackberry
C. occidentalis Common hackberry
Cercis siliquastrum Judas tree
Chamaecyparis lawsoniana Port Orford cedar
Crabapple
Cryptomeria japonica Japanese cryptomeria
Cupaniopsis anacardioides Carrot wood
× *Cupressocyparis leylandii* Leyland cypress
Cupressus arizonica glabra Arizona cypress
Elaeagnus angustifolia Russian olive
Eucalyptus cinerea Silver dollar tree
Ficus carica Edible fig
Fraxinus angustifolia
Fraxinus uhdei Evergreen ash
Geijera parviflora Australian willow
Ginkgo biloba Maidenhair tree
Gleditsia triacanthos Honey locust
Gymnocladus dioica Kentucky coffee tree
Ilex aquifolium English holly

English ivy (Hedera helix)

I. opaca American holly
Jacaranda mimosifolia Jacaranda
Juglans californica hindsii California
  black walnut
Liquidambar styraciflua American
  sweet gum
Liriodendron tulipifera Tulip tree
Macadamia
Maclura pomifera Osage orange
Magnolia
Maytenus boaria Mayten
Melaleuca styphelioides Black tea tree
Metasequoia glyptostroboides Dawn
  redwood
Morus Mulberry
Persimmon
Pinus canariensis Canary Island pine
P. monticola Western white pine
P. nigra Austrian black pine
P. patula Jelecote pine
P. sylvestris Scotch pine
P. torreyana Torrey pine
Pistacia chinensis Chinese pistache
Pittosporum rhombifolium Queensland
  pittosporum
Pseudotsuga menziesii Douglas fir
Pyrus Pear
Quercus ilex Holly oak
Q. lobata Valley oak
Quillaja saponaria Soapbark tree
Sapium sebiferum Chinese tallow tree
Sequoia sempervirens Redwood
Sophora japonica Japanese pagoda tree
Taxodium distichum Bald cypress
Ulmus parvifolia Chinese elm

Vines

Hedera helix English ivy
Wisteria sinensis Chinese wisteria

Shrubs

Acacia longifolia Sydney golden wattle
A. verticillata
Brugmansia Angel's trumpet
Buxus sempervirens Common boxwood
Calycanthus occidentalis Spice bush
Carpenteria californica Bush anemone
Cercis occidentalis Western redbud
Clerodendrum bungei Cashmere
  bouquet
Cotinus coggygria Smoke tree
Erica arborea Tree heath
Exochorda racemosa Common pearl
  bush
Hibiscus syriacus Rose of Sharon
Hypericum beanii St. Johnswort
Ilex × aquipernyi Holly
Lonicera nitida Box honeysuckle
Mahonia
Myrica pensylvanica Bayberry
Nandina domestica Heavenly bamboo
Phlomis fruticosa Jerusalem sage
Prunus caroliniana Carolina laurel cherry
P. ilicifolia ilicifolia Hollyleaf cherry
P. i. lyonii Catalina cherry
Rhus aromatica Fragrant sumac
Rosa Rose
Sambucus canadensis American
  elderberry
Shepherdia argentea Silver buffaloberry
Vitex agnus-castus Chaste tree

Maidenhair tree (Ginkgo biloba)

Angel's trumpet (Brugmansia)

Rose

Smoke tree (Cotinus coggygria)

Japanese maple (Acer palmatum)

Root Rots

Several *Phytophthora* and *Pythium* fungi are common in western soils; one of the most common of these fungi is *Phytophthora cinnamomi*. All thrive in poorly drained, overmoist soils where soil air is in short supply. Collar, foot, root, and crown rot are some of the names their damage goes by, but "water mold root rots" best describes the way these organisms work. Telltale signs include stunting, yellowing, wilting, and leaf drop; in time, the plant succumbs.

If your garden has poorly drained "heavy" soil, steer clear of plants that require well-drained soil, good aeration, or infrequent but deep watering. These are the plants that are most susceptible to water mold organisms. Rhododendrons and azaleas are classic examples, as are California natives *Ceanothus* and flannel bush *(Fremontodendron)*. You can build raised beds for such plants, but the simplest solution in the heavy soils is to grow plants that have no special drainage requirements.

Texas Root Rot

You find this soilborne disease in the semiarid and arid Southwest at elevations below 3,500 feet—from California's Imperial and Coachella Valleys through Arizona and New Mexico and eastward. The fungus *Phymatotrichum omnivorum* destroys the outer portions of roots, cutting off water to the plant. The first sign of trouble is a sudden wilting of leaves in summer, with the leaves remaining attached to the stems. At this point, at least half the root system has already been damaged.

The fungus thrives during periods of high temperatures in highly alkaline soil that's deficient in organic matter, but fortunately, you can combat the fungus by improving your soil. Control measures consist of reducing soil alkalinity (adding soil sulfur is one approach) and incorporating rapidly decomposing organic matter. As with other soilborne diseases, though, the best way to avoid the problem is to grow resistant plants.

PLANTS RESISTANT TO TEXAS ROOT ROT

(* indicates plants immune to the disease)

Trees

Acacia farnesiana Sweet acacia
Celtis pallida Desert hackberry
Cercidium Palo verde
Chilopsis linearis Desert willow
Citrus (on sour orange rootstock)
Cupressus Cypress
Elaeagnus angustifolia Russian olive
Eucalyptus
Juglans major Nogal
Lagerstroemia indica Crape myrtle
Lysiloma microphylla thornberi
    Feather bush

Morus alba White mulberry
Pinus halepensis Aleppo pine
Platanus Plane tree, sycamore
Prosopis Mesquite

Shrubs, Vines

Caragana arborescens Siberian
    peashrub
Dodonaea viscosa Hop bush
Jasminum Jasmine
Juniperus Juniper
Larrea tridentata Creosote bush
Lonicera japonica Japanese honeysuckle
Nerium oleander Oleander

Punica granatum Pomegranate
Pyracantha Firethorn
Rosmarinus officinalis Rosemary
Sambucus mexicana Blue elderberry

Accent Plants

Agave*
Bamboo
Cacti
Cortaderia selloana Pampas grass*
Ensete ventricosum Abyssinian banana*
Fouquieria splendens Ocotillo
Palms*
Strelitzia reginae Bird of paradise*

Bamboo

Agave

Verticillium Wilt

Verticillium species cause widespread damage in the West, especially in California. The fungus invades and plugs the water-conducting tissues in the roots and stems. The first symptom often is a wilting of one side of a plant. Leaves yellow, starting first at their margins and progressing inward, and then turn brown and die—usually upward or outward from the base of the plant or branch. Fungal development is favored by cool, moist soil, but wilting of foliage often doesn't occur until warm, sunny days cause leaves to transpire water faster than the diseased roots and stems can supply it. The fungi persist in the soil, even in the absence of susceptible plants. There is no cure for infected plants, so where the fungus is present, grow only resistant plants. Tomatoes are notoriously susceptible; resistant kinds are identified by a "V" next to the plant's name.

PLANTS RESISTANT TO VERTICILLIUM WILT

Trees

Betula Birch
Carpinus Hornbeam
Cedrus Cedar
Cercidiphyllum japonicum Katsura tree
Citrus
Cornus Dogwood
Crataegus Hawthorn
Eucalyptus
Ficus carica Edible fig
Gleditsia triacanthos Honey locust
Ilex Holly
Juglans Walnut
Liquidambar styraciflua American
    sweet gum
Malus Flowering crabapple
Morus Mulberry
Pinus Pine
Platanus Plane tree, sycamore
Pyrus Ornamental pear
Quercus Oak
Salix Willow
Sorbus aucuparia European
    mountain ash
Tilia Linden
Umbellularia californica California
    laurel

Shrubs

Arctostaphylos Manzanita
Buxus Boxwood
Ceanothus Wild lilac
Cistus Rockrose
Cornus Dogwood
Hebe
Helianthemum nummularium
    Sunrose
Ilex Holly
Lantana
Nerium oleander Oleander
Pyracantha Firethorn

Perennials, Bulbs

Alcea rosea Hollyhock
Alyssum
Anemone Windflower
Aquilegia Columbine
Begonia (semperflorens) Wax begonia
Dianthus Pink
Erysimum Wallflower
Gaillardia × *grandiflora*
Geum
Gypsophila paniculata Baby's breath
Helleborus Hellebore
Heuchera Coral bells

Iberis sempervirens Evergreen candytuft
Iris
Mimulus Monkey flower
Nierembergia Cup flower
Oenothera Evening primrose
Penstemon Beard tongue
Platycodon grandiflorus Balloon flower
Potentilla Cinquefoil
Primula Primrose
Ranunculus asiaticus Persian ranunculus
Vinca minor Dwarf periwinkle
Viola Violet

Annuals

Ageratum houstonianum Floss flower
Calendula officinalis Calendula
Dianthus barbatus Sweet William
Gaillardia pulchella
Iberis Candytuft
Impatiens Balsam
Nemesia strumosa
Portulaca grandiflora Rose moss
Scabiosa atropurpurea Pincushion flower
Tropaeolum majus Garden nasturtium
Verbena × *hybrida* Garden verbena
Viola Pansy, viola
Zinnia

Garry oak (Quercus garryana)

Hollyhock (Alcea rosea)

Bearded iris

Young seedlings of flowering annuals and perennials need protection from the sun until they can establish their roots in the ground. This is especially true if they have been planted during warm weather. Methods of protecting young seedlings are shown at right. Also, harden off seedlings for a week or so by exposing them to increasing intervals of time outdoors.

The bark of young trees is sensitive to sunburn, even in cool weather. Strong sunlight can kill exposed bark, causing it to split, which weakens the wood beneath. Likewise, the bark of recently pruned trees (especially evergreens like citrus and avocado) is highly sensitive. Protection can be provided by painting the trunk or branches white or wrapping with a light-colored commercial tree wrap, available at nurseries.

Sun

The sun is a powerhouse that fuels plant growth. But too much sun can damage plants and also make the outdoors unbearable for people. Summer sun also heats up houses, requiring additional air conditioning, which raises electrical bills and overtaxes the West's supply of power. Fortunately, there are some easy ways you can reflect or block the sun's heat. You can provide shade for patios and plant wisely to block or filter the hottest sun.

Plants that are adapted to the climate in which they are grown are seldom damaged by the sun if they are well maintained and well irrigated. But seedlings or plants that have recently undergone changes in growing conditions, such as transplanting or heavy pruning, can be harmed or even killed by strong sun. Signs of such damage include scorched leaves (especially at the edges), leaf drop, blistered fruit, and split or cracked bark.

Plants that face south, southwest, or west, or those that receive plenty of afternoon sun are in the most danger of sunburn. And those that are placed beside heat-reflecting driveways and patios or that are in exposed positions are more vulnerable.

Hot Spells

Periods of intense heat in late spring and early summer can hit plants when they are at a vulnerable stage. They are still producing tender new growth and haven't yet become conditioned to hot, dry weather. Take steps to protect them.

Before the heat. On warm summer days, plants wilt slightly because their leaves lose water faster than their roots can take it up. During the night the plants recover—if their roots have water to absorb. Make sure that water is available to the entire root zone (usually the entire area beneath the leaves) so that plants can recover after an extremely hot day. When you irrigate, give plants plenty of water—don't just sprinkle. Roots that were encouraged by winter rain and previous watering will have spread deeply into the ground and will help a plant survive through hot weather.

Mulching helps soil retain moisture and cools roots near the surface. For shallow-rooted plants such as azaleas, begonias, and camellias, mulch is essential. Apply an organic material such as compost or ground bark in a layer at least 2- to 3-inches thick around the root zones of these plants.

Shade Nomenclature

Partial shade. As the sun arcs across the sky, different areas of the garden are exposed to direct sun for part of the day and bathed in shade for at least half a day (or three hours during the hottest part of the day).

Filtered or dappled shade. As sunlight passes through the canopy of a tree, the leaves create a pattern of light and shadow, or dappled sunlight. This filtered effect can also be created by overhead lath. In general, filtered shade will support many plants that grow in partial or light shade.

Light or open shade. This bright, fairly even shade is found in gardens that are open to the sky but bathed in shadow cast by surrounding tall trees, walls, or other structures.

Full or deep shade. This is found where there is little or no direct sunlight, such as beneath a dense evergreen tree. The low level of light restricts the choice of plants.

During a hot spell. When temperatures begin rising toward 100°F/38°C, it's important to cool off plants and protect them from the sun's scorching, intense direct rays. Newly planted flowers and vegetables need the most help. Sprinkle throughout the day until shade covers the leaves or the sun goes down. If a sudden rise in temperature finds you without any kind of protection, throw a sheet or some newspaper over vulnerable plants until cooler weather arrives.

The soil in containers quickly dries out. Moving planters and pots into the shade can be easier than trying to keep them wet throughout the day.

Shading Plants

A bamboo mat or window shade can guard a tree trunk from sun. Simply wrap the mat around the tree and tie it in place.

Plant grafted trees with the bud union (where the tree has been grafted onto the rootstock) away from afternoon sun.

Floating row covers protect against both heat and cold. Lightweight cloth filters sun, saving seedlings from scorch.

Lightweight window screen can provide temporary shade for new plantings. Prop it against a stake or board.

Sturdy frame of 2-by-2s supports 4-inch lath. Wire sections together at top; move as needed to shield young plants.

Shade cloth supported on stakes protects plants from too much heat; the protection is especially valuable for seedlings.

Natural Cooling

Planting shade trees is one of the best ways to cool your home and garden. Public-utility companies have estimated that properly positioned trees can cut home energy costs for summer cooling by more than 20 percent.

Nature's Air Conditioners

For most houses, the ideal shade tree has a slightly spreading canopy and reaches between 25 and 45 feet in height. If the tree is deciduous, the sun can shine through its leafless canopy in winter, warming the home (and thus reducing heating bills) during the cool months. Ten good candidates are listed on the opposite page.

The east-facing and west-facing sides of the house are the most important ones to shade. Trees on the east side block the morning sun, while ones on the west side shade your house during the hottest part of the day—the afternoon. Trees should be planted no closer than 5 to 10 feet from the foundation of the house, depending on the size of the tree; larger trees must be farther away. At that distance, roots won't burrow down to damage the foundation, and the canopy will still be able to reach far enough to shade some of the roof. In most cases, you will have to plant several trees on each side of the house to provide adequate shading. Direct

E

In the morning, three trees planted on the eastern side of the house help keep the interior cool.

In the late afternoon, two trees planted on the western side help keep the interior cool. A third tree partially shades the patio.

N

As a bonus, tall, narrow trees such as giant redwoods planted in a row help block prevailing wind.

Prevailing winds

Seasonal Shade Patterns

This chart shows how much shade is cast by trees of various heights during winter and summer.

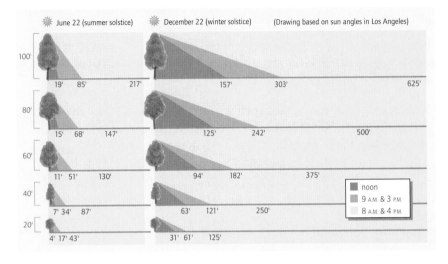

☀ June 22 (summer solstice)   ☀ December 22 (winter solstice)   (Drawing based on sun angles in Los Angeles)

■ noon
■ 9 A.M. & 3 P.M.
□ 8 A.M. & 4 P.M.

100'
19' 85' 217' | 157' 303' 625'

80'
15' 68' 147' | 125' 242' 500'

60'
11' 51' 130' | 94' 182' 375'

40'
7' 34' 87' | 63' 121' 250'

20'
4' 17' 43' | 31' 61' 125'

sun shining through windows can warm the inside of a house in a hurry. Try to position your trees where they'll shade windows but won't block desirable views from inside.

Reflected heat can increase warming of your home during the day; stored heat released from the paving at night can slow the cooling of your house. Shading your air conditioner can also reduce its workload and cut energy consumption.

THE WEST'S BEST SHADE TREES

Shade trees that best suit size and climate conditions in most Sunset climate zones are listed below. Before making a selection, ensure that the species is adapted to your region and will not outgrow your site.

Callery pear
Pyrus calleryana
'Chanticleer'
Moderate, 25–40 ft.
White flowers, fall color,
   resists fireblight

Chinese pistache
Pistacia chinensis
Moderate, to 60 ft.
Fiery fall color, shapely
   with age

Eastern redbud
Cercis canadensis
Fast, 25–35 ft.
Striking flowers,
   few problems

European hackberry
Celtis australis
Moderate, to 40 ft.
Deep-rooted, few
   problems

Flowering plum
Prunus cerasifera
'Thundercloud'
Moderate, to 20 ft.
Early bloom, some fruit

Ginkgo
Ginkgo biloba
Slow, 35–50 ft. or more
Golden fall color, female
   trees drop messy
   fruit

Goldenrain tree
Koelreuteria paniculata
Slow to moderate,
   20–35 ft.
Summer flowers, fall
   fruit; prune to shape

Lacebark or Chinese elm
Ulmus parvifolia
Fast, 40–60 ft.
Handsome bark,
   long leaf season

Locust
Robinia
 'Purple Robe'
Fast, to 40 ft.
Lingering flowers,
   aggressive roots

Olive
Olea europaea (fruitless
   varieties)
Slow to 25–30 ft.
Evergreen; older
   specimens have
   great form, beauty

Olive (Olea europaea)

Wildlife

Many western gardeners share their land with wild creatures, but whether or not you consider them pests depends on what you grow. Even birds occasionally wear out their welcome when they peck holes in your heirloom apples. You have three choices when dealing with wildlife: erect barriers, live with them, or deliberately invite them in.

Deer are especially numerous where countryside and suburbia intersect. They eat a variety of plants (roses and vegetables are particular favorites), establishing regular trails and browsing mainly at dawn and dusk. Deer are notorious for dietary preferences that differ from place to place.

What to do. The *Sunset Western Garden Book* lists plants that are best bets in deer country, but reliable deer-proofing calls for fencing. To protect an entire garden, install a barrier at least 7 feet high, higher on a downslope. Where space is available, you can erect two parallel 4-foot-high fences with a 5-foot space between them. (Deer can jump high or wide, but not both.) Surround individual plants with wire cylinders; even larger roses can be protected in this way until they exceed browsing height. For plants shorter than 3 feet, cylinders must exceed the plants' mature heights; for taller plants use a 4- or 5-foot-high cylinder. In springtime, bucks sometimes damage tree trunks by using them as "scratching posts," so surround the trunks with cylinders of wire mesh.

Gophers and moles live and tunnel underground. Gophers generally live in colonies, digging tunnels 6 to 18 inches deep, pushing up mounds of dirt. They eat roots, bulbs, and occasionally foliage. Moles burrow tunnels just below the soil surface, heaving up small plants, severing tender roots, and creating air pockets. Moles are especially disruptive in lawns. On the plus side, their diet consists of larvae and other subsurface bugs.

What to do. Traps and repellents are available (refer to the *Sunset Western Garden Book* for specifics). Protect individual plants with planting baskets of $\frac{1}{2}$-inch hardware cloth. For raised beds, securely attach a wire screen across the bottom. Unless your mole population is extensive, it's simplest to watch for tunneling, then firm soil around disturbed plants.

RIGHT *Sturdy fencing and wires keep predators out of this kitchen garden. Vines can be grown on the arbor well out of the reach of hungry deer.*

Rabbits are opportunists that dart into gardens to eat young seedlings and tender shoots—as well as summer flowers, shrubs, vegetables, and fruit tree bark.

What to do. Clean up thickets and brush piles where rabbits nest. Protect vegetable and flower gardens with 2-foot-high fences of 1-inch wire mesh that extends 6 inches below ground. Where rabbits gnaw on tree bark in winter, surround trunks with a 2-foot wire cylinder, securing it firmly to the ground.

Raccoons are nocturnal bandits who raid koi ponds and dig holes in their search for grubs. They eat many fruits and vegetables, especially corn and melons. Raccoons also overturn garbage cans in search of edible material.

What to do. Eliminate the foods that attract raccoons. Control lawn grubs with parasitic nematodes or a registered pesticide. Harvest ripe fruits, and pick up fallen fruit. Secure garbage containers, and keep kitchen waste out of the compost. Do not leave pet food outdoors. Protect ponds with electric fences or securely fasten sturdy wire mesh over the pond. Prune back tree limbs and woody vines that provide access to the roof or attic.

Squirrels are acrobatic tree-climbers that bury acorns and other nuts in pots and garden beds. They'll also nibble tender buds of camellias, grape vines, and fruit trees, as well as fruits, nuts, and sometimes roses.

What to do. You can limit your garden's appeal by excluding nut- and fruit-bearing shrubs and trees. Discourage digging in containers with a mulch of flattened river rocks or with a wire mesh. If squirrels have nibbled on plants, drape bird netting over the affected plants or wrap individual fruits with nylon stockings. To protect entire fruit or nut trees, place a flared metal collar around the trunk at about 4 feet above ground.

LEFT *Place bird and squirrel feeders under trees for protection from hawks and other flying predators.*

TOP *Gopher-proof bed lined with hardware cloth will keep out underground rodents.*

MIDDLE *Wire mesh deters rabbits and birds and is lightweight enough that it won't harm plants.*

BOTTOM *Netting held aloft with flexible stakes keeps birds off salad greens.*

Welcoming Wildlife

To many gardeners, birds and butterflies are more than a garden's finishing touches—they're essential to maintaining plant health, and they bring beauty and motion to the garden. You can greatly enhance your garden's attractiveness to these flying friends—and lure particular types—by choosing plants they favor.

Butterflies and hummingbirds feed on nectar. Fortunately, suitable plants include many popular garden ornamentals such as columbine, delphinium, and beard tongue. A number of these favorite plants feature flowers in red or blue, so a nectar-rich garden is sure to be colorful. For an extensive list of suitable hummingbird- and butterfly-attracting plants, see the *Sunset Western Garden Book*.

ABOVE *Hummingbirds find certain plants irresistible; Agastache 'Desert Sunrise' ranks high on that list. The plant flowers from midsummer through fall.*

LEFT *A monarch butterfly alights on an onion plant that has been left to flower and set seed; edible and ornamental members of the* Allium *family attract not only butterflies, but also bees and birds.*

RIGHT *Perennials in hues of pink, red, and blue attract birds and butterflies.*

BELOW *Brimming with plants that attract bees and other beneficials, the insectory garden at Benziger Vineyards in Glen Ellen, California, is as well tended as the wine grapes. The grasses and perennials were chosen specifically so that their bloom times attract beneficials needed to help control harmful insects in the vineyards.*

The Benefits of Bees

Before a flower can set seed or form fruit, it needs to be pollinated. Though some plants are pollinated by bats, birds, butterflies, moths, and wasps, most of the work is done by bees.

Bees are in serious trouble, though. Their numbers are in sharp decline, mainly because of shrinking habitat. Here's what you can do to promote a bee-friendly environment in your garden.

Provide food. Grow plants that bear flowers with plenty of nectar and pollen. Some native bees and plants, including penstemon and salvia, seem to be made for each other. Old-fashioned, heirloom-type flowers like bee balm, black-eyed Susan, cleome, sunflower, and zinnia are also excellent choices; they have more pollen and nectar than highly developed hybrids. Lavender, rosemary, thyme, and many other herbs have blossoms that bees favor. And it's helpful to include a large range of colors in your garden, especially blue, violet, white, and yellow. Aim to have something in bloom from early spring to late fall so that winged visitors are never without nourishment.

Furnish housing. One of the biggest challenges bees face is finding suitable nesting sites. We're not suggesting you house honeybee colonies; that's for professionals. But the majority of our approximately 4,000 species of native bees (honeybees are actually a European import) are solitary—essentially, single mothers raising their young alone. Having no hive to defend, they're not aggressive and rarely sting.

About 70 percent of native bees are ground nesters. A small patch of bare earth in a sunny spot—as little as one square foot—is all they need. The remainder are mostly wood nesters: they'll occupy holes in trees bored by beetles, or they'll move into nesting blocks like the one shown at left. The female bees will lay their eggs in the holes, then seal them; their offspring will emerge next spring to carry on.

Supply damp soil. Ground-nesting bees prefer soil that's soft enough to dig in. To provide it, periodically moisten an area of bare earth, or let a faucet drip slightly onto the ground.

Avoid pesticides. Nonselective pesticides don't just kill pest insects, they kill bees, too. Instead, provide a rich array of native plants to attract beneficial insects like lacewings and lady beetles, which devour aphids, mealybugs, and whiteflies.

Learn more. The Xerces Society (*www.xerces.org*), a nonprofit organization working to protect bees and other invertebrates, is a great source of additional information.

ABOVE LEFT *One way to give bees a boost is to create safe housing for them on your property. Madeleine McClendon personalized this bee box for her garden.*

BELOW *Busy collecting pollen from a verbascum flower (Verbascum bombyciferum 'Arctic Summer'), this bee is evidence of a healthy garden. Yellow is one of the colors that attracts bees.*

Attracting Birds

Birds (other than hummingbirds) separate into fruit-eaters and seed-eaters. To growers of stone fruits (peaches and cherries, for example) and pome fruits (apples and pears), certain fruit-eating birds are a yearly nemesis, zeroing in on ripening fruits. The only ways to prevent damage are covering a tree with bird netting or enclosing individual fruits in mesh bags. But in the majority of gardens, these fruit predators merely provide entertainment—enhanced if you plant ornamental fruiting plants sure to please them.

Seed-eating birds, on the other hand, are largely benign—unless, perhaps, you're growing sunflowers for seeds. While these birds usually find a variety of seeds to consume, you can guarantee their presence if you include plants they especially prefer and allow them to go to seed toward the end of their flowering period.

LEFT *The common yellowthroat is often found in marshy or streamside habitats, but it will visit drier areas if there is dense undergrowth where it can forage for insects.*

LEFT *House finches are regular visitors to bird feeders and nesting boxes. They favor berries and seeds, and sometimes help themselves to nectar from a hummingbird feeder. This one fancies penstemon buds.*

FRUIT-BEARING PLANTS

Trees

Arbutus unedo Strawberry tree
Carpinus Hornbeam
Celtis Hackberry
Cherry
Cornus Dogwood
Crabapple
Crataegus Hawthorn
Elaeagnus angustifolia Russian olive
Ilex Holly
Plum
Sassafras albidum Sassafras
Sorbus Mountain ash

Shrubs

Amelanchier Juneberry
Arctostaphylos Manzanita
Aronia Chokeberry
Berberis Barberry
Callicarpa Beautyberry
Cornus Dogwood
Cotoneaster
Heteromeles arbutifolia Toyon
Ilex Holly
Juniperus Juniper
Ligustrum Privet
Lonicera Honeysuckle
Mahonia
Photinia
Pyracantha Firethorn
Rhamnus
Ribes Currant, gooseberry
Vaccinium Blueberry and huckleberry
Viburnum

SEED-BEARING PLANTS

Trees

Abies Fir
Acer Maple
Alnus Alder
Betula Birch
Larix Larch
Liquidambar styraciflua American sweet gum
Picea Spruce
Pinus Pine
Pseudotsuga menziesii Douglas fir
Quercus Oak
Thuja Arborvitae
Tsuga Hemlock

Perennials

Aquilegia Columbine
Coreopsis
Digitalis Foxglove
Echinacea purpurea Purple coneflower
Rudbeckia
Solidago Goldenrod

Annuals

Calendula officinalis Calendula
Centaurea cyanus Cornflower
Coreopsis
Cosmos
Eschscholzia californica California poppy
Gaillardia pulchella
Helianthus annuus Common sunflower
Lobularia maritima Sweet alyssum
Nigella damascena Love-in-a-mist
Scabiosa atropurpurea Pincushion flower
Tagetes Marigold
Tithonia rotundifolia Mexican sunflower

Water

Dry summers, recurring drought, and a limited supply of water for a population that is constantly growing are just a few of the reasons that water is the West's most precious resource. Water conservation should be a part of every westerner's lifestyle. After an especially wet winter, it may be tempting to revert to endless green lawns and lush gardens. But keeping the big picture in mind can help you make smart landscaping decisions.

Most westerners live in a desert or semiarid climate. Aside from a few areas, mainly the narrow coasts of Washington, Oregon, and Northern California and major mountain ranges, the mainland Western states typically receive less than 10 or 11 inches of rain annually. And what nature doesn't supply, irrigation must.

Periods of extreme drought are part of the West's natural cycle. Tree ring studies show droughts that have lasted for more than 50 years. In 2002, when Colorado experienced the worst drought on record, lawn watering was banned for a time. And in recent years, serious droughts have hit Arizona, Montana, New Mexico, Utah, and even Washington State. Snow pack and runoff are unpredictable. And it's a certainty that other droughts will occur.

We're rapidly outgrowing our supplies. Experts expect California alone to add 24 million people by 2040. Considering that each resident uses 26,000 or more gallons per year, the supply challenge is clear. In some areas, groundwater supplies are dwindling. Overdrafting (pumping out more water from subterranean aquifers than is replenished) is a chronic problem.

The quality of groundwater is also worrisome. Toxic wastes are being detected in well-water supplies all over the West.

Clearly, the responsibility for using water wisely rests with all of us. But with smart landscape design and gardening practices, we *can* make a difference. The reward is a beautiful landscape that practically takes care of itself.

LEFT *Cottage-garden abundance can be found even in a dry, high-country New Mexico garden— if you choose your plants carefully. Sedums, yellow-flowered yarrow, pink* Penstemon palmeri, *and orange* P. pinifolius *get just moderate watering, yet provide plenty of color.*

Low-cost Solutions

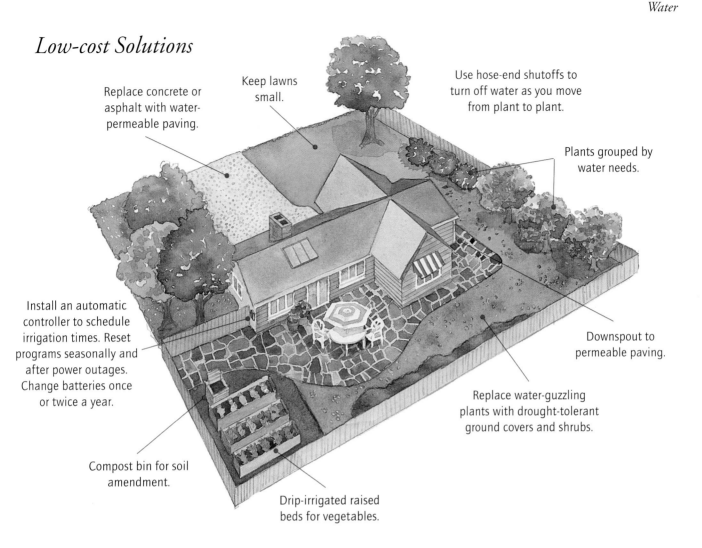

Replace concrete or asphalt with water-permeable paving.

Keep lawns small.

Use hose-end shutoffs to turn off water as you move from plant to plant.

Plants grouped by water needs.

Install an automatic controller to schedule irrigation times. Reset programs seasonally and after power outages. Change batteries once or twice a year.

Downspout to permeable paving.

Replace water-guzzling plants with drought-tolerant ground covers and shrubs.

Compost bin for soil amendment.

Drip-irrigated raised beds for vegetables.

No-cost Solutions

- Water properly to encourage deep rooting, which makes plants less susceptible to drought.

- Water plants only when needed and wet the soil only to root depth. (Check moisture in the soil by pushing a soil probe into the ground.) Most plants die from overwatering, not underwatering.

- Water when the temperatures are cooler and the air is still, usually at dawn.

- Adjust automatic irrigation systems to put water where it's needed—around plants, not around driveways, fences, house walls, or the street.

- Mow your lawn higher.

- Control runoff on slopes (see page 318).

- Don't apply water faster than the soil can absorb it. If necessary, pulse-irrigate—first water plants for

5 minutes, turn off the water for 10 minutes, then water for 5 more minutes.

- If you hire landscape professionals for watering and maintenance chores, let them know water conservation should be a priority.

- Sweep rather than hose down sidewalks.

- If you water with hose-end sprinklers, use a timer so you won't forget to turn the water off.

- Plant in fall, so winter rains will encourage root growth.

- Mulch to reduce weeds and moisture loss.

- Remove weeds. They steal water needed by ornamentals.

Choosing an Irrigation System

An irrigation system should fit the lay of your land and the arrangement of your plants. But you should also choose a system that doesn't demand more time than you have to spend in the garden. A poorly designed system results in unhealthy plants and lots of wasted water.

A wealth of equipment—from microsprinklers to automatic timers to soil moisture sensors—can help you water your garden efficiently, even when you're out of town.

Sprinklers

The more you know about sprinklers, the more water you can save. All sprinklers apply varying amounts of water within their spray pattern. That usually leads to wasteful runoff and at least some plants that are over- or underwatered. Another problem is that many sprinklers apply water faster than the soil can absorb it, leading to runoff. The best solution is to slow the delivery rate so the soil can absorb more of the water it receives. Or water in intervals, each time just to the runoff point, with a period between so the water can soak in.

Cut water use by choosing low-volume sprinkler heads. For more even coverage, look for matched-precipitation sprinkler heads. These guarantee that a half-circle head will deliver just half as much water as a full-circle head, rather than the same amount of water over a smaller area. Use specialty nozzles specifically designed for irregularly shaped or very small areas.

Low-flow Irrigation

A *soaker hose* is a long tube of plastic or canvas that seeps or sprinkles water along its entire length. It's great for watering trees (place it in a circle around the tree within its drip line). You can also lay several between rows of vegetables.

Drip irrigation describes the low-pressure application of water not only by controlled drip emitters but also by soaker tubing and miniature sprayers and sprinklers. You control watering by varying the time the system runs or by varying the delivery capacity (in gallons per hour; gph) of the emitters you use. And to regulate the volume of water to each plant, you select the type and number of emitters for each one.

Most nurseries and home centers carry drip-irrigation kits and components, as do stores that specialize in irrigation equipment.

Water use	Plants
High water use	Lawns, vegetables
Medium water use	Most plants: dahlias, roses, camellias, gardenias, daylilies, *Agapanthus*
Low water use	Natives: ceanothus, manzanitas Mediterraneans: lavender, rosemary Wildflowers: California poppies

To water efficiently, arrange plants in groups based on their water needs.

Vegetables

- Hand-water with basins and furrows.
- Use soaker hoses on flat ground.
- Install a drip-irrigation system with an emitter line for closely spaced plants and individual emitters for widely spaced vegetables.
- Position plants with similar watering needs together. Bigger plants need deeper irrigation than do small plants or seedlings. Edibles that are flowering for setting fruit need more water.

Annuals and Perennials

- Overhead watering may cause flowers to droop or spotting on the petals; certain species are more subject to leaf disease if not watered at the base.
- Underground sprinklers with pop-up risers work in extensive flower beds. Risers should be tall enough that their spray is not blocked by foliage.
- Choose drip emitter lines for beds with closely spaced plants, and use individual emitters for widely spaced plants.

Ground Covers

- Use underground sprinklers; select stationary heads for plantings more than a foot tall, and low precipitation–rate heads for ground covers on a slope.
- Drip emitters are suitable for shrubby ground covers.
- Drip minisprays work well for mass plantings of small ground covers.

Trees and Shrubs

- Use soil basins to direct water to roots and avoid runoff.
- Soaker hoses work for occasional deep watering of established trees.
- Drip-irrigation systems with emitters or microsprinklers are most efficient, especially on sloping ground.

Roses

- Underground sprinklers with flat-head sprayers run early in the day keep leaves dry, helping to prevent disease.

- Soaker hoses work well on level ground.
- Drip irrigation with emitter line works well with closely spaced bushes. Or use individual emitters for any bush.

Natives and Drought-adapted Plants

- Use ooze-type soaker hoses at low pressure.
- Use low-flow drip with a manual shut-off valve.
- Natives and drought-adapted plants need little to no water after they are established.

Lawns

- Hose-end sprinklers can work well for a small lawn.
- Underground sprinklers attached to a controller water a large or small area more precisely.

This irrigation schedule illustrates the maximum weekly water needs of some lawns in Northern California. The sprinkler run time (the minutes column) is based on an application rate of 2 inches per hour spread out over a week.

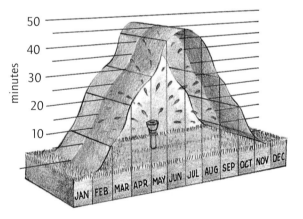

Seasonal Watering

In spring and fall, plants need about half as much water as they do in June, July, and August. At the summer solstice (June 22) near Portland, Oregon, for example, 14-hour days and intense sun increase water needs for most plants. At the winter solstice (December 22), 9-hour days and a lower, less intense sun angle mean decreasing water needs. Adjust watering schedules accordingly. (In many areas, you can stop watering altogether in winter when days are rainy and cool and plants are growing slowly, if at all.)

LEFT *Aromatic herbs such as lavender and thyme are the favored plants within this hot, sunny Sante Fe courtyard. Mixed with other low-water-use plants like lamb's ears and* Gaillardia, *they hug a dry creek bed, which helps collect sparse rainfall.*

Drought Strategies

When drought comes, and with it the possibility of local bans on lawn watering or punishing hikes in water bills, what can you do? It's too late at that point to install a water-conserving landscape, since even drought-tolerant plants need water to get established. But you can take steps to save the plants you have.

Save established trees and shrubs first. These are costly to replace and have the greatest impact on your landscape. (A lawn can be replaced in an afternoon from sod, but a 70-foot-tall redwood can take 20 years or more to replace.)

Reduce lawn watering. To stay green all summer, lawns need 1 to 2 inches of water per week. Turn on the sprinklers for about 10 minutes once a week, turn them off to let moisture soak in, then turn them on again for another few minutes. Or cut back to one inch of water every two weeks; under this regime, lawns turn straw-colored and go semidormant but bounce back quickly after weather cools in fall. Also, mow high and keep the mower blades sharp. Don't overfertilize; too much nitrogen encourages the production of thirsty new growth.

Cover pools. A pool cover can stop 90 percent of water evaporation waste, even allowing for times when the pool is in use. Many styles and materials are available, including translucent air-cell plastic types, sold at swimming pool supply stores. To avoid accidents, entirely remove any cover before jumping into the water.

Mulch. It bears repeating: a layer of mulch helps keep moisture in the soil. The best mulches don't compact easily, but allow sufficient air and water to reach plant roots. (For fabric mulches, see page 330.)

Water big trees in April and again in June. If the soil is dry at a depth of 10 to 12 inches (check it with a sampling tube), moisten the soil 18 to 24 inches deep. To increase water penetration before watering, drill 1-inch holes around the drip line and fill them with organic mulch, or use a spade or pitchfork to rough up the soil surface.

Coil soaker hoses around the tree at the drip line and half way between the drip line and the trunk; apply mulch over the root area, then allow hoses to run slowly overnight. For most big trees, you'll need about 10 gallons of water per inch of trunk diameter; riparian trees need twice that amount.

Water landscape plants growing in or near an unwatered lawn. Landscape plants used to having a well-watered lawn nearby likely have developed a dependency on that water and suffer when it is abruptly cut off.

Shallow-rooted shrubs. On azaleas, rhododendrons, and young camellias, watch for wilting or drooping of new growth. Build basins around them (make sure water won't pool around the trunks), and give them a deep soak in April with clear water (soapy water, on rhododendrons, can cause leaf burn).

Signs of Drought

Fruit trees. Most stone-fruit trees can survive some drought, although they'll produce smaller fruits, and fewer flower buds next year. But they'll be better off with a deep irrigation in April and again in June. (Citrus may need additional deep watering in summer; watch for wilting, yellowing, or curling leaves.)

Apply water slowly and deeply at the drip line with soaker hoses as described for big trees or make a basin 4 to 6 inches deep under each tree, extend it to the drip line (3 inches beyond if you can spare more water), and use a hose to fill the basin slowly.

Water Harvesting

Water scarcity calls for ingenuity. Harvesting, channeling, and storing rainwater in barrels or cisterns (large tanks or reservoirs) help keep gardens watered in times of drought. Harvested rainwater is a high quality "tonic" for house plants, seedlings, orchids, and other plants that may be sensitive to chemicals and salts found in some water supplies.

In the driest parts of the West, such as in the Arizona deserts, you can mimic nature by recreating desert washes in your garden. Normal rainfall is channeled from roofs through downspouts or along rain chains and along washes to planting areas. When heavy monsoons hit, the washes carry excess rains away from the house.

Natural washes contain various rock sizes: large ones, too heavy for the flow of water to move, stay in the center; small ones wash to the sides. Gravel settles in flat areas and bends, and in crevices between rocks. When making your own wash, work with at least three sizes of native rock that fit the scale of your garden.

An above-ground cistern catches and channels rainwater to a storage reservoir. Easy to install, it uses a simple screen system, set in the reservoir, as a filter.

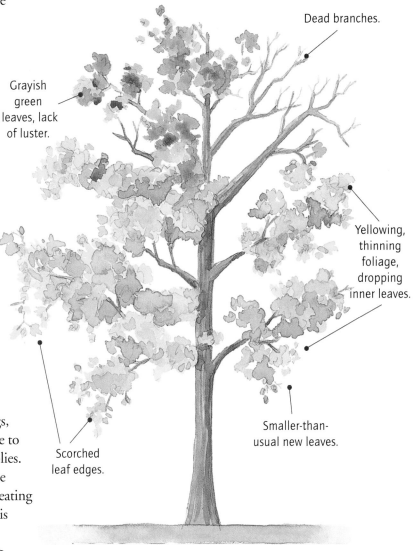

Dead branches.

Grayish green leaves, lack of luster.

Yellowing, thinning foliage, dropping inner leaves.

Smaller-than-usual new leaves.

Scorched leaf edges.

What Needs Water Most?

If you can give trees a deep irrigation in late spring, they'll be far better equipped to withstand another warm, dry summer.

Large landscape trees such as ash, birch, poplar (riparian trees that in nature grow near water), alder, coast redwood, magnolia, and Japanese maple are often the first plant specimens to show signs of drought stress. Weakened trees like Monterey pine may not die directly from drought but invite borers, which can finish them.

Water Quality

When you water and fertilize your garden, a nearby stream or the ocean a mile down the road may be the last thing on your mind. But gardening practices and the health of our streams and lakes are connected. Combined with heavy watering or significant rainfall, herbicides, pesticides, and fertilizers can run off your property and into storm drains where they flow, untreated, into lakes, streams, or the sea—polluting once-pristine bodies of water and even causing closure of beaches. Groundwater supplies can also be polluted by these contaminants.

To help prevent such pollution, avoid overwatering after applying pesticides or fertilizers, and don't apply pesticides or fertilizers before rain. Bag or compost leaves and plant trimmings; otherwise, winds can blow them into the storm drains where they cause clogging and contribute to local flooding. If possible, use nontoxic or less toxic products to control insect pests, weeds, and diseases. If you must use chemicals, spot-treat troubled plants rather than blanket the entire yard, and use the product only as directed on the label. Never dispose of lawn or garden chemicals into storm drains or into the trash. Take unwanted products to a household hazardous waste collection center.

Salmon-friendly Gardening

Salmon swim thousands of miles through the ocean, past predators and fishing nets, around locks and up waterfalls as they make their way back to the streams and quiet pools where they hatched. They start and end their lives in inland waters from California through Oregon, Washington, Idaho, and British Columbia. Unfortunately, when they arrive to spawn the next generation, they may find their spawning areas contaminated with garden chemicals, filled with silt, washed away, or paved over.

You can keep salmon habitats pristine with thoughtful gardening practices that reduce runoff, conserve water, and keep chemicals out of the water.

Build healthy soil with compost. Porous soil filled with beneficial organisms allows rainfall to infiltrate it, rather than running off into streams. And established plants growing in healthy soil need little water, fertilizer, or pesticides.

Choose the right plants. They should be adapted to your garden's conditions. Native plants, especially, thrive with little additional water or care.

About Monsoons

Late summer is monsoon season in the Southwest. Clouds suddenly darken desert skies (often in the afternoon) and dump heavy rain. Then, almost as suddenly, the rain stops, leaving garden plants freshened and their leaves quivering with moisture. The clouds disappear, unveiling the hot sun again. While not true monsoons, which are more common in tropical climates, these rains—the result of warm, moist air carried northward from the Gulf of Mexico—can be a gardener's best friend. They can irrigate your garden with high quality water. But you must catch, store, and disperse this sudden bounty of rainwater using washes, cisterns, and other techniques.

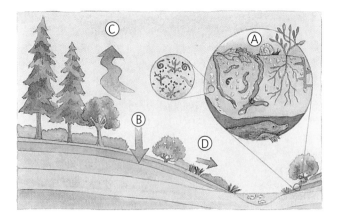

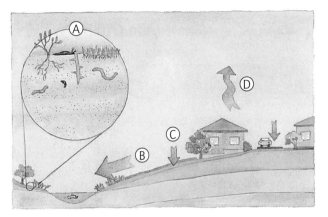

Native soil. In an undisturbed stream ecosystem, there is a healthy covering of organic matter and topsoil filled with beneficial organisms, moisture, and air (A). This protective layer allows about 35 percent of the surface water to be directly absorbed into the ground (B). A further 50 percent is released back into the atmosphere by plants (C) and the soil through the process of evapotranspiration. Only 15 percent of the water runs off into nearby creeks and rivers (D).

Disturbed soil. When vegetation and topsoil are removed (as typically occurs in new housing developments), the result is often a very thin layer of topsoil directly on top of subsoil, which contains little organic matter (A). This surface is virtually impervious; up to 70 percent of surface water runs off into streams (B), carrying with it pollutants harmful to fish: sediments, pesticides, fertilizers, and animal wastes. Only 15 percent of rainwater is absorbed into the ground (C). Fewer plants and more paving release less evapotranspiration (D).

Water wisely. Minimize or eliminate lawns, which need lots of water to look good. Water plants deeply and infrequently to encourage deep rooting, and irrigate early in the morning when the air is still. Use soaker hoses and drip irrigation. Apply mulch around plants to reduce evaporation.

Think twice before using chemicals. Choose plants that are resistant to pests and diseases to reduce the need for chemicals, and hoe or pull weeds to minimize herbicide use. Use slow-release fertilizers that don't wash into streams as easily, or choose organic fertilizers and manage pests with traps and barriers.

Direct rainwater appropriately. Use porous paving materials such as gravel, or bricks in sand, to reduce runoff. And direct any runoff into dry creek beds or grassy swales.

Protect shoreline habitat. Disturb as little native soil as possible during new construction. Preserve a buffer of native trees, shrubs, and ground covers by streams and lakes to prevent erosion, attract beneficial insects, and provide shade and shelter to salmon.

BELOW *Chinooks need to spawn in larger, deeper streams than other types of salmon.*

Wind

Strong winds can truly raise havoc in the garden. Irrigation from sprinklers blows everywhere but on plants, foliage dries out, and trees grow irregularly, their limbs subject to breakage.

But if you live in one of the West's many windy areas, you can protect your garden and its plants. Listed below are some temporary solutions to wind problems.

Stakes and ties. Make sure plants are properly staked and tied, especially newly planted trees. Tie loosely, using flexible materials that don't cut into the trunk or branches (see page 183).

Temporary windbreaks. When the ground is frozen, cold winter winds can dry out plants, even though the ground contains plenty of moisture. At other times, new plants may need wind protection to help get them established. You can redirect blowing snow or sand with snow fences. For temporary windbreaks, encircle plants with wire or plastic screen and fill in around it with straw; or protect it with burlap, shade cloth, or lath supported on a sturdy frame.

Mulches. To prevent excess drying of the soil around plants, mulch with organic matter such as straw, ground bark, or bark chips (the larger sizes are less likely to blow away). Cover the mulch with chicken wire, landscape fabric, or burlap, pegged at the corners to hold it down securely. Or place a layer of gravel, rocks, or moist soil over the mulch. If you soak the mulch thoroughly before a windy period, it is less likely to blow away.

Watering. In windy areas, drip irrigation, soaker hoses, and bubbler sprinkler heads are more effective than overhead sprinklers. For lawns, use sprinklers that apply water in heavy streams close to the ground, and, if possible, wait until wind dies down to irrigate.

After a strong wind, irrigate trees and shrubs. Newly planted lawns may need sprinkling several times a day during extremely windy periods. Set container plants in a protected area; soak thoroughly and sprinkle overhead. To prevent moisture from evaporating too quickly from clay pots, set each one in a larger pot, or plunge single pots in the ground.

LEFT *Rooftop gardens are subject to gusting winds that can be hard on plants and people. Clear glass barriers block wind without obscuring city views.*

A properly placed windbreak of trees or shrubs buffers cold winds and diminishes blowing dust, which in turn slows soil erosion. It can lower home energy consumption and make gardening easier. A windbreak also reduces noise, which makes the outdoors more pleasant.

If positioned perpendicular to prevailing winds, a windbreak reduces winds on the leeward side (the side facing away from wind) by up to 50 percent, depending on the density and height of the plants used. In open areas (a Wyoming ranch, for example), maximum wind reduction occurs on the leeward side for a distance of 10 to 20 times the height of the tallest trees. To protect homes in residential areas, windbreaks should be planted no farther away than four times the height of the tallest tree.

The ideal windbreak consists of fairly fast-growing, upright trees or shrubs that can be planted close together. Suitable species include some eucalyptus, junipers, pines, pittosporum, privet, and poplars.

Western Winds

What matters to gardeners—and to garden plants—is when winds come and how strong they are. In many areas, fortunately, winds are generally predictable.

Coastal winds. As the land heats up on clear days during the warm months, the air over it also heats and rises. To replace it, cool, humid air flows onto the land in a northwesterly direction from the ocean. Called "sea breezes," these steady winds start in midmorning, reach their peak in the afternoon, and taper off in the evening. As the land cools after sunset, the flow reverses and cooler, drier air runs down canyons and valleys and out to the sea—but only if it becomes cooler than the ocean. These "land breezes" are most pronounced in winter and in California, where the ocean is relatively warm.

Storm winds. Pacific storms that strike the coast are fronted by strong southerly winds. As these winds are squeezed between the advancing storm and the coastal mountains, they intensify.

Ice storms, Santa Anas, and chinooks. When air pressure builds in the intermountain states during fall and winter, it pushes past the Sierras, Cascades, and Rockies toward lower-pressure areas to the east and west. In the Northwest, this creates powerful ice storms as winds roar out of the Columbia Gorge and Fraser River Valley. In Southern California, it creates Santa Anas—hot, dry winds. On the eastern flank of the Rockies, these winds are milder and known as chinooks.

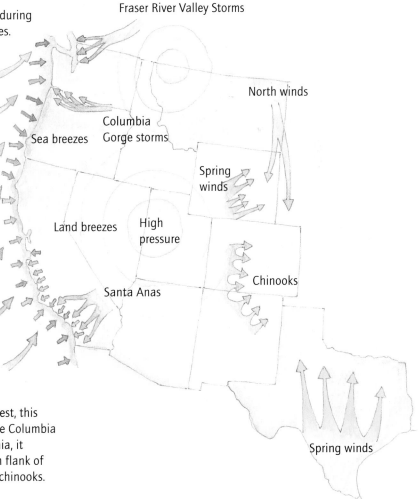

Fraser River Valley Storms

North winds

Columbia Gorge storms

Sea breezes

Spring winds

Land breezes

High pressure

Chinooks

Santa Anas

Spring winds

Planting in Windy Areas

By the very nature of their growth habits—tall and spreading—trees are highly susceptible to wind damage. Special care should be taken when planting trees in windy locations to make sure they become firmly rooted and develop a strong structure. Regularly examine mature trees and take steps to prevent a tree or broken limbs from falling—both can be extremely hazardous to people and property.

The first step is to choose a species that can withstand windy conditions (below). When choosing a tree at the nursery, select one with a strong trunk that doesn't need much staking for support. The canopy should be symmetrical, making up about two-thirds of the height of the tree. Look for specimens with branches along the entire trunk; these will further strengthen the tree as it grows. Be sure to avoid any root-bound trees grown in containers.

As you set the tree in the hole, position the side with the most branches into the wind. If planting a bare-root tree, place the largest roots toward the wind to improve anchoring. Stake the tree securely (see page 183).

Young trees growing in windy sites can be stunted by as much as 25 percent and usually grow lopsided, most of their branches and foliage growing away from the wind. Consequently, they need careful pruning to develop a strong structure and a pleasing shape. Mature trees also need regular pruning to withstand strong winds. Consult a certified arborist for help.

TREES AND SHRUBS FOR WINDY AREAS

Trees

Acacia
Acer campestre Hedge maple
Broussonetia papyrifera Paper mulberry
Calocedrus decurrens Incense cedar
Casuarina Beefwood
Chamaecyparis lawsoniana Port Orford cedar
Chilopsis linearis Desert willow
× *Cupressocyparis leylandii*
Cupressus Cypress
Elaeagnus angustifolia Russian olive
Eucalyptus
Fraxinus 'Fan West'
F. velutina 'Rio Grande' Fan-tex ash
Lagunaria patersonii Primrose tree
Ligustrum lucidum Glossy privet
Maclura pomifera Osage orange
Melaleuca
Olea europaea Olive
Palms
Parkinsonia aculeata Jerusalem thorn
Picea abies Norway spruce
Pinus Pine
Pittosporum (except *P. phillyreoides*)
Populus Poplar
Prosopis glandulosa Honey mesquite
Pseudotsuga menziesii Douglas fir

Quercus ilex Holly oak
Schinus molle California pepper tree
Sequoia sempervirens Redwood
Tamarix Tamarisk
Thuja occidentalis American arborvitae
T. plicata Western red cedar
Ulmus pumila Siberian elm

Shrubs

Arbutus unedo Strawberry tree
Arctostaphylos Manzanita
Artemisia
Baccharis pilularis Dwarf coyote brush
Berberis Barberry
Buxus Boxwood
Callistemon Bottlebrush
Ceanothus Wild lilac
Chamaecyparis False cypress
Cistus Rockrose
Correa Australian fuchsia
Cotoneaster
Dodonaea viscosa Hop bush
Elaeagnus
Escallonia
Euonymus japonicus Evergreen euonymus
Griselinia littoralis
Hakea suaveolens Sweet hakea
Juniperus Juniper
Lantana

Laurus nobilis Sweet bay
Lavandula Lavender
Lavatera Tree mallow
Leptospermum Tea tree
Leucophyllum Texas ranger
Ligustrum japonicum 'Texanum'
Myrica california Pacific wax myrtle
Nandina domestica Heavenly bamboo
Nerium oleander Oleander
Pittosporum
Prunus (evergreen)
Pyracantha Firethorn
Rhamnus
Rhaphiolepis
Rhus Sumac
Rosmarinus officinalis Rosemary
Westringia fruticosa Coast rosemary
Xylosma congestum

Rockrose (Cistus) *and lavender*

Trees: Seven Danger Signs

Tree experts agree that most storm damage to trees is predictable. These signs indicate trouble.

Too dense a crown. A top-heavy canopy of foliage can act like a sail, catching wind and causing the tree to blow over or limbs to break. To thin the foliage, remove at least half the volume of leaves. (Arborists say that you should be able to see light through the tree canopy.)

Too wide a crotch. An almost horizontal limb can break under wind, snow, or the weight of rainwater on foliage. Shorten or remove the limb if it isn't too large to handle, or have a professional install a cable.

Dead or weakened wood. In winds, these branches often break. Prune them off yourself if they are small enough and low enough to handle; otherwise, hire a professional.

Too narrow a crotch. A narrow crotch can split. If the limb isn't too large to handle, you can prune it off; otherwise, call a professional to install cables to prevent splitting.

Climbing ivy. As the plant grows, its stems will girdle the tree trunk, interfering with the uptake of nutrients and water. Ivy foliage adds weight and harbors pests. Remove all the ivy as far up as you can, and keep it from growing up in the future.

Shallow or weak root system. A tree is susceptible to blowing over if the root system is weak. Thin foliage if necessary to allow wind to blow through the canopy. Water deeply and infrequently to encourage deep rooting.

Trunk cavity. The bigger the cavity, the more it can weaken the tree. Carve out rotted wood and smooth the edges of the bark.

Seacoast Gardening

As the Pacific coastline stretches from the Mexican border to the tip of Alaska, it embraces climates that range from balmy to frigid. Regardless of the temperature, all seacoast gardens are subject to special conditions: salt-laden winds, fog and humid air, and low sun intensity. In addition, many coastal soils are sandy, even somewhat salty, and retain little water. Those special conditions call for special plants. Fortunately, western gardeners can choose from among a wide variety of tough customers that will thrive in the seacoast environment. Some plants in these lists—ceanothus, *Myoporum*, rosemary, and statice, for example—will endure direct hits of spray-laden wind. Others, such as rockrose, will be damaged by direct salt spray but still revel in the more sheltered portions of a coastal garden.

FACING PAGE *Sturdy perennial and grasses like pheasant's-tail grass* (Stipa arundinacea) *tolerate coastal conditions.*

BELOW Lavatera maritima *forms a blooming privacy screen in this sheltered Laguna Beach garden. Homeowner Rana Malas designed the garden with a Mediterranean flair, so it includes other tough coastal customers such as lavender, rosemary, and a clipped olive tree.*

Summer Fog

San Francisco Bay area gardeners know all too well about "June gloom." Just when you think beach weather should begin, the fog arrives. If you're lucky, sun may break through by noon. Summer fogs also frequently cloak the redwood and Sitka spruce belts in Oregon, Washington, and the Southern Californian coast. This phenomenon develops when soaring inland temperatures cause warm air to rise, creating a vacuum underneath. That pulls cold, foggy air in off the ocean, making the pea soup that sets off fog horns from Morro Bay to Cape Flattery. As the fog drifts inland, it warms and dissipates.

In this moist, mild climate, you can forget about heat-loving melons, for example, and only early tomatoes stand a chance of ripening there. Among citrus, lemons are dependable—especially if planted in a heat trap against a south-facing wall. Vegetable growers are able to harvest winter vegetables well into spring—some even into summer. Rose blossoms can be bigger and longer-lasting along the coast, but foliage diseases (chiefly powdery mildew, black spot, and rust) also thrive in the humidity. Rather than fight disease with sprays, plant disease-resistant roses such as 'Ballerina', 'Color Magic', 'Honor', 'Ingrid Bergman', 'Olé', 'Paradise', 'Pascali', 'Sun Flare', and 'Voodoo'.

Even with the difficulties coastal gardeners face, inland gardeners truly envy the fog-belt successes of fuchsias, begonias, and a host of plants from cool-maritime climates in New Zealand, the Canary Islands, and southern Chile—as well as tender plants from cool tropical highlands.

LEFT *Blue pride of Madeira is a familiar site in coastal gardens; it tolerates poor soil, wind, and fog.*

BELOW *Perched on a hilltop overlooking the Strait of Juan de Fuca, Marni MacNeill's garden boasts a colorful array of annuals and perennials, thanks to careful soil preparation and plenty of gravel mulch.*

PLANTS FOR COASTAL GARDENS

Trees

Albizia distachya Plume albizia
Casuarina stricta Mountain she-oak
Chamaecyparis lawsoniana Port Orford cedar
Cordyline australis
C. indivisa Blue dracaena
Corynocarpus laevigata New Zealand laurel
Cupaniopsis anacardioides Carrot wood
Cupressus macrocarpa Monterey cypress
Eucalyptus ficifolia Red-flowering gum
E. leucoxylon megalocarpa Large-fruited yellow gum
E. rudis Flooded gum
Ficus rubiginosa Rustyleaf fig
Melaleuca quinquenervia Cajeput tree
Metrosideros excelsus New Zealand Christmas tree
Myoporum laetum
Pinus contorta contorta Beach pine
P. halepensis Aleppo pine
P. heldreichii Bosnian pine
P. muricata Bishop pine
P. nigra Austrian black pine
P. pinaster Cluster pine
P. roxburghii Chir pine
P. torreyana Torrey pine
Pseudotsuga menziesii Douglas fir
Quercus ilex Holly oak
Sequoia sempervirens Redwood
Tsuga heterophylla Western hemlock
Vitex lucens New Zealand chaste tree

Shrubs

Acacia longifolia Sydney golden wattle
A. verticillata
Arbutus unedo Strawberry tree
Atriplex Saltbush
Calocephalus brownii Cushion bush
Calothamnus Net bush
Carissa macrocarpa Natal plum
Cistus Rockrose
Coprosma
Corokia cotoneaster
Correa Australian fuchsia

Cytisus Broom
Dodonaea viscosa Hop bush
Echium candicans Pride of Madeira
Elaeagnus
Escallonia
Euonymus japonicus Evergreen euonymus
Euryops
Garrya elliptica Coast silktassel
Gaultheria shallon Salal
Genista Broom
Griselinia
Hakea
Halimium
Hebe
Juniperus Juniper
Lagunaria patersonii Primrose tree
Laurus nobilis Sweet bay
Lavatera assurgentiflora Tree mallow
Leptospermum Tea tree
Lonicera nitida Box honeysuckle
L. pileata Privet honeysuckle
Melaleuca (most)
Myoporum
Myrica californica Pacific wax myrtle
Photinia × fraseri
Pinus mugo mugo Mugho pine
Pittosporum crassifolium
P. tobira Tobira
Prunus laurocerasus English laurel
Rhamnus alaternus Italian buckthorn
Rhaphiolepis
Rhododendron occidentale
    Western azalea

Rhus integrifolia Lemonade berry
Rosa rugosa Ramanas rose
Rosmarinus officinalis Rosemary
Viburnum davidii
Westringia fruticosa Coast rosemary

Vines, Ground covers

Abronia Sand verbena
Arctostaphylos uva-ursi Bearberry
Arctotheca calendula Cape weed
Atriplex semibaccata Australian saltbush
Baccharis pilularis Dwarf coyote bush
Bougainvillea
Carpobrotus Ice plant
Ceanothus gloriosus Point Reyes
    ceanothus
C. griseus horizontalis Carmel creeper
Cotoneaster dammeri
    Bearberry cotoneaster
Delosperma Ice plant
Drosanthemum
Erica × darleyensis
Fallopia baldschuanica Lace vine
Juniperus (many) Juniper
Lampranthus Ice plant
Lavandula angustifolia English lavender
L. × intermedia 'Grosso' Lavandin
Muehlenbeckia complexa Mattress vine
Osteospermum fruticosum Trailing
    African daisy
Solandra maxima Cup-of-gold vine
Tecoma capensis Cape honeysuckle
Vinca minor Dwarf periwinkle

Bulbs

Hyacinthoides non-scripta English bluebell
Muscari armeniacum Grape hyacinth
M. latifolium Grape hyacinth
Narcissus Daffodil
Tulipa Tulip

Perennials, Annuals

Aloe arborescens Tree aloe
Aurinia saxatilis Basket-of-gold
Carex Sedge
Centaurea cyanus Cornflower
Cerastium tomentosum Snow-in-summer
Cortaderia selloana Pampas grass
Chrysanthemum
Erigeron glaucus Beach aster
E. karvinskianus Mexican daisy
Eriogonum Wild buckwheat
Eschscholzia californica California poppy
Euphorbia
Felicia amelloides Blue marguerite
Impatiens sodenii Poor man's
    rhododendron
Limonium perezii Statice
Lithodora diffusa 'Grace Ward'
Pelargonium Geranium
Phormium tenax New Zealand flax
Santolina chamaecyparissus Lavender
    cotton
Sedum spathulifolium 'Cape Blanco'
    Stonecrop
Tropaeolum majus Garden nasturtium

Sedge (Carex)

Euphorbia

New Zealand Christmas tree (Metrosideros)

planning

Evaluating the Site

Whether you're facing an empty lot or renovating an established garden, start by taking stock of key elements. First among these is your climate. The *Sunset Western Garden Book* assigns climate zones to all areas of the West and indicates whether a plant will thrive in the average conditions found there. These zones take into account not just temperature, but also latitude, elevation, and prevailing winds. Within your property, you are also likely to find microclimates: areas that are a little warmer or cooler, wetter or drier, or more or less windy than others.

Your garden's soil will also determine which plants will do well. Soils are usually described as sandy, clay, or loam. Sandy soil drains fast and doesn't hold nutrients well. Clay soil holds nutrients and water, but not air—so it gets hard as a brick when dry. The perfect garden soil is loam—a light, crumbly mixture of approximately equal parts of sand, silt, and clay, with a healthy component of organic matter. All soils benefit from organic matter, which holds water, nutrients, and air—and is loose enough for roots to penetrate easily.

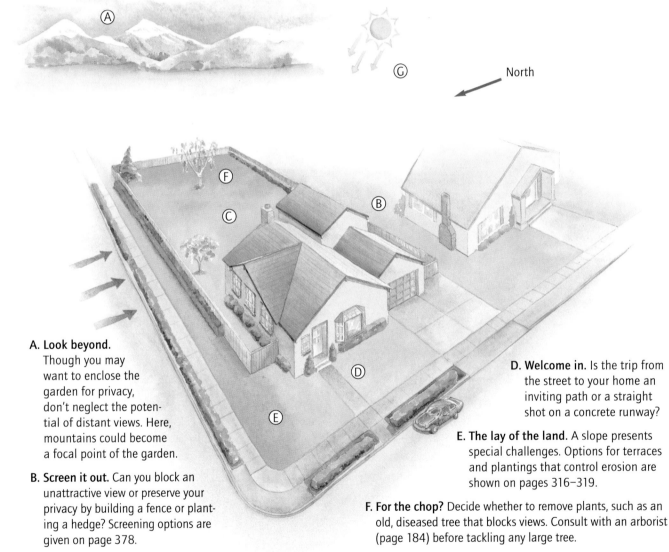

North

A. Look beyond. Though you may want to enclose the garden for privacy, don't neglect the potential of distant views. Here, mountains could become a focal point of the garden.

B. Screen it out. Can you block an unattractive view or preserve your privacy by building a fence or planting a hedge? Screening options are given on page 378.

C. So long lawn. Do you really need a huge expanse of turf? Lawns require a considerable amount of time, effort, and money to keep looking good. See page 208 for alternatives to traditional lawns.

D. Welcome in. Is the trip from the street to your home an inviting path or a straight shot on a concrete runway?

E. The lay of the land. A slope presents special challenges. Options for terraces and plantings that control erosion are shown on pages 316–319.

F. For the chop? Decide whether to remove plants, such as an old, diseased tree that blocks views. Consult with an arborist (page 184) before tackling any large tree.

G. North or south? A south-facing exposure will receive more sunlight and be the hotter part of your garden—perfect for a vegetable garden. Areas facing north, especially those in the shadow of the house, call for shade-tolerant plants.

Tracking the Sun

Remember that the angle of the sun dramatically affects the shade patterns in the garden during different seasons—exaggerating sun in summer and shade in winter. It's good to know these patterns before planning a major feature such as a seating arbor, greenhouse, or swimming pool.

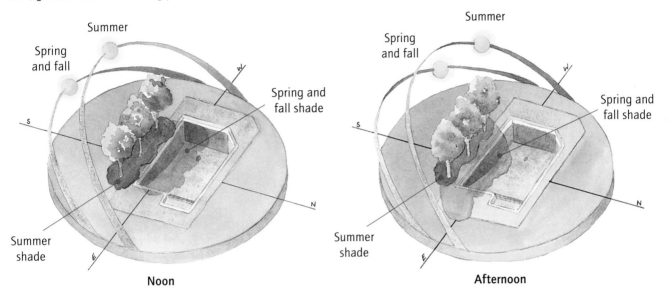

Noon

Afternoon

If you are just starting out in a new garden—or if your plants are struggling—it's a good idea to check the pH of your soil. Some plants have specific acid/alkaline requirements. In arid parts of the West, soils tend to be alkaline (pH above 7); where there's abundant rain and snow, soils tend to be more acid (pH below 6). It's possible to change your soil's pH; for example, you can make soil more alkaline by adding lime or make it more acid by adding peat. However, in many cases, it is easier to choose plants that are adapted to your soil than to try to change the soil to suit the plants (see page 331).

In most parts of the West, we can count on dry summers, recurring drought, and a limited supply of water for a growing population. Because water conservation should be a part of every westerner's lifestyle, landscapes must be as water-thrifty as possible. Another environmentally conscious—and labor-saving—approach is to consider which plants and materials in an existing garden you can keep or reuse.

Making It Official

How can you find out about zoning or other laws that might affect your landscaping?

- Your *property deed* gives you the exact location of property lines, easements or rights-of-way, building restrictions, or tree-removal restrictions.

- The local *building* or *planning department* can confirm setback requirements; height limitations for fences, buildings, or other structures; safety codes for pools and spas; tree or historic preservation ordinances; and building codes and permits.

- Contact your municipal *utility company* to find out the location and depth of underground utility lines, as well as building or planting limitations under power lines. Your *water company* may have restrictions on water use or restrictions on the size of lawns.

- The *neighbors* almost certainly have opinions regarding views into and beyond your property and your mutual need for privacy, light, and wind. They may also have concerns about existing trees and other plants, structures, and shared walks and driveways. Homeowners' associations may also have landscaping rules and requirements.

Setting Goals

Close your eyes and picture your dream garden. How do you want to use your outdoor space? Would you like a patio for entertaining and outdoor dining? A swimming pool, small pond, or other water feature? Or simply a secluded retreat? Raised beds for a kitchen garden? A gazebo? Planting beds for colorful, annuals and perennials? A lawn for kids to play on? A wildlife habitat area? A flower border, edged with winding stone paths? Dream big, then edit—be realistic about the space required and about your site's potential.

Looking Good

Your garden's style is as distinctive and personal as your wardrobe or your interior design—and so it deserves the same consideration. Do you want your garden wild, with native shrubs and rambling vines, or tailored, with a white picket fence around a square lawn? The images in this book and gardens you visit can serve as inspiration but, if you are unsure where to begin, look to your house architecture for some initial direction. A Spanish-style house, for instance, lends itself to a Mediterranean garden with lavender, citrus, and a fountain, while a cedar-shingled house in a Northwest forest might be most at home surrounded by rhododendrons, vine maples, and conifers. In the Southwest, adobe might pair best with desert-adapted palo verde trees, cactus, and wildflowers. A modern home might inspire you to create a showcase for art and sculptural plants.

Working Hard

As a final practical note, consider how much upkeep you're willing to take on. To reduce the amount of time and effort your garden will require, avoid high-maintenance features such as lawns, sheared hedges, or trees that drop leaves in autumn. A formal rose garden is lovely, but it can mean a tremendous amount of pruning, tidying, and tending. Also consider installing time-saving devices such as an automatic irrigation system (page 348).

FACING PAGE
Designed for outdoor living and recreation, this Southwestern garden provides a cozy seating area by a fireplace to warm swimmers after evening dips. The scene is just as inviting as any indoor room.

ABOVE *Plant-lovers can find a way to pack even the smallest space with greenery. The front yard pictured here is edged with an abundance of shrubs, vines, and perennials.*

LEFT *There's no reason an edible garden has to look like a barn-yard. These beds brimming with leafy vegetables blend with colorful flowers around carefully tended gravel paths. The result is a feast for the eyes as well as for the table.*

367

Making a Plan

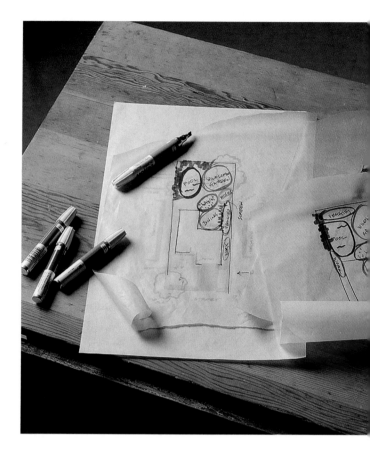

Once you have some features and an overall style in mind, it's time to put your ideas on paper. You don't need a professional site plan, but it's helpful to have an overview of your lot in order to see how your desired elements will fit into the space.

You'll save time if you can find a deed map that gives actual dimensions and the orientation of your property, or architectural plans that show the site and its buildings. Otherwise, you can measure your property yourself and transfer the dimensions to a base plan, preferably on graph paper.

On the next three pages, a plan for the lot shown on page 364 is developed through the typical stages. You may find that using a similar approach will help you to refine your own ideas. First, draw (or obtain) a scaled plan of your property. Next, use a "bubble plan" to rough in the various elements of your potential new landscape (see facing page). Finally, you may wish to produce a detailed plan showing all the elements in place (see pages 370–371).

Working with Professionals

There's a lot of satisfaction in leading a visitor through your garden and saying, "I did it all myself." The fact is, though, that even if you have the time, skill, and energy to do all the designing, planting, and building yourself, there are times when you need to enlist the help of professionals. But who should you call, and when should you call them?

If you'd like your garden to include a patio, deck, pool, drainage system, or outdoor kitchen, a *landscape architect* can be a big help. Landscape architects are licensed to design exterior structures, solve site problems, and give advice on siting service lines, entries, driveways, and parking areas. For individual services or simple consultation, landscape architects usually work at an hourly rate. Or you may sign a contract for an entire package, from conceptual plans to construction drawings and supervision of the project.

The terms *landscape designer* and *garden designer* apply to professionals who may be self-taught or may have the same academic credentials as a landscape architect, but lack a state license. They are more likely to work on smaller, strictly residential projects.

If your plans call for major construction—beyond the bounds of do-it-yourself projects—you may need the services of a licensed *landscape contractor*. Such professionals may be trained in methods of earthmoving, construction, and planting.

And if you can't tell the difference between a daffodil and a dogwood, you can find experts who work primarily with plants. A *horticulturist* is trained in the selection and care of garden plants. *Arborists* are trained in the care of trees and other woody plants. Other valuable sources of information are the staff people who work at reputable local nurseries and garden centers. Some nurseries may also offer design services but beware of free design services, as the designer may be obligated to work only with materials offered by that particular nursery.

Finally, don't hesitate to visit the website of your local Cooperative Extension Service. These government-funded agencies are especially helpful when it comes to choosing plants that will do well in your area; they can also offer advice on pest and disease control.

Drawing to Scale

To get started, enlist a helper and head outside with a measuring tape and a sketch pad. Make a rough sketch of the property's outline, then measure all boundaries and dimensions of the lot, as well as the outlines of the house and other structures. Take your time and measure spaces between things carefully; your sketch may look a little odd, but it will all make sense later on. Mark the location of windows and doors on your house, as well as any existing paved areas or structures that you plan to leave in place. Also mark only those trees and shrubs that you'd like to keep. Use a compass to determine north; this will help you identify exposures and patterns of sun and shade. It's also a good idea to indicate the direction of prevailing winds throughout the year. If there are any particularly high or low points on your site, indicate those on your plan.

Once you've made your measurements, you're ready to draw a base plan for your garden that is to scale—essentially a "bird's eye" view of your garden. Just choose a scale (*x* number of feet per square) that allows you to fit the entire plan on a single sheet of paper. Start by drawing the outer borders of the property, and then fill in the details.

Bubble Plan

With your scale drawing in hand, you can use a "bubble plan" to indicate roughly the different elements of your new garden. Either make several photocopies of the base plan to sketch on, or use tracing paper laid over the base plan.

Each bubble—actually a rough circle, square, or oval—represents a particular activity or garden feature that you want to include in your design. Bubbles may overlap where spaces merge; where separate spaces are called for, draw a line to suggest a screen or barrier. Your site assessment will come in handy at this point. Locate your vegetable garden, for instance, where it will get sun for most of the day.

Try out several different arrangements before choosing the one that works best for you. This will form the basis for your final plan.

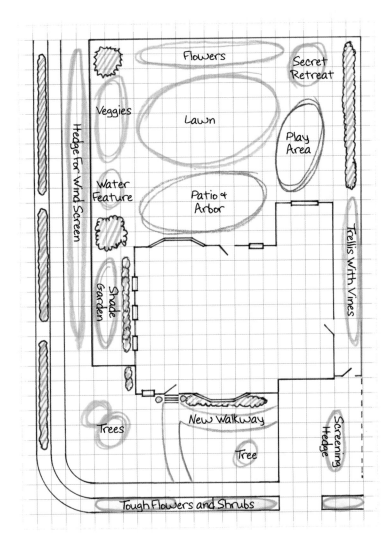

One Garden, Three Ways

Once you've decided on the basic elements of your garden, you can refine your plan. To get a feel for how you might arrange those elements, you can mock up the design on your property with stakes, strings, or markings. To give your design a unified feel, repeat simple shapes when laying out beds, borders, walkways, and lawns.

In this version of the plan, flowing organic and circular shapes are employed.

- A curving lawn that incorporates the kids' play area is complemented by the rounded shape of the deck.

- Vegetable rows are laid out in an oblong bed, and a natural-looking pond mimics the lawn's shape.

- A concrete path winds through the shade garden.

- A few shrubs and a small, curved bench make up the retreat area.

- Mulched paths in all areas complete the casual feel of this backyard's design.

- In the front yard, a curving path makes for a gracious entry.

Another version of the same basic plan uses triangular and hexagonal shapes.

- The lawn's irregular form wraps around the angular deck.

- A raised bed for vegetables and a formal reflecting pool are shaped like elongated hexagons.

- Stepping-stones form pathways throughout the back garden.

- The retreat area includes a hammock nearly surrounded by a hedge.

- In the front, a straight concrete path leads directly to the front door.

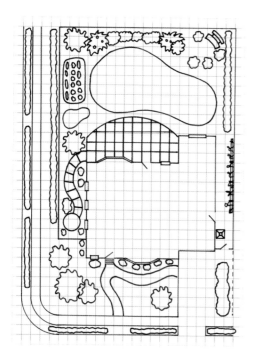

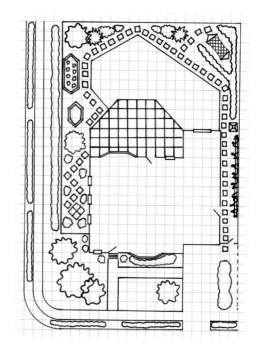

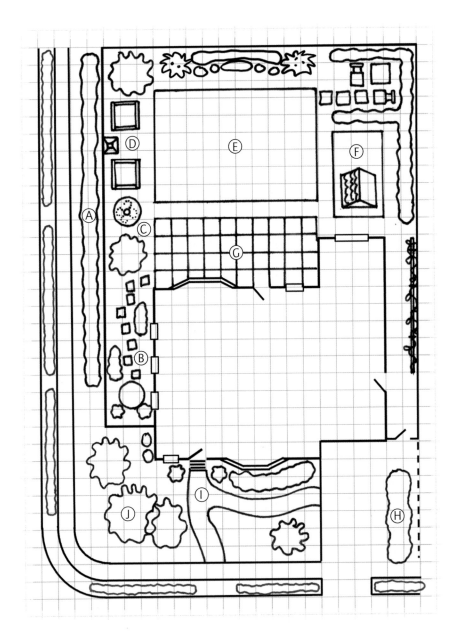

This backyard design is based on right angles, for a clean, modern look.

- The rectangular lawn will be easy to mow; the deck design is easier (and likely cheaper) to build than the previous two.

- A recirculating fountain provides the sound of flowing water.

- The kids' play area is defined by a sandbox and playhouse set apart from the lawn, and the retreat includes two chairs and a small table enclosed by a low flowering hedge (an extension of the existing hedge that is kept clipped at a higher level).

- Two raised beds for vegetables are easier to reach into, and the compost bin is located where it is convenient to the kitchen, vegetable beds, and lawn (where much of the raw material will come from).

- Gravel pathways connect the different areas, with stepping-stones leading through a fragrant ground cover in the secret retreat and through low, lush plantings in the shade garden. The curving front walk from the first version is retained.

A. Planting a hedge on the hill along the street will block the wind and the noise of traffic. Because it's on the north side of the property, it won't cast shade anywhere inside the fence.

B. A shade garden is suitable for the north side of the house. It's visible from indoors, so it's also a good place to display a piece of garden art.

C. A fountain placed here can be seen from indoors as well as on the patio.

D. This south-facing spot offers plenty of sun for a cutting or vegetable garden.

E. Smaller lawns mean less mowing, fertilizing, and watering.

F. A children's play area is sited where it can be safely supervised from the patio and house.

G. A patio is shaded from the hot sun by an arbor.

H. Part of the driveway could be replaced with a hedge for screening.

I. A new walkway to the front door features a graceful curve.

J. Trees in the front yard will help block wind and reduce the area of a high-maintenance lawn.

ABOVE *Rhythm. A path that zigzags between angular flower beds lead the eye through a Phoenix, Arizona, garden (designed by Christy Ten Eyck) to views of distant Camelback Mountain. The beds also confine thirsty plants to small areas—a necessity in this dry region.*

RIGHT *Focal point. Sculpure, a great bench, even a gazebo can draw attention to the corner of a garden. The bold stone orb pictured here accents a small orchard in a Eugene, Oregon, garden. The blue wall and gravel ground cover enhance its presence.*

RIGHT *Symmetry is created when matching or similar elements are balanced on either side of a central axis (the centerline of a composition, such as a view or a walkway). Symmetry tends to make a garden look more formal, such as in this design, where lavender shrubs and olive trees are evenly arrayed on either side of entry steps and pathway.*

LEFT *Simplicity is the result of restraint and repetition. In this grassy garden, large drifts of similar plants create a soothing and restful composition, punctuated with just a few accent plants.*

Design Basics

When thinking about your garden, keep in mind some of the basic principles of design. In a well-designed garden, all the parts work together to read as a whole rather than as a hodgepodge of disparate elements. Each part—whether a deck, planting bed, water feature, or seating area—is in *proportion* to the rest of the garden and in *scale* with the house and property. A sense of rhythm is achieved by *repetition* of plants, colors, and materials—and enhanced with occasional *accents* that contrast with their surroundings. In addition to these basics, professional designers employ an assortment of tricks to overcome typical landscaping challenges or to make the garden more attractive and livable. You can learn a lot by studying gardens that you visit or see in magazines, as well as those pictured throughout this book. Try to relate the elements that make these gardens work to the examples shown here, and then apply them to your own garden.

Design Tricks

ABOVE *Conceal parts of the garden to create mystery or to make small landscapes appear larger. Here, large clumping grasses partially obscure elements.*

FACING PAGE *Borrowed scenery. A garden can seem more spacious if you draw in views from beyond your property line. Here, an allée of Agapanthus leads toward and frames the wooded hillside beyond.*

LEFT *To add drama in a small space, place a large, showy plant—such as this angel's trumpet—in a prominent spot.*

BELOW *Create a series of garden "rooms." Sonny Garcia and Tom Valva's San Francisco garden measures just 50 by 30 feet, but it seems larger thanks to four levels connected by a series of stairways.*

Outdoor Rooms

Think of your garden as an outdoor room that needs a floor, walls, and a ceiling. The "floor" may include a lawn, a planting area, a pathway, a patio or deck—even a pool. Garden floors can provide an unbroken carpet of green foliage or an elaborate planting of brightly colored flowering plants. They can modify the climate: a large concrete slab will reflect the sun's heat, while dark pavement such as asphalt will collect heat during the day, then release it at night. In contrast, a ground-cover planting can reduce the air temperature by several degrees. Floors also play a protective role, covering the soil and preventing erosion by controlling runoff of excess water.

Where a sports or play area calls for a soft but sturdy floor, a lawn of turfgrass is the best choice. To keep a well-used lawn in top condition, however, calls for regular mowing, weeding, and watering. Also, most turfgrasses require steady moisture, and in the West, water is a limited resource. If the area is not to be used for activities, consider other ground covers or hard surfaces.

Raised beds, which make planting and harvesting vegetables easier, are located in a sunny, south-facing area.

A gently splashing fountain can be seen and heard from indoors and outdoors.

Stepping stones set among low ground-cover plants in the sideyard lead to a small private retreat.

376

Pavers used to edge a small
lawn link the hardscaping to
the front entry; the lawn provides
a soft surface for games.

A play area for kids features
a sandbox and playhouse in
the view of the main deck.

A wooden deck offers a transition between house and garden
and provides a practical surface
for outdoor entertaining.

Pavers provide a finished
look to the front walkway.

The Garden Walls & Ceiling

The "walls" of a garden provide enclosure, defining the space and offering privacy. Fences, hedges, concrete or stucco walls, and even small trees and large shrubs can shield your garden from the neighbors, or block the wind, sun, or unsightly views. The "ceiling" may simply be the bright blue sky or a canopy of trees, an arbor or pergola, or even an umbrella or fabric awning. Your garden may have several different ceilings, each with a different feel beneath. A dining area, for example, benefits from overhead shade, while an herb bed needs maximum exposure to sunshine.

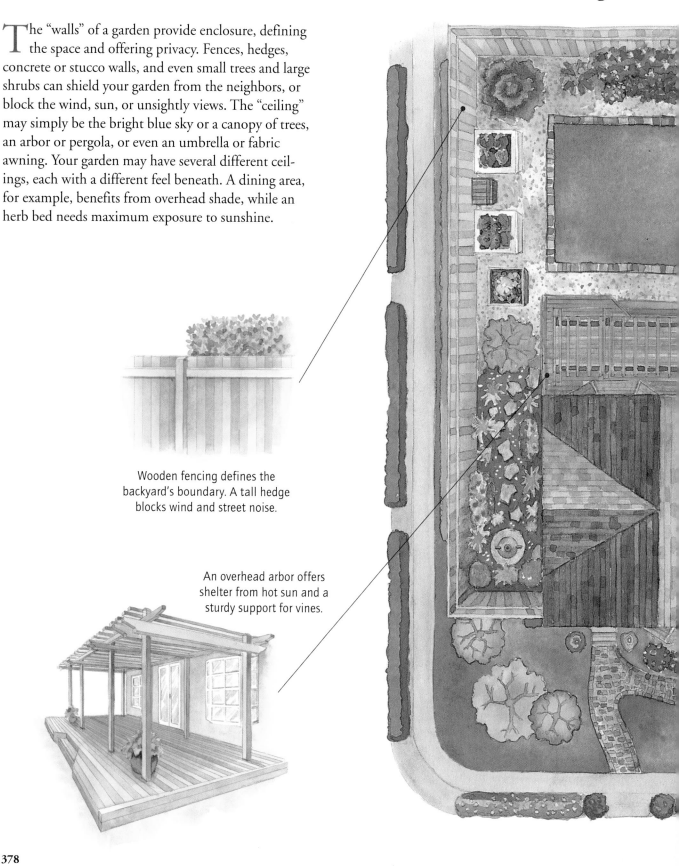

Wooden fencing defines the backyard's boundary. A tall hedge blocks wind and street noise.

An overhead arbor offers shelter from hot sun and a sturdy support for vines.

Tucked into a corner of the garden is a covered dining nook.

A colorful mural adds whimsy to the kids' play area.

To increase privacy, a trellis is added to the top of the fence.

A gated fence defines the garden's boundaries and provides privacy and security. It can also support vines, espaliers, or hanging pots.

Tall shrubs take the place of unneeded paved parking, providing extra shade and screening.

Getting Started

It can seem daunting to go from a bare dirt lot or an overgrown weed patch to an inviting garden—especially if you haven't tackled such a job before. This checklist will remind you of the steps involved.

- ☑ Determine your climate zone (see Evaluating the Site, page 364) . You'll save a lot of time, money, and frustration by choosing plants that are proven performers in your area.

- ☑ Get to know your soil. Is it predominantly sand, clay, or loam? To find out, thoroughly wet a small patch of soil, then about a day later, squeeze a handful firmly in your fist. If it forms a tight ball with a slippery feel, you have clay soil. If it feels gritty and crumbles apart when you open your hand, it's sandy. A slightly crumbly ball is closer to loam. You can test your soil's pH (acidity or alkalinity) using a test kit sold at nurseries. Or you can get a more precise picture of your soil by hav-ing it tested by a commercial soil laboratory (contact your local Cooperative Extension Agent). See Soil, page 328.

- ☑ Take note of your garden's sun exposure. Is your site open to the sun all day, or is it largely in the shade? Which areas are sunny in the morning and shady in the afternoon, and vice versa? Where do the house, trees, or other large structures cast shade in winter when the sun is lowest? See Tracking the Sun, page 365.

- ☑ Make a note of any special conditions. If you're planting where deer browse, for instance, you'll either need to include a deer fence in your plan or start assembling lists of plants that deer are less likely to eat (see Wildlife, page 340). If your garden is on a steep slope, you might plant shrubs and ground covers or plan for terraces to mitigate the abrupt grade. See Slopes, page 316.

- ☑ When thinking about the style of your garden, consider the architecture of your home and its surroundings. Casual or formal? Tropical or Mediterranean? Traditional or avant garde? See Setting Goals, page 366.

- ☑ Check local zoning and other laws if you plan to do any major construction, and contact your water and utility companies with any questions about underground cabling or water use. See Making It Official, page 364.

- ☑ Jot down a few ideas about how you'd like to use your garden space. Do you plan to use it for entertainment, relaxation, or both? Do you want to grow vegetables and herbs for the table, or would you rather compose a pretty picture of colorful leaves and flowers? Will kids and pets be playing in the garden?

- ☑ Consider how you might recycle materials like old flagstones or even broken concrete. If you discover large stones when you begin digging a flower bed, you might use them to border a path or even build a small rock garden. If you're tearing down an old fence, you could use the boards to build a compost bin.

☑ Draw a site plan of your property. Start by measuring the outer boundaries and make a rough sketch as you go. Include all the features of the garden, and indicate your home's doors and windows. See Making a Plan, page 368.

☑ Using these measurements, draw a base plan to scale so that you can play with different configurations. You can lay a piece of tracing paper over your base plan and see where, for instance, you'd like to locate the pool or rose beds. An herb garden needs full sun, and it would be nice to have it near the kitchen. Where is the best place for the bench? See Drawing to Scale, page 369.

☑ Remember some of the basic principles of design. Include focal points like a special tree or a piece of art at the end of a sight line. Strive for of symmetry and balance, even with something as simple as matching plants on either side of the entrance. Keep proportion in mind; don't try to fill a large space with dozens of annuals when a single shrub might suit the space. To achieve a sense of unity and rhythm, repeat a few favorite plants through the garden, and punctuate your composition with accents. See Design Basics, page 372.

☑ Choose the surfaces for your garden's "floor." Your local nursery can advise you on turf grass your area, for instance, but it's up to you to decide between stepping stones, gravel, or mulch for any paths. Would you like to cover a patch of ground with a few decorative boulders, or would a fragrant ground cover or a bed of perennials suit you better? Should your pool be surrounded with plain concrete or decorative pavers? See Outdoor Rooms, page 376.

☑ Next think about up and over the garden. A fence may be the quickest and most obvious way to gain privacy, but a hedge or even a small tree can also do the job. Would you prefer to shade a dining area with a simple umbrella or an arbor draped with flowering vines? See Outdoor Rooms, page 378.

☑ To get a sense of how your plan will look in reality, mock up the design. Lay out a hose where a curved flower bed might be or use wooden stakes and string for a hedge's outline. Use colored powder, such as limestone, flour, or gypsum, to sketch out free-form shapes on the ground. Bamboo poles can represent tall elements and help to see how shadows will fall. Use a beach chair to test out locations for a garden bench, and see how it feels to sit there at various times during the day.

☑ Remove any dead or unwanted plants from the garden. If you have diseased trees, it's a good idea to consult an arborist about whether they can be saved. Some plants that seem sickly might recover if moved to a more suitable spot; ferns that look burned and parched might recover nicely if moved to a shadier, moister part of the garden. And don't be in a hurry to dig up all the beds if you're not sure what's planted in them; a collection of beautiful bulbs might just pop up next spring where you saw only a bare patch of ground.

☑ Before setting plants in the ground, finish any construction or other large-scale projects, such as installing boulders or changing the grade. Also, install lighting and irrigation systems. Then begin planting. Set out trees and shrubs first, then fill in perennials, annuals, and bulbs.

Your front garden is the most visible part of your property, and ideally it should balance a feeling of welcome with a degree of privacy. A well-planned front garden is true to your home's architectural style and to your family's personality. The plantings are carefully chosen, and the pathway and front door are easy to locate and well lit for night use. Whether a casual cottage garden, or a natural-looking composition of boulders and shrubs around a redwood deck, your front garden tells the world that you take as much care with the outside of your home as you do with the inside.

LEFT *Golden Mexican feather grass, rusty red kangaroo paws, and the fluffy maroon flower heads of fountain grass complement the warm hues of this Mediterranean-style house in Santa Monica, California. Artful pruning of the jacaranda tree allows screening for upstairs windows without completely blocking the light.*

LEFT *To unify this house with its small front garden, the blue-gray hues of the window awning and painted trim are repeated in the bold forms of palm fronds, agaves, and ground-cover succulents.*

BELOW *A well-planned composition of color and texture softens the paving and adds interest to a small entry courtyard.*

One Front Yard, Two Ways

Cottage corner (below) As soon as you step out of the car onto a soft and fragrant ground cover (A), you feel how welcoming this front garden really is. Entries from the sidewalk and driveway (B) are framed by vine-covered arches. Meandering mulched paths (C) take you through a plant-lover's collection of flowering shrubs, perennials, and annuals—all in a happy jumble. On the other side of the driveway, blooming vines cover a trellis (D), with flowery perennials below.

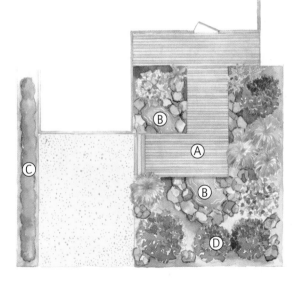

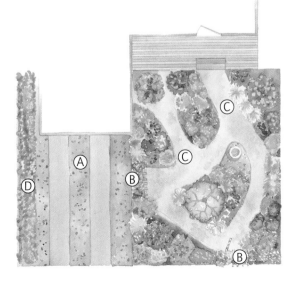

Rugged and rustic (above) Large shrubs and boulders surround a spacious redwood deck (A) raised slightly above ground level. Two small ponds (B) look perfectly natural among the stones, and a simple line of narrow evergreens anchors the opposite strip along the gravel driveway (C). Though this garden is more private than the other one, with shrubs screening the view from the street (D), the view from the driveway suggests spaciousness.

spaces: sideyards

The typical sideyard may be only a few feet wide and quite shady, but don't be discouraged by a dim, narrow space. There's almost always space for plants, or to tuck in extra storage, or even to make a hidden retreat.

Simple solutions include stepping-stones interplanted with low-growing, shade-tolerant ground covers, perhaps edged with a mix of ferns and moss-covered boulders. There may be just enough room for a few potted plants with a path winding between them. If unattractive block walls separate your side yard from your neighbor's, place flower boxes on top and fill them with cascading plants. You can create an espalier by training plants on a trellis

ABOVE *A double-wide pathway of stone pavers set in gravel is made foot-friendly with mounds of greenery. An exotic umbrella draws the eye to the end of the space.*

LEFT *Offering maximum utility in a minimum of space, this sideyard includes a wall-mounted sink, a seating area, and even an outdoor shower—all beneath vine-covered arches.*

FACING PAGE, ABOVE *Color is key in this slender passageway. Rich-hued walls play off the more muted tones of the rusty-leafed succulent Kalanchoe orygalis.*

FACING PAGE, BELOW *Designer Theresa Clark made the most of a narrow space between a hillside and this Rancho Santa Fe yard. The combination fountain/dipping pool runs nearly the width of the space, and a substantial fireplace of matching pavers is tucked into a corner.*

or on wires attached to the wall. Or mount hanging baskets or flat-backed terracotta pots on the wall or fence. A neglected fence out of public view might be just the spot to let kids paint their own mural, or to hang a collection of found art.

Take advantage of an out-of-the-way spot by putting a compost bin in a side-yard, or use the area to store extra pots, watering cans, and potting soil. Or pave the area with bricks and build a handsome recycling center. Add a series of arching trellises covered with vines to create a green canopy overhead. Use your imagination and turn a neglected outdoor hallway into an attractive and functional part of your landscape.

Even though it's often one of the most visible features of the property, the driveway is often overlooked as a potential area for landscaping. Remember that the driveway is really part of your home's entry. If the parking is accessible and the walk to the entry is pleasant, then your home extends a gracious welcome to your guests before you have even opened the door.

To begin with, consider how many parking spots you need; not enough space means constant shuffling, too much and you'll have a valet lot. Although parking in front of the house is logical, it can detract from a home's curb appeal, so consider adding a handsome wall or a row of tall shrubs to screen the area.

Driveways don't have to be just gray rivers of poured concrete. You can dress up existing concrete by having it stained, bonded, or top-coated in a color and finish that

ABOVE *A contemporary driveway, designed by Henning-Anderson, Oakland, California, has overlapping sections of granite, stained concrete, and multihued gravel for textural interest. A strip of white concrete works as a drainage channel; a stained concrete pad directs visitors to the front door.*

FACING PAGE, ABOVE *To make an interesting entry out of a bare concrete slab, designer Cevan Forristt broke up the old driveway and rearranged the pieces in a concrete-and-granite patchwork, then framed it with larger blocks of granite.*

FACING PAGE MIDDLE *Tropical plantings provide lush barriers between closely spaced driveways in a new development.*

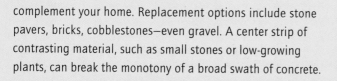

complement your home. Replacement options include stone pavers, bricks, cobblestones—even gravel. A center strip of contrasting material, such as small stones or low-growing plants, can break the monotony of a broad swath of concrete.

Soften the edges of the driveway with shrubs or flowers, making sure there's plenty of clearance for people getting out of their cars. Give visitors a good first impression with fragrant or colorful planting beds to greet them.

Narrow Strips

The poor cousin of the neglected driveway is that parched ribbon of unclaimed territory along the side-walk out front. Planting trees in these areas requires careful consideration, as the plants may have invasive roots that can buckle concrete sidewalks and others grow too tall to fit beneath overhead power lines. Instead, dress up a narrow curbside with a variety of rugged perennials, bulbs, grasses, and small shrubs that are unfussy about soil and need little water. In the Tucson garden at right, tough yet sculptural opuntias and yuccas mingle with softening vines and ground covers.

spaces: backyards

While the front yard is the public face of your property, the backyard is where you can let your hair down. Do you want a serene retreat where you can sit quietly in the dappled shade, or an outdoor gathering place with a patio, pool, and maybe even a fireplace? Do you plan to display a collection of delicate specimen plants—or will your backyard be a playground for kids and pets? You may want a traditional lawn surrounded by shrubs and flower beds—or perhaps you'd prefer no lawn at all, but mulched paths winding among native plants?

When planning your backyard, keep in mind how it will look from indoors; generally, houses have plenty of doors and windows opening to the back. Think of your backyard as an extension of your home. This private area is like another living space, so make it a place you, your family, and guests will want to be. Pay careful attention to traffic patterns and access, using pathways to direct people to destinations in the garden. The main thing is to have an overall concept in mind that you'll enjoy seeing through. And don't worry if your plan changes; just enjoy the journey as your backyard garden evolves.

RIGHT *In order to screen off a large contemporary home from its neighbors, landscape architect Mia Lehrer turned a bare lot in Beverly Hills into this woodland. Bands of blue fescue are interspersed with sections of lawn around a grid of 'Natchez White' crape myrtle.*

FACING PAGE *Colorful, sculptural elements are used as accents in a lively and livable backyard. To unify the space, the stone grid of the walkway is echoed in the metal wall and in an arbor over a pool deck.*

One Backyard, Two Ways

Inviting nature (below) A small pond (A) is sited across the garden from a raised birdbath. Located in sight of both, a gazebo (B) offers a quiet place to sit and watch the birds. Taking the place of a traditional lawn is a meadow planting (C) bordered by flagstone paths (D) and landings.

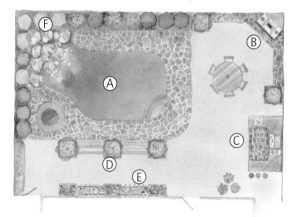

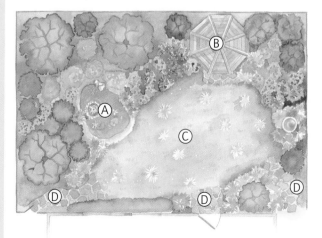

Outdoor living room (above) Family fun and outdoor entertaining are the main priorities in this backyard, which features a swimming pool (A) and a large patio with a fireplace (B) and kitchen area (C). Wooden planter boxes hold small trees, and three boxes are joined together to form benches (D). Wooden trellises hold vines above the house windows (E), and an L-shaped hedge (F) offers privacy from the neighbors.

Among the earliest known gardens were courtyards: Egyptian paintings show oases of repose and refuge open to the sky above yet protected and defined by surrounding walls. Whether graced by a splashing fountain, furnished with comfortable chairs and a dining table, or simply populated by a collection of container plantings, a courtyard garden offers a world of gardening opportunities in a modest space.

ABOVE *Different leaf colors and textures lend tropical touches to this Del Mar courtyard, which is also filled with dry-climate plants such as lavender, salvia, and santolina—all of them in pots of various sizes. A high-rising fountain makes an impressive focal point.*

RIGHT *Taking a cue from surrounding hills, this inviting dining area is filled with lush plantings of deep green and gray. The warmer tones of the paving and tile roofs enhance the feeling of a cozy enclosure.*

LEFT *A defining feature of the Eichler home is the atrium; the outdoors is brought quite literally into the center of the house. Here, large windows on all sides make this a natural area for showcasing choice plants and a couple of stylish chairs.*

BELOW *At night, a San Jose yard designed by Cevan Forristt is transformed into a paradise. Lanterns provide soft lighting, exotic plantings fill beds. Water trickles along the top of the wall and into the pond.*

Not every gardener has a plot of land, but that doesn't mean you can't create a lovely garden. An assortment of containers on a balcony or rooftop can hold a beautiful display, from clipped topiary to rotating displays of flowering annuals or herbs for snipping off fresh leaves. Add a couple of chairs and a small table, and you've got a little piece of paradise perched on high. Gardening up high, however, does take a little extra planning.

If choosing containers, remember that terracotta pots are fairly heavy and, being quite porous, they tend to dry out quickly unless glazed. Wood is a durable choice that is somewhat lighter but is also porous unless sealed. Plastic or resin containers are lightest and most moisture retentive. Make sure all containers have good drainage, and pay close attention to where the water will drain—liners or saucers may be needed to protect the roof or floor.

Safe distribution of weight is an important concern. Your landlord, contractor, or homeowners' association can advise you about weight limits for recently built structures. If you live in an older building or plan to amass a large collection of heavy pots and furniture, it is well worth the cost to get a survey from a structural engineer.

LEFT *A floor of organic blue shapes and pristine white walls give this San Francisco rooftop, designed by Topher Delaney, a retro feel. The metallic furnishings and rugged palms stand up to foggy weather.*

FACING PAGE, BELOW *A lot of country charm is packed into this small space on a Denver rooftop. Lightweight furniture and a few large pots are arranged on the wooden decking; hanging baskets and spilling annuals fill the vertical spaces.*

BELOW *The sophisticated terrace was inspired by a Mexican beach resort. Landscape designers Pamela Berstler and Alex Stevens embedded blue pool tiles in the concrete to give the impression of swirling water. A built-in daybed provides comfortable seating.*

Pots Up Top

It's important to choose the right potting mix for rooftop containers. For plants that will stay in the same pot or planter for a year or more, soil-based mixes are best. Lightweight soilless mixes are best for annual plantings, hanging baskets, and where weight is an issue. Specific mixes for aquatic plants, cacti and succulents, and acid-loving plants like azaleas and camellias are widely available, and some mixes contain water-retaining gel and fertilizer.

Match the container to the plant: keep in mind the plant's mature size, growth rate, and root structure. Don't put a small plant in a big container; for the most part, plants do not thrive when there is too much extra soil around their root ball. All container plants need regular water and feeding to thrive, but rooftop and balcony gardens are more exposed to wind and sun, so be sure to choose plants that can tolerate these conditions.

BELOW *The centerpiece of this rooftop garden in Seattle is a large galvanized metal planter overflowing with an untamed mix of trees, shrubs, perennials, and creeping ground covers.*

FACING PAGE, TOP *This San Francisco roof terrace, designed by Andrea Cochran, holds a series of undulating aluminum containers filled with billowing grasses and massed succulents. Checker-plate aluminum, precast pavers, Trex recycled lumber, and Mexican river pebbles form the floor of the garden. At night, fiber-optic lighting makes the space glow.*

BELOW AND LEFT *It took careful planning to ensure that this Vancouver roof deck could support the weight of Glen Patterson's transplanted garden. Custom soil mix and artificial stone kept the weight down, while steel reinforced the roof. The result is an urban oasis of conifers, Japanese maples, rock-garden plants, and even a pond filled with koi.*

makeovers

Eastern Influence, Western Exposure This front yard was dominated by overgrown shrubs that blocked the windows and shaded the tiny lawn. The new Asian-style garden, framed by a stylish low fence, features a dry stream bed and a curving path of fieldstones. Low-maintenance plants such as heavenly bamboo, mugo pine, and fortnight lily offer a variety of textures and colors.

before

- The simple architecture lends itself to a streamlined Asian design.

- Large pots are strategically grouped to block the area where trash cans are stored. Another acts as an attractive focal point next to the entry gate.

- A wooden pergola brings the garden right up to the house without blocking the window.

- Soil excavated for the dry stream bed was used to form small mounds that add interesting changes of level.

- Large stones are carefully placed and serve as sculptural elements.

after

after

Lusher Look When Claudia and Kurt Armann purchased their new home, they knew something had to be done about the uninspired front yard. Replacing the boring patch of lawn with a colorful combination of succulents and drought-tolerant perennials gave them the lush look they were after. After only two years, the fruits of their do-it-yourself labors are stunningly evident.

before

- The bold forms of agave and cycads balance the existing queen palm and bird of paradise.

- The new garden needs irrigation only about once a month, in contrast to the thirsty lawn that was there before.

- Birds, butterflies, and bees are attracted to the profusion of flowers, offering a lively show visible from the porch and large front windows.

- Before, the garden palette was largely green. Now, vibrant threads of pink and purple are offset by shades of gray and enlivened with touches of yellow and orange.

- A variety of textures—from soft rosemary to spiky cycads—guarantee interest even when nothing is in bloom.

- California poppies and Mexican sage contrast beautifully in color and texture.

makeovers

Scenic Remake The goal of this front garden's transformation was to reflect its surroundings. Before the makeover, the flat lawn and white picket fence were more in the style of an East Coast cottage. Landscape architect Jeffrey Gordon Smith's design enhanced the Arts and Crafts style of the home and echoed the topography of the surrounding terrain.

before

- The fence was discarded in favor of a stacked-stone wall and steps that look as if they might have been quarried from local hills.

- The entire front yard is elevated to lead the eye up to the house and then to the scenic hills beyond.

- A pleasing symmetry is attained with nearly identical plantings on either side of the path.

- Soft, mounding plants soften the rough edge of the stones and contrast with spiky accents such as red-hot poker and pride of Madeira *(Echium)*.

- Colors for the new paint and trim match tones within the flagstones. A bright pumpkin-colored front door provides a warm welcome.

- In the backyard, a shallow stream cascades over a stone wall that matches the retaining wall in the front yard.

after

Natural Connections A shady side yard offered little but a straight runway of pavers leading from the front yard to the back. A shelf precariously attached to the fence made the passage even narrower, and sun-loving plants failed to thrive in the shadows. A new and wider path leads through bright hanging baskets and a variety of colorful shade-lovers.

before

after

- Irregular stepping-stones of Mariposa slate replace boring concrete pavers.

- Ferns, coleus, and shade-tolerant bamboos surround a collection of potted orchids that is brought outdoors during the warm season.

- The poorly sited shelf was removed to make the space easier to navigate, and a new potting area was added elsewhere.

- Hanging baskets of begonias make maximum use of the vertical space.

- A thick layer of bark chips keeps moisture in and weeds out.

- Whimsical stencils populate the wooden fence with iguanas and butterflies.

makeovers

Borrowed Space The U shape of this 1950s suburban ranch house created a deep central courtyard that was awkward and little used, so architects Scott Strumwasser and Tash Rahbar came up with an ingenious solution. They created a spacious family room between the flanking wings and added a raised patio opening onto the lawn and pool.

after

- Trees that had originally been planted too close to the house were taken out, and a new one planted in a more suitable spot in the lawn.

- The patio was raised to the level of the interior floors to give the feel of an outdoor living room.

- Using the same stacked-stone facing on the patio and the hot tub creates unity of design.

- Large pots filled with ornamental grasses and small shrubs help to tie the house to the garden.

- Outdoor lighting subtly highlights the pool and house, further connecting the indoors and out.

- High ceilings and glass doors help bring the outdoors in.

after

Applied Geometry This urban backyard had lots of room but lacked a useful design. To create an outdoor living space, the owners installed an elegant fieldstone patio featuring a raised pond and a dining area. The space is surrounded by densely planted perennials and shrubs for privacy.

before

- Attractive containers hold impatiens, caladiums, and fuchsias; these color accents can be changed with the seasons.

- The pond's octagonal shape is repeated in the pattern of the fieldstones that form the floor of the dining area.

- Wide top stones atop the low wall form an inviting place to sit.

- Bright highlights in varying textures are provided by golden forms of creeping Jenny, sedge, and potato vine.

- Sound and motion are supplied by a bubbling fountain and darting fish; both invite the indoor viewer to come outside.

- Opening directly onto the patio, French doors frame a view of the pond.

makeovers

Faux Natural To transform a dark Washington backyard into an inviting area for entertaining, Natyam Schraven and his wife, Leslie Werner, started by removing a few trees and pruning others to let in more light. Next, they added a naturalistic pond fronted by a curving deck, and finally added lush plantings that thrive in dappled shade.

before

- The cedar used to construct the deck blends beautifully with the wooden exterior of the house.

- Concrete "boulders" that form the edges of the pond have been carefully sculpted and spattered with paint to give them a more natural look.

- Planting pockets in the pond make water gardening easier than if the entire bottom were soil.

- Poles holding colorful flags add vertical pizzazz.

- Grassy plants, ferns, and sprawling ground covers all help to soften the pond's edges.

after

after

New Life for a Bog This two-level backyard with a low-lying soggy spot presented the homeowner with more than the usual gardening challenges. Her solutions include a bog garden and new steps connecting a wide gravel terrace and a meandering path leading through a casual collection of plants to a comfortable bench on higher ground.

before

- The vibrant blue of bench and steps draws the eye from the foreground to the farthest reaches of the garden.

- Japanese irises and calla lilies are great choices for planting in a sunny wet area.

- A concrete birdbath provides a simple focal point.

- Low, spreading plants spill from the upper to the lower level, masking the hard edge of the retaining wall.

- Placing the bench at the back of the property encourages a stroll through the garden.

- Tucked into the surrounding foliage, a simple wooden bench makes an inviting retreat.

after

Easy-Care Color Looking out onto her backyard in Los Altos, California, Betty Norlander saw weeds thriving and ornamental plants struggling in the heavy clay soil—but she also saw potential. She turned to garden designer Gay Bonorden Gray to help her transform the space into a low-maintenance, high-interest flower border.

before

- Amended with compost, the soil is now light enough to grow a variety of plants successfully.

- Trellises fixed along the fence add vertical interest to the garden's walls, with or without vines growing on them.

- In spring and summer, pink roses create a ribbon of color through silvery gray lamb's ears, society garlic, and artemisia. Evergreen plants like heavenly bamboo and phormium carry the show through winter.

- A drip irrigation system provides regular, efficient watering.

- Most of the plants need only some cutting back in winter or dividing every few years.

- Pink 'Flower Carpet' is a freely blooming rose that stays low, rarely topping 3 feet tall.

- A low redwood deck provides an elegant stage for the contemporary outdoor furniture.

- A little asymmetry makes all the difference here. The strip of gravel separating deck and lawn is in the unexpected shape of an elongated triangle.

- Large stepping-stones cut a straight path through the manicured lawn; their simple square shape reinforces the space's modern look.

- Arching phormiums and sculptural succulents fill chic metallic containers.

- Against the restrained palette of the house and furniture, the lawn seems a brighter green.

- A small stone-framed goldfish pond completes the modern look.

An Inviting Family Garden. When designer John Jennings and landscape architect Sasha Tarnopolsky set out to remodel the Spanish-style cottage they had just bought, they knew they wanted a modern look inside and out. In the backyard, they transformed a jumbled mess into a sleek, open patio and lawn to accommodate their toddler and two lively dogs.

before

after

How sweet it is at the end of the day when work is done and a comfortable chair awaits in the garden—or just beyond.

Pat Kuleto's Sage Canyon Ranch, Napa Valley

subject index

Italics indicate a page with photos or diagrams.

plant index

Italics indicate a page with photos or diagrams.

photography credits

T = top; B = bottom; C = center; L = left; R = right; M = middle

Melanie Acevedo/PictureArts: 111T, 275ML. **Agence Images/ Beateworks.com:** 262T. **Aquascape Designs, Inc.:** 146T, 151MR. **Peter Arnold, Inc./Alamy:** 261TR. **Scott Atkinson:** 107. **Joyce Baker:** 403B. **Botanica/PictureArts:** 5B, 250 crossover. **Paul Bousquet:** 151BR, 208T, 216, 225, 244B, 367B, 392R. **Brand X Pictures/Alamy:** 359R. **Marion Brenner:** 44, 45, 46 both, 47 both, 60 crossover, 62, 63 both, 134BR, 135 all, 148 both, 149 all, 158B, 211TR, 218B, 239R, 254BR, 272B, 297BR, 396BL, 396BR, 399R. **Marion Brenner/Picture Arts:** 406 crossover. **Rob Brodman:** 287BR. **Nicola Browne:** 336. **Burke/Triolo Productions/Picture Arts:** 192T. **James Carrier:** 129BL, 271BL, 277TL. **Jennifer Cheung/ Steven Nilsson:** 4TR, 178 crossover, 233BL, 266MR, 266BL. **Jennifer Cheung/PictureArts:** 283T. **Connie Coleman:** 162T, 194. **Grey Crawford:** 6TL. **Claire Curran:** 111B, 114R, 115T, 133B, 195BR, 222T, 231, 234BL, 255, 285R, 288T, 294T, 318B, 324TR. **Robin Bachtler Cushman:** 120, 161, 163, 171B, 213B, 218T, 221B, 228TR, 247BMR, 259B, 264BL, 289BL, 372B, 403T. **Lilly Dong/Picture Arts:** 164 R. **D.A. Horchner/Design Workshop:** 20, 21 both, 28, 29 all, 207, 316. **Andrew Drake:** 141T, 253TL, 271TR, 375TR. **Jack Dykinga:** 166B. **Linda Enger:** 385T. **Rob Fiocca/PictureArts:** 271BR. **Roger Foley:** 401T **Fotosearch:** 320. **Frank Gaglione:** 138BL, 138BR, 139BL, 139BM, 139BR. **The Garden Picture Library/**

Alamy: 157B. **David Hewitt/ Anne Garrison:** 126. **Andrea Jones/ Garden Exposures:** 4TL, 8 crossover, 92 both, 93, 253BR, 269T, 392TR crossover. **Fiona Gilsenan:** 141B, 144BL, 186B, 199R, 270T, 309TL, 310 all, 311BL, 311BM, 311TR, 321 all, 329, 332, 333 all, 334L, 335 all, 342B, 343T, 360B, 361 all. **David Glomb:** 293. **John Granen:** 5TR, 104, 298 crossover. **Art Gray:** 7. **Steven Gunther:** 15, 16, 17 both, 18, 19T, 22 both, 23 both, 38, 39 both, 56, 57 both, 70 crossover, 71BR, 76TL, 77, 78 all, 79, 80 crossover, 81 both, 82, 83 both, 86 crossover, 87 both, 99T, 103T, 118L, 122T, 131BR, 134T, 140T, 157T, 165B, 172T, 190, 192B, 193, 198, 203B, 205 both, 222B, 223B, 226T, 239L, 263TR, 265TL, 268B, 276R, 279L, 290B, 291 both, 308, 312, 322 both, 324TL, 324BR, 334R, 356, 373R, 382, 383L, 384B, 385B, 387MR, 388, 390T, 393, 397T, 398B. **Jerry Harpur:** 108TL, 150, 164L, 169, 171T, 175T, 177B, 276L, 278B, 282T, 290TL, 360T, 372T, 375BR, 380. **Philip Harvey:** 275TR, 368. **H. Ross Hawkins:** 342T. **Cheryl Himmelstein:** 110. **Saxon Holt:** 2, 12, 13 both, 24, 25, 30 both, 31, 72, 73 both, 88, 89 all, 108MR, 115B, 140B, 144T, 152, 189R, 209 both, 217T, 220T, 223T, 230, 234T, 235, 236, 240BL, 240BR, 241, 247BR, 254TL, 280BR, 287BL, 309BL, 318T, 358, 373L. **Lisa Hubbard/PictureArts:** 102. **George H. Huey:** 352. **Sandra Ivany/PictureArts:** 99B. **Muffy Kibbey:** 269B. **Jacqueline Koch:** 34B, 35B, 40, 41, 143B, 204, 297TR. **Caroline Kopp:** 260R,

261BR, 290TR. **Ernst Kucklich:** 189L. **Mark David Levine:** 153B, 167. **Janet Loughrey:** 114L, 142L, 176T, 188, 196B, 206, 210, 217BR, 228B, 233T, 243B, 278T, 289R, 341BL. **Allan Mandell:** 33 both, 34T, 35T, 58, 59 all, 162BL, 162BR, 180R, 181, 196T, 211B, 238, 247T, 253TR, 306, 307TR, 315, 375L. **Charles Mann:** 3, 132L, 146B, 174BL, 176B, 202 both, 212, 217ML, 220B, 247BML, 249, 280TR, 303T, 346, 350. **Tom Mannion:** 401B. **J.B. McCarthy:** 166T. **Jim McCausland:** 32, 279R, 292. **David McDonald:** 326 crossover. **E. Andrew McKinney:** 113 all. **Terrence Moore:** 6BL, 123B. **Clive Nichols:** 10 both, 11 both, 54 both, 55 both, 142R, 151T, 259T, 267T, 273T. **George Olson:** 348L. **Karin Payson:** 125. **Anthony Peres:** 400B. **Victoria Pearson/Picture Arts:** 6TL, 137T, 174BR, 264BR. **Norm Plate:** 1, 26, 27 both, 36, 37 both, 48 both, 49, 64, 65, 74, 75 both, 84, 85 both, 103B, 116 both, 118R, 147BL, 155B, 160, 168, 173B, 177T, 182, 195T, 199L, 208B, 211TL, 214, 252, 256 both, 259B, 263TL, 263B, 265B, 281, 283B, 286T crossover, 289MR, 297TL, 307C, 309R, 319B, 340, 366, 367B, 370, 383R, 384T, 386, 387BR, 391B, 394. **Norman A. Plate:** 330, 348TR, 387TL. **Janet Rademacher:** 248B. **Sandra Lee Reha:** 94 both, 95 both. **Lisa Romerein:** 4BL, 19B, 96 crossover, 132R, 143T, 268T, 405BL, 405BR. **Susan A. Roth:** 134BL, 174TR, 203T, 233BR, 244T, 304TR, 341MR. **Mark Rutherford:** 109 all. **Jeremy Samuelson:** 105, 155T, 158T, 175B, 254MR, 264TL, 270B,

389, 390B. **Jeremy Samuelson/ PictureArts:** 117B, 137B, 139TR, 257, 274, 282B. **Christine Schmidhofer:** 295B, 296T. **Evan Sklar:** 122B. **Carl and Lynne Steffens:** 129TM, 129TR, 129C, 129BM, 129BR. **Holly Stewart:** 266TL, 395T. **Thomas J. Story:** 5TL, 52 both, 53, 117T, 127 both, 130, 131TL, 131TR, 144BR, 154, 156, 159BL, 159BM, 159BR, 221T, 224, 226B, 227, 228TL, 245R, 247BL, 261TL, 277BL, 277MR, 277 lower R, 277BR, 280TL, 294B, 307TL, 314, 317T, 323 both, 331, 341TR, 341BR, 343B, 344B, 359L, 362 crossover, 381, 399L, 404T. **Tim Street-Porter:** 42 both, 43TR, 50, 51 all, 66, 67 both, 68 both, 69 both, 90, 91 all, 98, 119, 123T, 136, 138T, 153T, 170 both, 172B, 173T, 180L, 213T, 242T, 262B, 265TR, 267B, 272T, 286L, 311BR, 313, 319T, 339, 354, 374. **Tim Street-Porter/Beateworks. com:** 108BL. **Tim Street-Porter/ PictureArts:** 165T. **Martin Tessler:** 121 both, 186T, 273B, 296B, 395BL, 395BR. **E. Spencer Toy:** 245L, 317B, 328L. **Luca Trovato/ PictureArts:** 284. **Mark Turner:** 240TR, 242B, 243T, 295T. **Mark Turner/PictureArts:** 101. **Deidra Walpole:** 344T. **Andy Wasowski:** 248T. **Simon Watson/PictureArts:** 6 lower L, 285L. **Marvin Wax:** 391T. **Peter O. Whiteley:** 6ML, 133T, 328T. **Bob Wigand:** 147TR, 159T, 200, 258T, 260L, 303B, 345 both. **David Winger:** 304TL, 304MR. **Ben Woolsey:** 402B. www.brandoncole.com: 353. **David Zaitz:** 300.

designer credits

T = top; B = bottom; C = center; L = left; R = right; M = middle Adams Design Associates: 126. Tracy LaRue Adams, Duo Design Group: 116B. Carol & David Ager: 279R. Suzanne Arca: 140B. Greg Asbagh: 15, 16, 17 both, 190. Sandy Atherton, Atherton and Lewis: 367T, 383R. Robyn Atkinson: 143B. Autumn Skies Landscapes: 217T. AZ-Home Landscape: 174TR. Peter Bailey: 18, 19 both. Doug & Sue Band: 380. Barton-Leier Gallery: 141B. Shari Bashin-Sullivan, Enchanting Planting: 24, 25, 168, 319B. Michael Bates: 247BR. Pat Bauer Design: 282T. Tom Berger, The Berger Partnership: 116T. Julia Berman: 217ML. Lynne Blackman: 279L. Jane Bogle: 280TR. Roberta & Scott Bolling: 247BMR, 264BL. Marcus Bollinger: 182. Steve Bollinger: 174BL. Sharon Brasher: 162T. John Brown: 157B. Les Bugajski: 162BR. Debra Burnette: 385T. Carlotta in Paradise: 346. Bob Carlson, Pacific Northwest Construction: 104. Olga Cattolico: 324TR. Jack Chandler: 2, 12, 13 both, 30 both, 31, 254TL. Jared Chandler: 63 both. Chip-N-Dale's Custom Landscaping: 193. Linda Chisari: 291B (landscape design). Bob Clark: 211TR. Robert Clark & Archie Days: 267. Theresa Clark: 80 crossover, 81 both, 82, 83 both, 103T, 118L, 165B, 203B, 359L, 384B, 385B. Clemens & Associates: 36, 37 both. Linda Cochran: 176T, 196B, 217BR, 233T, 278T, 280BR. Andrea Cochrane: 266TL, 395T. Greg Corman: 263B. Stacey Crooks, Crooks Garden Design: 32, 33 both, 34 both, 35 both. Christine Curry Designs: 269B. Tim Curry: 122B. Ginny Davis: 144T, 152. Francine Day, Tom Zachary Landscape Architects: 228B. Jeffrey L. Day, Min/Day with BurksToma Architects: 133T. Bruce de Cameron, Great Gardens, Inc.: 244B. Topher Delaney: 4TL, 8 crossover, 92 both, 93B, 171T,

269T, 278B, 280TL, 392T crossover. Claire Dohna: 253TL. Stephen K. Domigan: 146B. Marcia Donahue: 253BR, 254BR. Pamela Dreyfuss Interior Design and Exteriors Landscape Architecture: 127 both. Andrew Duff: 151T. Barbara Duno: 64, 65, 199L, 212. Mary Effron Landscape Design: 122T, 360T. Steven Ehrlich Architects: 6TL, 108BR. Élan Landscape Design and Build: 402B. Ellerie Designs & Jeanne McNeil and Associates: 326 crossover. Julie Ellison, Art of Gardens: 94 both, 95 both. Enchanting Planting: 317T. Puck Erickson, Arcadia Studio: 195T. Richard Faylor: 48 both, 49. Fire Magic, Robert H. Peterson Co.: 126 (barbecue). Flower to the People: 393. Cevan Forristt: 155B, 256T, 283B, 289MR, 387TL, 391B. Rachel Foster: 403T. Sonny Garcia: 169, 375BR. Carol & Jerry Garringer: 259B. General Electric: 126 (refrigerator). Michael Glassman & Associates: 314. Andrew Glazier, Wild West Gardens: 52 both (landscape design), 53 (landscape design). Robert Glazier, Hill Glazier Architects: 52 both, 53. Franz Goebel: 118R. Brenda Gousha, Sisters Specialty Gardens: 294T. Gay Bonorden Gray: 404T. Isabelle C. Greene: 276L. Ursel Gut: 290TL. Stefan Hammerschmidt: 70 crossover, 71BR. Benjamin H. Hammontree: 244T. Francesca Harris, FHIG, Inc.: 295B. Richard Hartlage: 175T. Helene Henderson: 198. Henning-Anderson: 386. Herschberger Design: 20, 21 both, 207. Paul Hervey Decorative Products: 259T. Tom Hobbs: 177B. Kristin Horne: 134BL. Huettl-Thuilot Associates: 318T, 323 both. Ilga Jansons & Mike Dryfoos: 54 both, 55 both. John Jennings & Sasha Tarnopolsky, Dry Design: 405BL, 405BR. Anni Jensen: 220T. John Kaib: 289BL. Judy Kameon, Elysian Landscapes: 39 both. Rebecca & Chuck Kaye: 239L. Cory Kelso, Cory's Cottage

Garden: 86, 87. Rob King, Clemens Associates: 173B. Vi Kono, Creative Designs: 211B, 292. Joan Kropf: 171B. Ed & Nancy Lane: 350. David Larkins, LRM Architects: 86, 87. Terry LeBlanc: 196T. Mia Lehrer + Associates: 134T, 157T, 192B, 205 both, 222B, 268B, 373R, 388. Marni Leis Design: 296T. Mark David Levine: 153B, 167. Gina MacDonald: 84, 85 both. Tom Mannion: 401T. Jean Manocchio, Belli Fiori: 245L. Steven Martino and Associates: 22 both, 23 both, 336. Jim Matsuo: 164L. Nancy McCabe: 134BR. Carol McElwee: 90, 91 all, 213T, 272T. Nancy McFadden: 163. Richard McPherson: 209T. Meerkerk Rhododendron Gardens: 194. Frank Mitze: 111B (bamboo fence). Jane Mooney/Tatton Park: 142R. Christine Moore: 322 both. Laura Morton: 42 both, 43TR, 123T, 265TR, 267B, 286L. Mosaic Garden Design and Construction: 372B. Martin Hakubai Mosko, Marpa Associates: 208B. Eric Nagelmann: 56, 57 both. Mario Navarro & Craig Prunty, All Oregon Landscaping: 315. Noble Design Studio: 166T. Marietta & Ernie O'Byrne: 289R. Alejandro Ortiz Architects: 110. Dan Overbeck: 177T, 387BR. Pamela Palmer, Artecho Architecture & Landscape Architecture: 383L. Ken Parker Collection: 276R. Glen Patterson: 186T, 395BL, 395BR. Karin Payson Architecture: 125. Craig Pearson: 265B. Phoebe Noble garden: 329. Birgit Piskor: 58, 59 all. Polyscapes Landscape Construction & Design: 117T. Nancy Goslee Powers: 98, 136, 319T, 339, 374. Progressive Construction: 126 (builder). Janet Rademacher: 248B. Mike Ransom, Robert Howard Associates: 151BR. Lisa Ray: 60 crossover, 62. Nancy & Steve Reid, A Gardener's Dream: 163 (greenhouse design). Paul Repetowski: 297TR. RHS Chelsea: 108TL. Elizabeth Robechek,

Clemens & Associates: 4BL, 96 crossover. Chad Robert: 281 (exteriors). Pam Roy, Planscapes: 394. Greg Rubin, California's Own Native Landscape Design: 240BR, 285R. Santa Fe Permaculture: 249. R. Michael Schneider, Orange Street Studio: 76TL, 77, 78 all, 79. Sallye Schumacher: 3, 176B. Richard Shaw: 316. Jeanie Sims: 216 (landscape architect). Sisters Specialty Gardens: 133B. Smith & Hawken: 277BL. Jeffrey Gordon Smith: 290B, 324TL, 398B. Sonoran Desert Designs: 74, 75 both. Spears Architects and Stephen Watkins Design: 268T. Scott Spencer Garden Design: 172T. Rob Steiner: 291T (landscape architect). Diana Stratton: 88, 89 all. Peter Strauss: 66, 67 both, 68 both, 69 both. Scott Strumwasser & Tash Rahbar, Enclosures Architects: 400B. Bud Stuckey: 294B. Sunshine Greenery: 382. Bob Swain: 10 both, 11 both, 273T. Freeland & Sabrina Tanner: 245R. Freeland Tanner, Proscape Landscape Design: 72, 73 both, 272B. Betty Taylor: 26, 27 both. Christy Ten Eyck: 202B, 372T. Michael Thilgen: 240BL. Patrick Tighe, Tighe Architecture: 7. Bernard Trainor: 44, 45, 46 both, 47 both. TSO Construction and Tom Farrage and Company: 7. Kanau Uyeyama: 296B (architect). Philip Van Wyck, Van Wyck & Associates: 166B. Greg Vasilieff, Western Gardens Landscaping: 255. Ron Wagner & Nani Waddoups: 238. Bruce Wakefield: 206. Terry Welch: 253TR. Luane Wells: 150. Peter O. Whiteley: 144BR. Tom Wilhite: 364, 370 both, 371, 376–379 all, 389 both, 396BL, 396BR. Nick Williams & Associates: 131BR. David Stark Wilson, Wilson Associates: 5TR, 298 crossover. Chris Winters: 366. Jeff Zischke: 256B, 263TL, 286T crossover.